That Guy Fae The Corries

Ronnie Browne was born in Edinburgh in 1937 and has lived in or near the city all through his life. Best known as a folk singer, especially as one half of The Corries, he is also an accomplished portraitist. In these roles he has travelled the world and is a popular and unmistakable figure. Closely associated with Scotland's anthem, Flower of Scotland, he has led the singing at many international sporting events and gatherings. Ronnie Browne has made many musical albums not only with The Corries but also in his own right.

More information and downloads are available at
www.corries.com

That Guy Fae The Corries

Ronnie Browne

SANDSTONEPRESS
HIGHLAND | SCOTLAND

First published in Great Britain
and the United States of America in 2015
Sandstone Press Ltd
Dochcarty Road
Dingwall
Ross-shire
IV15 9UG
Scotland.

www.sandstonepress.com

Editor: Robert Davidson
Index: Roger Smith
Technical Support: David Ritchie

The publisher acknowledges support from Creative Scotland
towards publication of this volume.

ISBN: 978-1-910985-06-9
ISBNe: 978-1-910124-37-6

Front image by Trevor E. R. Yerbury
Book design by Raspberry Creative type, Edinburgh
Typesetting by Iolaire Typesetting, Newtonmore
Printed and bound by CPI Group (UK) Ltd, Croydon CR0 4YY

Acknowledgements

To Matthew MacIver, whose infectious enthusiasm and encouragement finally forced me to put pen to paper.

To the Hand of Fate which must surely have decreed that I keep Pat's and my own diaries together for all these years to form the nucleus of this book.

To Eileen Hetterley (Kinnear) for her invaluable scrapbooks, (and her big brother Bill, for his smile).

To Gavin, Maurice and Lauren for filling in details of family life overlooked by the diaries.

Special mention to Gavin for his technical knowledge of 'dropboxes', 'PDFs', 'backups', 'jpegs' and all that stuff which is 'way over the head of this old man.

To Robert Davidson and his team at Sandstone Press for their patience during the past year.

And, finally, to all you bums on seats out there for your support over, what seems, the most of my life.

List of illustrations

14. The Corrie Folk Trio and Paddie Bell sing in The Hoot'nanny Show, 1963.
15. Circ. 1968. Roy, with his first wife, Vi, mother of his two girls, Karen and Sheena.
16. Circ. 1968. With Gavin, Pat and Lauren.
17. In the seventies, (l. to r.), Jim Wilkie, Brian Wilson (M.P. to come), and Dave Scott, founders of The West Highland Free Press.
18. 1973? Lauren, Maurice and Gavin in Petticoat Lane, London.
19. The Corries, a publicity shot.
20. Family and friends gather round for the 1977, 'Peat Fire Flame' album cover shot.
21. 'Where did that note go, Roy?'
22. I interview Lonnie Donnegan in our 1983 award-winning STV series, 'The Corries and other Folk'.
23. My first solo commitment as Founder Member of The Beechgrove Garden Club.
24. My two Grand Slam Commemorative paintings and members of the 1990 Squad.
25. The 1991 Official S.R.U. Calendar.
26. 'Ah cannae hear ye!'

SECTION TWO: colour

1. 'O.K. Roy, so it's a combolin! Now, do you really expect me to actually play it?'
2. Lee, Roy and me at Eyemouth Harbour.
3. I wonder if this was 'Killiecrankie'?
4. 1991. My first solo publicity shot.
5. The Java St Andrew Society Ball, 1993. Pat, (purple gown), is led to the top table on the arm of the Canadian Ambassador.
6. 'My hero!' I wish.

7. Work in progress.
8. The family. Standing, (l. to r.), Maurice, me and Gavin. Seated, (l. to r.), Kate, Maurice's wife, (divorced), holding their second, Michael, Lauren, holding Gavin's first, Rebecca, Pat, holding Maurice's first, Karlyn, and Michelle, Gavin's wife (heavily pregnant at the time with Jessica, their second). Confusing, isn't it.
9. With Craig Brown in Vienna, 1996, for the world qualifier versus Austria, when the S.F.A chose 'Flower of Scotland' as their anthem for the first time.
10. I know you'll never believe it, but Stephen beat me.
11. At a charity event with Brian Leishman, a real gentleman in the Rog Whittaker mould and business manager of the Edinburgh Military Tattoo for 25 years.
12. Pat and me with Prince Philip for the Duke of Edinburgh Awards.
13. Oliver Reid 'disrobes' in Peebles.
14. I sing 'Flower of Scotland' in 1998, at the Ross Bandstand with the Royal Scottish National Orchestra and Chorus, conducted by a very excited Jerzy Maksymiuk.
15. 'Hey you wi' the Hong Kong tartan jacket, ye've had enough tae drink. Ye're gettin' no more.'
16. Lauren with Paulo Nutini.
17. 'And we'll all go together, to pull wild mountain thyme.'
18. The Black Douglas.
19. Robert the Bruce in my car.
20. (l. to r.) Rebecca, Michelle, Gavin and Jessica.
21. Maurice with Karlyn and Michael.
22. Lauren with her 'Sunshine Project' children.
23. Pat and me. Guess where?

Prologue

We were in a dressing-room in the Royal Albert Hall, London, which as most people know was designed to resemble the Colosseum in Rome. Its seating capacity at the time was 8,000, although nowadays it has been reduced, so forgive me when I say that we were very proud to be playing to a full house that night.

My brother-in-law, Lee Elliot, was our road-manager and was taking our instruments on stage to lean them against the assortment of chairs that were already assembled behind the microphones. Most of his task had been completed and only the combolins were left to be tuned. These were multi-instruments, designed and made by my partner in The Corries, Roy Williamson, and were always last to go on stage.

It was, of course, close to curtain up, and as Lee came in to the dressing-room for the last time, I asked, 'Okay Lee, how's it looking out there?'

He replied with a growl, 'Aw' ye need now is the lions!'

Chapter One

My first encounter with felines was when I was about three years old. It's also the first memory I have of the start of my existence here on Earth. I was sitting on the cobbles of Moncrieff Terrace in Edinburgh, which was the site of the family home, upstairs at No. 3, and there, stretched out in front of me was a dead cat. I was happily smearing powdered glass into the blood of the animal with a stick, and obviously making a fine old mess.

You may well ask what a three-year-old was doing there in the street, alone and unsupervised, but the year was 1940 and, in those days, there weren't the same dangers for youngsters. I was plastering away when my brother Ian, three years my senior, rounded the corner on his way home from Sciennes Primary School, saw what I was about, and ran upstairs to tell our mother, shouting all the while how much trouble I was in. Inevitably, the window was thrown open and Ma screamed at me to come up immediately. Not thinking what all the fuss was about, I quickly headed upstairs to find myself lying over my mother's knee and having my arse skelped very hard with an open palm. Maybe that's why I seemed to spend the rest of her life not getting on with Ma. Or is that what you call bearing a grudge? Give her her due, she was never one to say, 'Just wait till your father gets home'. Maybe she realised that he wouldn't have meted out such physical punishment, being less of a disciplinarian.

Apart from a skelped arse, I don't remember as much about my mother as I do about my father in these very early years. It was because of my father that Ian and I were the most popular boys in the district. Not that we possessed scintillating personalities, it was more that my father was a lorry driver during the Second World War and, for a part of that period, he transported loads of Bourneville chocolate round the country. During those years of rationing, chocolate was at a premium, but not for the Browne boys. Keep sweet with us and you were fairly sure to get a few bars now and then.

My father was called John Albert Browne and my mother was Anne. Although he was known to everyone else as 'Bert', or 'Bertie', I never ever heard my mother call him anything other than 'Daddy', although he always referred to her as 'Nancy', or 'Dear'. Ian and I called my mother 'Ma', and my father 'Pop.'

Pop was very good with his hands, and I was particularly fascinated to watch him re-soling and heeling our shoes on his cobbler's last. A last comes in various shapes and sizes and Pop's was a piece of heavy metal, curved at both sides. Imagine yourself sitting at a typical upright kitchen chair with your feet firmly planted on the floor and placing this heavy item on your legs with the curved sides down between your thighs. There's a square hole in the middle of this 'plate', into which is fitted another piece of spiked metal with a shoe-shaped top, over which the shoe to be mended is slipped. The necessary tools are: a hammer, a round-headed pair of pliers and a very sharp knife, steeply curved at the end to shape and shave the new leather. With a mouth-full of nails and a pot of glue melting on the gas cooker he was ready to go. Smelly and loud it was, but the end result was always well worth it. It may not have been much cheaper than sending the shoes to the cobbler, but my father found it infinitely more satisfying. As indeed I have, doing odd jobs round the house all my life.

One of the nicest things I remember was a wee motor-car he made by whittling a piece of wood to shape the body. To watch this car emerge from an ordinary slab of wood was, to say the least, exciting, but when he came to make the wheels, that was something else. He had a tin mould, which was in two pieces, into which he pressed some plastic wood. When this had dried, he pulled the two pieces apart to reveal, lo and behold, a perfect wheel. He drilled a hole in the centre and affixed it to the side of the car with a small nail. Once painted and polished, the finished object was just as valuable to me as any of the Dinky Toy Limousines I was given in later years.

Ma was no slouch with her hands either, regardless of her skelping ability. She had been in service as a cook in her early years and taught me how to boil and fry eggs, mix dough and flour for bread and cake-making, and place a porcelain funnel in the middle of the pastry top on a steak pie. She was a dab hand with an embroidery needle too, teaching me a bit of that craft, and many were the nights the family sat round a coal fire making rag rugs to set at the hearth, to stop the sparks burning into the 'good' carpet.

Ma was born in East Wemyss, Fife, on March 20th, 1898, and given the name of Annie Grant Stuart. Her father's name was James Phimister Stuart, Phimister denoting, according to my mother with a certain amount of pride, that we were from a bastard line of Bonnie Prince Charlie. Apart from the Prince, the only references I can find to her family are as coalminers. Her father, for instance, is identified on her birth certificate as a Colliery Engineman which, in my book, is more honourable than being a Jacobite.

I don't know a lot about her background, but I do know quite a bit about my father's, taken from a large, Victorian style Family Bible, together with a couple of military medals and the diaries of great-uncles.

Two years after Ma, in 1900, Pop was born on February 26th in 15 Oxford Street, Edinburgh, and given the name of John Albert Browne, exactly as his father before him, who was born in Blackness Castle, near Bo'ness. This is where the military connection comes in because, in 1862, when my grandfather first saw the light of day, Blackness Castle was an arsenal.

Both of my grandfather's uncles had come over from Limerick, in Ireland, earlier in the 19th century and joined the British Army. I inherited a Crimean War Campaign Medal from one of them, my great –great-uncle Samuel, and a couple of diaries from the other, another John, who was a Proof Sergeant at Woolwich Arsenal. John specialised in the newly acquired Lee Enfield Rifle which was replacing the defunct Brown Bess. In one of his diaries, he mentions meeting some of the crowned heads of Europe at the Paris Universal Exhibition of 1867, where he was exhibiting and demonstrating the new rifle. The medal he received was eventually handed down to me.

In the other of the two diaries he tells of a trip to America where he proof tested 37,000 rifle barrels, travelling extensively across that country. At the beginning of the diary, he writes of a storm which delayed his departure from Liverpool for America, and records his daily expenses together with a tale of dalliance with a Lady of The Night. This last has been all but obliterated in black ink by one of his more prudish Victorian successors. I have placed all of this material, which is of historical interest in military terms, within the Military Museum in Edinburgh Castle.

Born in 1900, Pop would have qualified to fight in the First World War, but the only thing I know for sure is that he and another soldier escorted a prisoner in handcuffs from somewhere in Scotland to Belfast. He and his companion were saved from a lynch mob in Ireland by the prisoner himself, because they had got on very well together on the journey. Later, I'll recount his abilities at 'spit and polish', and as a sharpshooter.

My father was the youngest of four. Robert in 1887, Fanny in 1888, Juliet in 1890 and then, after a rest of ten years, my father in 1900. So, I really did have an Aunt Fanny. She never liked me and I reciprocated. Fanny married a tall, approaching rotund, quiet, very gentle man called John Low but they never had children. You can imagine Fanny's excitement when, in 1934, her younger brother's son was born, my brother, Ian. She welcomed him with open arms and treated him as her own. However, when in 1937 the Usurper, me, came along, her comment to my mother was, 'I don't know why you did that Nancy, one is more than enough.'

In this way began a stand-off between us which ended about nine years later when I stopped visiting her on Sunday afternoons, as Ian and I were always encouraged to do. We were on our way from Buccleuch Street, via Rankeillor Street to her home at 44 St. Leonard's Street, when I stopped in my tracks and left Ian to carry on alone, his warnings that I would be in trouble again ringing in my ears.

In spite of not liking my Aunt Fanny, I did feel compassion for her because she had a club-foot and walked with a severe limp. Might that have been why she received a sympathy vote when my grandmother died and left her everything? As I remember, she was always very well dressed and gave the impression of being better off than us. I have to say though, that I never once heard any word against her from Pop. I wouldn't have heard a word from my Uncle Robert either, because we rarely saw him, except in the street now and again when he would slip us a threepenny bit each.

I don't know what my Aunt Juliet thought about anything because she emigrated to America and married a guy called Charlie Walter in New York in 1912. I never met her, but after her death in 1948, Uncle Charlie, who had become the Mayor of Flemington, New Jersey, visited us briefly and presented me with my first pair of running-spikes, encouraging immensely my blossoming interest in athletics.

I always sensed that I wasn't wanted by Fanny. When, as a toddler, I visited 44 with the family, I used to crawl under her table to take refuge from I know not what, but that was my position always in the room, watching legs walk by. A kitchen-cum-living-room with two windows looking out on to St Leonard's Street, it had a sink in one window and a cupboard in the corner with a gas cooker beside it. In front of the cooker, in a way that seemed ludicrous to me when I got older, a very ornate upholstered easy chair. Crowding the middle of the room was a large mahogany dining table, under which Fanny stacked her laundry basket. It was to this basket, and its content of clothes for the Steamie, that I clung for comfort. Why should I remember it so clearly? Maybe a psychologist could explain.

I think Uncle Johnnie sensed the inequalities in Fanny's affections for Ian and me and didn't like it, because I remember only kindness from him. I called him Poltis but cannot remember why. He must have been a bit older than his wife because, by the time I was visiting under my own steam he had retired from his job at Nelson's Printing Works and become the Weekend Watchman. We would accompany him to the top of Preston Street where Nelson's stood, right opposite my school, and do his rounds with him. The Finished Book Rooms in the print works had, attached round the walls, a system of rollers set at a slight angle. The books would be stacked on boards and laid on the rollers to slide gently towards the packing department. With no one else present, Ian and I would sit on the boards and have fun guiding ourselves round before continuing with Poltis on his rounds.

One office scared us though. For some reason, a lattice blind was always hanging on the window, which meant that the room was in half-light. Seated at the large desk in the middle of the room, in what you might call the customer seat, was a full-sized dummy of a lady dressed in a long skirt, shawl and bonnet. It was really ghostly, particularly since an eerie silence prevailed throughout, it being Sunday. Although going into the room scared us, we couldn't wait to go in and be scared, and there was always an ice-cream for us on the way home.

Uncle Johnnie Low possessed a skill that I never tired

6

watching him perform. He would take a sheet of blank paper and, freehand, without using a ruler, draw perfectly straight lines, exactly equally spaced down the length of the sheet. I tried many times, but with no success, and I've never seen it done again by anyone.

A few years later Fanny died, and my mother suggested that Poltis should come and stay with us. Even my young mind couldn't understand why he accepted, because no one could possibly have put up with her house-proud ways, and so it proved. It lasted two days. Poltis moved into lodgings and spent the rest of his life mostly at his bowling club in the Meadows.

At this point, closing this chapter of early memories, I find there is something I must get off my chest. I don't know when a wee boy is supposed to get interested in his bodily bits and pieces, but my friends and I did from an early age. For instance, most of my pals told me that they had, a 'willie', or a 'queer-thing', or, a 'cock', or, what I really wanted, a 'tadger'. But no, according to my mother I had a 'wumpy'. Oh dear, Ma! Where did a *wumpy* come from? If that had come out in front of my friends, pardon the pun, I would have died of shame. There are some things you can never forgive your parents.

Chapter Two

Wouldn't it be nice to have total recall? Unfortunately, I don't. The only other thing I remember about my stay in Moncrieff Terrace is Frankenstein. Why I would be taken to see a Frankenstein film at the tender age of four or five I can't imagine, but I clearly remember the monster standing at a window in a burning building and his face melting in the flames. It being wartime, there were sandbags in the streets, stairways and shelters, and on the second landing in our stair, the door of the flat at the end of the corridor had a fan-light above it. A couple of sandbags had been placed behind the glass and their silhouette reminded me of Frankenstein's head. That sight scared me so much that, every time I passed I didn't just walk but ran like the wind. Thankfully, we moved.

I do remember quite clearly my first skelped arse at 23a St. Leonard's Bank. Across my mother's knee again, I was feeling very aggrieved, because, as the blows descended, I looked up at a medal suspended on white tape from the mantelpiece. At Preston Street School I had won the medal as dux of the class at the end of my first year and couldn't quite equate my skelped arse with having won a medal for excellence.

St. Leonard's Bank is an Edinburgh street that borders The King's Park. No. 23a was the basement of the building, and, as we ascended the stairs, at the top we were confronted by the glorious sight of The Lion's Head, the extinct volcano which dominates the Edinburgh landscape. Directly across from our

8

house stood Jeannie Deans' Cottage in what was known as The Plantation. That's where the park ranger, Mr McCann, lived with his family. I went to school every morning with the son of the house, Eddie, and that's where I fell in love for the first time. Can you fall in love at age six? I don't know, but that's the best way I can describe my feelings for Eddie's big sister, Maureen. She would never have known because I was too young and shy to speak to her and, anyway, she would not have taken any notice of the snotty kid from across the street. Years later, when I was performing in the *Hootenanny Show* for The BBC in The Place, Victoria Street, I popped into a pub down the hill from the venue, there to find Maureen serving behind the bar. I did speak to her at that time, not that she remembered me, and I found that those first stirrings didn't bother me anymore. Oh fickle heart!

We were in St Leonard's for only a couple of years before moving to No. 3 Buccleuch Street, which was still in the catchment area for Preston Street School. I don't remember Ian being at Pressie, as the school was called, so I assume he stayed on at Sciennes when we moved.

Eddie McCann and I, Billy Hall and Sandy Henderson, all vied for the dux medal over the next few years until we went together to Secondary, and it was during that time that my father took an interest in the match-stick men I had started to draw. I thought that Eddie's more filled-out drawings of Cowboys and Indians were better than my efforts, but Pop encouraged me to start to copy things, the first of which was a Birthday Card showing a simple round face. Over the years this led to bigger and better things until I was completely embarrassed in my final year by the Headmaster, Mr Moffat, insisting that I take a pastel drawing of *Christ Leading the Children* to show round all of the classes.

That work of art led to the first of the two nervous breakdowns I've had in my life, maybe three. This is not something I have spoken of in public before, but it's not the kind of thing you shout from the stage of The Usher Hall. More of those later. First, let's return to when I first realised that I didn't have only one brother, Ian, but another brother and a sister, Big Jim Stuart and Jenny Collie.

As I've said, my mother was born in Fife, where she spent her early years. She appears to have been a bit unfortunate as a teenager because she had two children who didn't know who their father was and had always resented it. Separately, in later life, they told me this. They did not appear to be the off-spring of the man she married when she was 21 years of age in 1919: P. F. Gray, Coalminer. In her divorce papers from this man, dated December 6th, 1930, she is described as a Housekeeper (Spinster), both parties resident at the same address, 55 Bow Street, Denbeath, Fife. Neither of the children is mentioned.

What I find interesting in the papers is that my mother is noted as 'Pursuer' against Peter Forbes Gray as 'Defender', with Rose Janetta, Spinster, 267a Canongate, Edinburgh, and Margaret Briggs 'presently an inmate of Dysart Combination Poorhouse, Thornton, Fife' as 'Co-defenders'.

I showed these papers to my niece, May, the daughter of my brother, Big Jim, but she was as bewildered as I because she understood that my mother had been married, but had never entered the home of her husband because he wouldn't allow her to bring her two children with her.

What I did glean was that my mother, when she was a bit older, left Jim, who was born on December 18th, 1914, when she was 16 years of age, and Jenny, in Buckhaven in the care of her step-mother, whom I knew in childhood as Aunt Betsie. Ma had come to Edinburgh to work in service as a cook on the Wauchope Estates where she met my father who worked as a chauffeur. He helped her with her divorce from Peter Gray, and they were married on January 30th, 1932.

This was confusing for a wee boy, with parents I always felt were very old, and a brother and sister who were both old enough to be my parents, a fact magnified by the knowledge that Jenny's daughter, Norma, my niece, was but one year younger than I. Also in the mix: my cousin, Betty Stuart, also resident in Fife, had a wee boy called Bobby before marrying a man called Vatrick whose name we were never allowed to mention because (this was said in the quietest of quiet whispers): 'He's Polish, you know.'

Years later, Betty and Vatrick attended a Corries concert in Kirkcaldy's Adam Smith Hall and I went to their flat after the show, there sampling Vatrick's home-made beer. In the ensuing conversation, and we weren't talking through drink, because Vatrick was not a drinker, I discovered that he was one of the most gentlemanly, politely soft-spoken souls anybody could meet. I therefore have no hesitation in shouting to the four winds to anyone who is listening that: 'HE WAS POLISH, YOU KNOW!'

Ian and I would be taken by train to spend school holidays with Big Jim, as we always called him, and his wife, Peggy, at 19 Pirnie Street, Methilhill, Fife. We slept on a mattress in the living-room and were fascinated by the life of a miner, which is what Jim was. I used to run to the corner store to buy anthracite for his lamp, although the smell turned my stomach. Jim could not get home quickly enough from his shift to entertain us by accompanying music on the radio, tapping out a rhythm on his teeth with the stem of his pipe.

When we weren't digging into the pit bings, burnt waste from the mines, to release the flames from the simmering shale underground, we were probably playing an exciting game in the air-raid shelter at the end of Pirnie Street. A circle of chairs would be laid out and the boys of the district would sit down leaving one chair free. The girls would stand behind all of the chairs and the girl behind the empty chair would wink at one of the boys she fancied. If he fancied her, he would make a dive for her empty chair and, if he made it, she would reward him with a kiss. If he didn't fancy the winker, but preferred the girl standing behind him, and she fancied him, he would make

11

not too much of an effort to get away, making it easy for her to hold him back so that she could reward him with a kiss. The boys would then change places in the chairs with the girls and the game would start all over again, the result being that, invariably, everybody was a winner. It was all very innocent, not like today, when the kids seem to dispense with the chairs, the winks and the kisses and cut to the chase and jump into bed. Thinking of my mother though, let's draw a veil at this point.

Visits to Aunt Betsie usually ended up in a run down to the Buckhaven beach and the small fishing boats to grab a live crab in one hand and a lobster in the other. Running back to Betsie's house we would drop the beasts into a big cauldron of boiling water on a large coal fire in the fireplace. On a shelf above the fire sat a two-foot tall glass dome, within which stood a glass ship in full sail with tiny blue-glass sailors clinging to the rigging. Those were our school holidays.

Most Sundays in Edinburgh, during school term-time, I would take a tram to my sister Jenny's house at 80a Great King Street, where I would play with her kids, Norma and Brian. Jenny married her husband, Johnnie Collie, before I was born. I have no recollection of him as a guest in our house, the reason being, obviously, that he and my mother didn't get on. He wasn't even Polish.

Uncle Johnnie, as I called him before I learned that he was actually my brother-in-law, had a brother, Bill married to Nan, and they of course became my Uncle Bill and Auntie Nan. Afternoon visits on Sundays to Jenny's house became alternate visits on Sunday evenings to Bill and Nan's, where we played cards and darts. I was always made to feel more than welcome there, the reason being, as they told me later in life, they felt a bit sorry for me. As they put it, 'Your mother was a bit quick with her hands.' My arse bore painful testimony to that.

Two tram-cars took me to Jenny's, a number 27 from Forrest Road, changing to a number 23 on Hanover Street at The

Mound (or was it the other way around?). At the tram-stop on Hanover Street stood a jeweller's shop. Down a flight of five steps, the window seemed always to display collections of Japanese Ivory chess-sets, carvings and, most fascinating of all to me, examples of Netsukes. A Netsuke is a small toggle, usually made of ivory or wood in the shape of human and animal figures, used to secure a purse or container suspended on a sash on a Kimono. Looking at these exquisite objects at such an early age began a lifelong interest in them and Japanese carvings in general. Strangely enough, the first carving which came into my possession was given by Jenny or, more precisely, through Jenny when she became manager of a hotel owned by a man called Murray.

Murray, and that's all I ever called him, was a very high and powerful Union Representative whose wife had been given, when she was a girl, an eighteen-inch tall Japanese wooden statue of *A Mendicant Priest* by a sea captain on his return from the Far East. She kept it all her life, finally placing it on a shelf in the hall of the hotel. As a teenager, I worked there after school, and did I not covet that standing figure? Murray never understood my liking for it since he thought it grotesque. When his wife died he passed it on to me. I'm sure that, if he were alive today, he would appreciate even more the profuse thanks I offered at the time because I have kept it all of my life. Indeed, it is standing on an intricately carved Japanese wooden table not six feet from where I am writing at this very moment, unlike some other carvings and chess-sets which I had to sell to help save our bacon when we fell on hard times.

I was to be in Buccleuch Street for the next four years, so, why don't I show you around?

Our flat was on the corner of Buccleuch Street and West Crosscauseway, sitting above an office/shop complex at Number 1 and entered through a stairway at Number 3. Walk into the stairway for about five metres and you have, facing you, a double glazed doorway which leads into the joiner's yard of a Mr Baillie. He encouraged me to come into his workshop to watch his men at work, sometimes to help by making a small cut on a plank, a start for the saw, or supporting a large piece of wood they were working on, or simply demonstrating the mechanics of circular saws and other equipment on the bench. Never was I made to feel that I was in the way. I would return the compliment by sweeping up sawdust and shavings or perhaps running an errand for one of the men.

Turn right at Baillie's door and proceed up the stairs to the first landing where ours is the first flat you'll see. Turn right again along the landing and you'll come to the next flat, cheek by jowl with ours, that of the Weinstein family. Say it in a whisper, (we seemed to do a lot of whispering), 'Of course, they're German Jews, you know.' Turn right again at their door and proceed further up the stairs to find, facing you, Tommy Hand's abode. Tommy had a Scottish Country Dance Band, and, since that was where they practised and rehearsed, we always heard a lot from them. Tommy's mother, Maggie Hand, lived opposite at Number 4 and she had a sure-fire cure for cramp of the foot or lower leg. Simply stick your foot down your toilet and pull the plug. I tried it once and, of course, my foot got stuck, so never again.

Mrs Turnbull and her son, Jimmy, are next to Tommy and are the last family in the stair. They were constantly visiting Mr Turnbull in hospital where he was suffering from, and here's another whisper, 'Sleeping Sickness.' Sleeping Sickness, I have since discovered, is caused by the bite of a Tsetse Fly which has its abode in Africa, so I assume Mr Turnbull was infected during a foreign campaign in the war which had just ended, or perhaps it was simply a euphemism for some kind of mental disorder. Whatever it was, I never saw hide nor hair of him all the time I lived in the district.

Okay, let's go into the flat.

Open the front door and you're in a narrow hall. On the

left is the door to the kitchen and, following the hall to the right, you come to the door into the toilet. That's all it is, just a toilet bowl, no bath, not even a hand-basin. You won't see any rolls of toilet paper either but just squares of newspaper tied together with string and hooked on a nail.

Facing you as you enter the kitchen are two windows. Moving to the right-hand one, the smaller of the two, you pass a standing cupboard and a sink with a short draining board. If you raise the window, you'll find a meat-safe. This is simply a box sealed to the window-frame and it has fine mesh panels at top and three sides. 'No fridge?' you ask. No, that was it!

Stand at the sink with your left shoulder towards the window, and you'll find your arse is jammed against the gas cooker. On the wall to the right is suspended a gas geyser water-heater with its tiny pilot-light glowing blue. Below that you'll find two glasses each containing, first thing in the morning, a set of false teeth, deposited there the night before by my father and mother.

Along the wall from the cooker is the large window which looks on Baillie's yard and, outside the window, a T-shaped clothes pulley. The next wall is filled with an open coal fire. Finally, you turn into an alcove with another standing cupboard. In the middle of the room stands a plain, scrubbed, white-wood table with a hinged flap at the window end, and four plain kitchen chairs rammed underneath.

Coming out of the kitchen into the hall, you'll find half-a-dozen coat-hooks. Ahead of you is a corner coalhouse and, as the hall turns sharp right, a door on your left into the lounge and a door in front of you into my parents' bedroom. Move into the lounge and you're in the room which is on the corner of the property, one window on the right looking on West Crosscauseway, the other on Buccleuch Street. In the middle of the room stands a mahogany oval table on a central column of three curved legs with casters. On the left are two large padded armchairs standing either side of an open fireplace and the door to my bedroom, which I share with Ian, on the end of that wall.

The window in my bedroom looks out on to Buccleuch Street, so let's open it and see what we can see. Directly opposite is a four-storey tenement, number 2. The tenement wall is attached to a high church wall at the start of Chapel Street which takes you right, and on towards Edinburgh University's McEwan Hall, where Graduation Ceremonies take place. Further along you would find the Royal Infirmary. To the left, the street snakes down to the Royal Dick Veterinary building which stands facing the Meadows, or, in our colloquial slang, the 'Meedies'. Both the Royal Infirmary and the Dick Vet have now moved to different sites.

Opening my parents' bedroom window you would be confronted with, on the left, Chapel Street Church, behind its high wall, and, on the right, another church, Buccleuch & Greyfriars Free Church of Scotland, in West Crosscauseway. The Chapel Street Church always had better *pooroots* than the Free Church. A *pooroot*, or 'pour out', was the traditional practice of bride and groom saving small change for their wedding day and throwing it from the window of their bridal carriage as they left the church to the eagerly awaiting local waifs. If we were really lucky, we might find the odd threepenny bit or sixpence amongst the pennies and halfpennies in the scramble.

The space between these churches of Chapel Street and West Crosscauseway was a cobbled triangular area dominated, and dissected, by a large cast iron horse-trough. This space was popular with us kids for playing *bools* (marbles), in the grooves between the cobbles, and *peevers* (hop-scotch), on the pavements in front of the churches. It was also a convenient space to light our bonfires each year, although, invariably, the fire brigade was called to douse them for fear of the heat breaking the glass in the windows of nearby houses. You would also see, in an open space just down from the Free Church, a concrete air raid shelter in the spot where the large space narrowed down to West Crosscauseway proper.

I've mentioned that we had no bathroom in the house and no fridge. In addition, we had neither freezer, washing machine, dish-washer, telephone, television nor Hoover. I can almost hear the youngsters saying, 'How could they survive without a mobile or iPad to break their fingers on?'

We did have a radio for entertainment, and Pop rigged up a loudspeaker attachment in our bedroom so that, late on a Saturday night, Ian and I could lie in bed and be scared by the very deep voice of a presenter called Valentine Dyall, who would say to his listeners after telling one of his famous ghost-stories, '. . . and this is your storyteller, the Man In Black, saying Good-night to you.'

At this point your story-teller, Ronnie Browne, starts the story proper of where I suppose, my life really began.

Chapter Three

I can't promise that everything will be in perfect chronological order, but what I can say, without any fear of contradiction, is that this is when what I'll call, 'The Weinstein Saga' began.

Within the first few days of occupying Buccleuch Street, Ma made the acquaintance of Mrs Turnbull upstairs, who suggested that perhaps in moving here we had bitten off more than we would be able to chew. When questioned further on the subject, Mrs Turnbull explained that her wee boy, Jimmy, had gone in fear of his life through all his young years because of the Weinsteins who lived below her. To an adult, I suppose, it wouldn't have seemed much, but to wee Jimmy it was really quite frightening to wake every morning to the banging of a brush on his floor from the flat below and a voice shouting to him to make less bloody noise. To be passed in the street and be given hostile, silent, malevolent stares from a close neighbour, as he was in the habit of receiving, and for that same neighbour, most times when he passed her door, to open it and glare at him, continuing that glare as he progressed upwards, could be most unsettling to a wee person.

A wee person he certainly was, because, although we were the same age, he was only half my size. Half my size he may have been but I think he must have had twice my brain capacity because, did he not end up in later life, a scientist? Where did I end up, but singing for my supper? Wait while I put my fiddle away. Jimmy used to tell me how he always ran past the Weinsteins' door. I remembered my own terror at the Frankenstein sandbags and fully sympathised.

Mrs Turnbull's warning proved prophetic because, only a few days later, *The Saga* began to unfold. As far as we could tell, Mrs Weinstein was housebound and at home by herself all day. Mr Weinstein was a butcher of sorts and out all day plucking chickens, if the feathers clinging to his clothing were anything to go by. It seems he held himself aloof from all the trouble that was to come our way because none of us remember hearing a word pass his lips. Come to think of it, I don't remember hearing much from Mrs Weinstein. Hilda, the daughter of the house, was a different kettle of fish. Also out all day, she was a scaffie or, to use more modern, politically correct nomen-clature, a street-cleanser. She was a thick-set lady (I use the term loosely), probably in her mid-twenties when we moved in, with thick, dark, somewhat windswept hair. She always wore trousers, which was unusual for women when I was a boy. Always too short, they exposed sturdy ankles, and she had very dark eyes that stared from a wild-looking countenance to terrify poor wee Jimmy.

How do bad relationships arise between neighbours? In our case, it was something as simple as a few of Mr Weinstein's feathers falling from his jacket and wafting over to our front door where they became lodged. Ma, being the house-proud woman she was (she changed her window-curtains throughout the house at least three times a year), would tidy them away at the earliest opportunity and, no doubt, complain to Mrs Weinstein. Possibly Mrs Weinstein would retaliate by telling my mother not to be so silly, I don't know. Whatever happened, bad blood did arise and continued and would erupt on occa-sions. Hilda would come in from work and her mother would describe one of these niggles with Ma, whereupon Hilda, perhaps being a bit over-sensitive, and maybe sensing some hint of persecution, would shout through our wall in a banshee wail, something like, 'Browneeeeeee!' (you will have noticed that my name is spelt with an 'e' on the end). 'Browneeeeeee, it's a damn disgrace! Ah'll thank you tae keep yer tongue off ma mother or you'll be sorry, Ah'm tellin' ye.'

Or sometimes when a washing had been put out on our pulley at the window, 'Browneeeeeee, it's a damn disgrace! That poor wee laddie's shirts are still filthy. You should be bloody-well ashamed o' yersels'.'

Years later, when the poor wee laddie had grown up and married in 1959, Pat and I were living round the corner at 5 West Crosscauseway, three flights upstairs, our kitchen window overlooking Ma's window and the Weinsteins'. Having had our first child, Gavin, in 1961, and returning home of a Sunday evening after a visit to my in-laws, the lights going on in the flat became the signal for, 'Browneeeeeee, it's a damn disgrace! Keepin' that poor wee bairn oot till this time o' the night, you should be bloody-well ashamed o' yersels.'

Of course, on many occasions, the police would be called but, in spite of their taking statements from neighbours who had heard the shennanigans, since no blows had ever been struck, and nobody had ever been harmed except by a bit of name-calling, it was always put down as 'a Domestic', and they would proceed to spend their valuable time on some other, more worthy crime.

Only once did it threaten to become really serious. It was Hilda's turn to 'do' the stair. She had brushed it down and doused it with hot water, mopping it all up into her bucket which, by the end of the operation, was a swirling, smelly mix of greasy water filled with used matches, fag-ends, chicken feathers, spiders entwined in their webs, old chips dropped from discarded fish-suppers, trodden-on sweeties with their sweetie-papers and, I've no doubt, although at my tender age knowing nothing about it, the odd spent condom. The bucket was balanced at the top of the stair on the corner of the landing with the mop beside it and Hilda with brush in hand, when my mother opened our door and made a comment such as, 'Well, I hope ye made a better job of it than ye did the last time!'

This was a red rag to Hilda, who raised her brush and took a swipe at Ma as she swiftly closed the door. The dent in the lower left panel was still there when I moved out years later. Just at that moment, Pop appeared halfway up the stairs coming home from work, dressed, as was his wont, in cap and scarf atop his air force blue, forces' supplement, double-breasted, belted overcoat and, peeking out from underneath, his highly polished working shoes. Realising that they were at it again, he exclaimed, 'Now ladies!', when , all of a sudden, the bucket was in Hilda's hands, and she shouted, 'An' as for you!!!!' and poor old Pop was covered, speechless, from head to toe in the matches, grease, spiders, et al, the condom hanging from the pipe which was never out of his mouth.

Realising that this time she had gone too far, Hilda grabbed mop, brush, and bucket and disappeared behind her door. After the Polis left an uneasy silence descended which lasted for fourteen years. Until it all started up again.

Unlike Jimmy Turnbull, I wasn't intimidated at all. Maybe I thought it was all too stupid, or maybe I was into so many other things it didn't touch me so much.

'We'll Dib, Dib, Dib.'
'We'll Dob, Dob, Dob.'
'Yes, Akela.'
'No, Akela.'
'Of course, Akela, I'll do a good deed for someone every
   day.'

By now I was a wolf cub, attached to the 79th Newington Boy Scout Troop with Headquarters in Nicholson Street Church, whose Church Hall backed on to the Church Hall of the Buccleuch and Greyfriars Free Church Hall. I've explained that it stood opposite our house, but the front of the church was round the corner from West Crosscauseway in Nicholson Street. Although I never saw my mother and father attend any of the churches, they encouraged Ian and me, nay, forced us, to join both the Cubs, and, in Ian's case, the Scouts, and we couldn't very well enjoy youth organisations without also going to the Sunday School and Church to which they were attached. I must say, I didn't mind at all. I enjoyed those days, as did my parents.

My mother took a delight in baking scones, tarts, cakes etc. for sale at fund-raising events for the Church, such as whist-drives and sewing-bees. On one occasion my father really went to town, displaying his artistic talents by making a costume for me to compete in a Cub fancy dress competition. He fashioned a sword out of a piece of wood with a scabbard made of hessian, as were the Viking tunic and chaps, tied round with tape. He took one of Ma's oval, metal, grooved jelly moulds and attached wings to the sides for a helmet. Who knows, maybe he got them from Mr Weinstein because, as you might know, there can be great cameraderie between men whilst their women-folk are at each other's throats.

My beard was made with upholstery horse-hair stuck to shaped canvas (Pop refurbished chairs as well), and my shield was made from a circle of wood with a dragon design picked out in round-topped upholstery tacks. He insisted that he be there to dress me on the night and to apply the finishing touches of make-up to face, legs and arms before I presented myself at the Church Hall. He forgot though, that Cubs are youngsters and the competition would take place early in the evening. By the time he got home from work, completed the costume and got us to the hall, it was all over. A compensatory 2/6 (two shillings and sixpence, 12 1/2p in today's money), was awarded, but I don't know if he thought it was worth all that effort. I'm sure he would happily have given up the money for the glory of winning.

Chapter Four

Alcoholic beverages were never seen in our house except at Hogmanay when every door was wide open to accept First Footers bearing small gifts of shortbread, black bun, and a lump of coal. A wee dram would be offered to accompany the tit-bits. My father's favourite tipple was Fowler's Wee Heavy, a very dark, strong ale made in Prestonpans and sold in a small bottle. Pop wasn't in the habit of indulging, so when he'd had a few of these wee devils, they went to his head in no mean fashion. This manifested itself in a first stage of false confidence, enough to make him want to stand up and sing his party piece:-

'Trumpeter, what are you sounding now?
Is it the call I'm seeking?'

When the second stage of inebriation kicked in he forgot the words, his knees buckled slightly and his head started to swoon, forcing him to grab for a seat. End of performance. This same scenario was played out every year and we never ever found out what the trumpeter was sounding.

In a whisper, naturally, with a slight cock of the head, a false, shy smile, and in a very posh voice, Ma would ask for, 'Just a small sherry, please.' It sounded as though she had already been at the small sherries on the quiet in the kitchen.

It was at these gatherings that I first started to sing in public.

23

I would stand up, crippled with embarrassment, and give out in a sweet, but trembling soprano:-

'Ave Maria . . .'

I always managed to finish the song, but couldn't sit down again quickly enough. I had a certain amount of confidence because I was now singing in a choir, but choirboy singing, surrounded and supported by all your chorister friends, is entirely different to singing solo.

St Peter's Episcopal Church had its home in Lutton Place, parallel to East Preston Street where Pressie stood, and so it followed that the school was a natural recruiting centre for cherubic choirboys such as myself and other reprobates like Sandy Henderson, Billy Hall and Billy Campbell. What appealed to all of us was, not so much singing in church twice on a Sunday, but the 2/6 we were paid each week for doing it, and also the Wednesday evening boxing club in the Church Hall following choir practice. I'll admit we all felt like ponces in our red surplices with the stiff, fluted white collars. It's amazing what we'll do for money all through life.

Singing in church on Sundays never interfered with listening to *Two Way Family Favourites* on the radio. If I had been a BBC programme planner then I have to say that I too would have ensured that the shows were slotted *between* church services. Presenting on that day meant a virtually captive audience. Lest you don't grasp the import of what I'm saying, since Sundays today are just like any other day of the week, when I was a boy very little was allowed to happen on the Day of Rest. People will tell you that you couldn't even whistle on a Sunday, and that's not far from the truth. I wore my good clothes only on that day.

These were the years just after the end of World War II, when many British and Allied troops were still billeted in Europe, particularly Germany, and aching to be home. Cliff Michelmore was there with them, while his wife to be, Jean Metcalfe, was back in London, together hosting this very sentimental radio request programme.

Favourites of 'Two-way' were *Les Compagnons de la Chanson* with their rendering of the song, 'Jimmy Brown'.

'There is a chapel, hidden deep in the valley,
Among the mountains high above . . .',

Vera Lynn herself sang,

'There'll be blue-birds over
The white cliffs of Dover . . .'

Josef Locke's weekly radio programme, *The White Horse Inn*, was where I picked up some of my first songs, such as 'Pedro the Fisherman', 'Goodbye', and 'Hear my Song, Violetta'. It was this last which saw me in my very first stage performance.

Each year the 79th Newington Scout Troup would mount one of the fund-raising ventures I talked of earlier. Of course, it wasn't all about money. It was just as much a consolidating event to strengthen the ties between the Cubs, Scouts, and, I should say, also the girls of the Guide Movement attached to Nicholson Street Church. Everybody was encouraged to take part and we did so enthusiastically. My contribution was to sing the song I had learned from Josef Locke, 'Hear my Song, Violetta', dressed in a tight-fitting shirt which nowadays would be called a T-shirt, with round neck and short sleeves, coloured in narrow stripes of pink and light purple. (A few years later I wore it when I first played rugby and it gave rise to my school nick-name of 'Pedro'.) I wore a garish pair of silk pantaloons with a wide sash at my waist and topped the lot with a black beret and a black curled false moustache.

Tightly gripping my mandolin I pretended to accompany myself (accompaniment actually came from a piano on the hall floor, stage right), whilst I sang the song, standing precariously on a four-wheeled wooden go-cart with a cardboard gondola silhouette nailed on. I was serenading Skinny Reid, standing in a make-shift wooden balcony halfway up the back stage wall that showed a painted scene of Venice. Skinny was bedecked in a long, blonde wig and full make-up, dressed in one of his mother's evening dresses with a couple of oranges stuffed down his chest to signify that he was, indeed, a damsel. My 'gondola' was attached to a pulley of ropes controlled in the wings by, two on each side, senior Rover Scouts, the Dryllie brothers and the Biggars, who pulled me across the stage. The show ran for a week and, on a couple of nights, as I reached my top note while passing Skinny, the gondola gave a wobble and I was almost tossed out. Was that wobble caused by the reverberation from my powerful voice, or was it a pre-arranged sideways tug on the ropes? Only The Rovers could say.

In another production, *Cinderella*, Ian took the part of Dandini, Prince Charming's right-hand man, in a powder blue costume with tights and high-heeled, buckled shoes. He wore a huge white curly wig and strutted around at rehearsals trying to impress the Guides. It was my turn for the oranges, I remember, but I don't recall a singing part.

A Sunday-school play marked my final exit from Nicholson Street Church. We had a Sunday School Superintendent called Mr Wishart who seemed to be into everything and he it was who took control of the play, acting as director, stage-manager, scene-painter, etc. At the end of one of the Acts he rushed out of the wings and burst through a door at the edge of the stage, only to be confronted by my friend Dinah. Just a wee girl, she was waiting for her cue at the top of a short flight of steps when Wishart crashed into her and, with a snarl, grabbed her by the shoulders and forced her back down the steps and against a wall, where he shouted at her to keep out of the way.

Dinah was shocked and not surprisingly, burst into tears. I witnessed the whole incident and thought to myself that, if this is the kind of behaviour we were to expect from this so-called 'paragon of all the virtues', then it wasn't for me. I stopped attending both Sunday School and Church. I realise now that it was probably worry and overwork that brought on his rage, but I was profoundly unimpressed at the time.

Like most wee boys I was given a certain amount of pocket-money. One day I visited our local sweetie-shop and there I bought a couple of packets of sweetie cigarettes, which came with two 'cigarette cards'. They showed images such as racing cars, ships, or famous footballers. I was flashing them about the house when my father reached over the table, grabbed my arm, took the cards and said, 'Where did these come from?'

I thought that I was about to get a row for wasting my money on such rubbish, so I made up a story. I told him that I had been given them by my class-mate, John Todd.

'Is that right?' said my father, 'and where does he live?' When I told him, Park Side Street, he said, 'Let's go then,' rose from his seat and started to put on his coat. Struck dumb, I followed him out of the house and ran along beside him. In Montague Street, half-way to Parkside, I piped up with, 'No, I've just remembered, it wasn't John Todd, it was George Valentine, and he lives down at Prestonfield'.

Completely unabashed, Pop stopped, said never a word, and started back towards our house. He had known I was lying from the word go and wanted to teach me a lesson, which he certainly had. That was his way though. One day when I was even younger, I was out walking with him when, on the pavement opposite the McEwan Hall, an old down-and-out stopped him and said, 'Could you spare a bob for a bite to eat, Guv?'

Pop dug in his pocket and fished out a shilling which he handed to the old guy. We walked on one way, the old guy in the opposite direction. After a couple of paces, Pop stopped and gently turned me round. Looking down at me, never saying a word, he put a finger to his eye for a second, took it away and pointed after the old man. I followed his gesture and watched as the old man turned into a pub.

Why had I lied in the first place? It was my pocket-money I had spent, and that's only to the tune of about four pence. It was perfectly legitimate for me to have done so.

A French psychologist once wrote a treatise on the works of the sculptor, Sir Henry Moore, in which he explained why Moore created the shapes and textures he did. He handed it to Moore to read. Sir Henry looked at the first couple of pages and shook his head, closed it and handed it back, saying that, if he knew why he did what he did, he was in danger of not wanting to do it anymore. If that psychologist is out there and possibly reading this book, perhaps he'd be kind enough to explain to me my actions that day, 'cos it's got me beat.

We used to play cards, gambling with cigarette-cards, hiding up a stairway. We also played a game called 'Droppie', where you held a card against a wall at about shoulder height and let it fall to the ground. This process was repeated again and again, each player taking a turn until one card dropped on top of another, at which point that 'dropper' collected all of the fallen cards.

Bringing these reminiscences to mind reminds me of one time I really did deserve a skelped arse.

When the war had finished, most of the air raid shelters were demolished. Ours in West Crosscauseway suffered that fate, leaving a flat piece of ground of about twenty square metres, a natural football pitch for us, much to the consternation of the householders who feared broken windows.

One day a lady, whose window we were playing far too close to, reprimanded us in a loud voice, calmly picked up our ball, deposited it in her shopping-bag and disappeared through her door. When we realised that we were not getting it back, I picked up a stone and threw it through her window. Where I got the gall to do it, I don't know, but over the loud crash of breaking glass we scattered to the four winds. Word went round that it was the laddie Browne who had done it, and a deputation of the lady and her husband duly presented itself at our door.

Ma and Pop invited them into the living-room where Ian, who was known more than I as the 'laddie Browne', was sitting with his legs crossed in my father's armchair. It was Ian who was accused. I was sprawled on the carpet reading a comic and, since he defended himself very well, kept my mouth shut. As my parents couldn't believe that I might have been the culprit (their younger son wouldn't do a thing like that), the incident passed with no one being called to account. Of course, Ian knew but didn't spill the beans, protecting me from what would have been a well-deserved punishment.

I wouldn't want you to think of me as a snivelling little lying coward although, obviously, I was on that occasion. So allow me to demonstrate how I made amends, at least in my own opinion.

Fourth year at Boroughmuir Senior Secondary School. Class 4A enters the science lab on the top floor of the building. Inflated balloons are suspended on strings from the gas jets on the work-benches around the room, the result of the previous class's experiment. Smartarse Ronnie, together with half-a-dozen other smartarses, goes round the pipes unhooking the balloons and watch them soar upwards to bounce on the ceiling of the Lab. It seemed funny at the time. But, once done? Yes, accept the consequences, which followed minutes later when the science teacher came in. She didn't have to ask who had done it; we saw the question in her eyes. I don't know if I consciously remembered the guilt and shame of all those years before and wanted to erase it in one glorious act of self-sacrifice, but I leapt to my feet and put up my hand. Unfortunately, I was the only one who did.

When I told Ian this story years later, he simply laughed out loud and told me how much I deserved the six-of-the-best I received from the headmaster, Bob Carswell. Watching the tongs of his leather Lochgelly belt descending, six times, all on the one hand, I reflected that there was no point really in everyone being punished if only one person could sop it all up. I felt really self-righteous, particularly when Ronnie Ronaldson told me that one of the girls in the class, Moira Ponton (to this day nobody knows I fancied her!), told him that, as far as she was concerned there was only one man in the class.

The Empire Theatre wasn't far from us and, as often as not, that's where we spent our Saturday nights. Ian and I would run up the road ahead of our folks and stand in the queue for the gods, the cheap seats. Ma and Pop would join us later at, usually, the head of the queue, buy the tickets, and then Ian and I would scamper to the top of the theatre and bag four seats at the front. Around this time the first nude performances began, in the form of 'living statues', where none of the nude figures was allowed to move a muscle. I remember thinking it strange that it was only women who were allowed to take their clothes off. On the way home we called in to May's Chip Shop on Bristo Street for a fish-supper and got home in time to listen to Valentine Dyall's ghost story.

Circuses used to come to perform in the Empire and the animals would be billeted at the bottom of Buccleuch Street. On their way back and forward during the week or so of performances, they would stop at the horse-trough at our triangular piece of the roadway for refreshment. I don't know if you're aware of what elephant dung does for rhubarb, but I'm an expert.

Ma was developing an allotment over in the Meedies, as people were encouraged to do after the war. Rationing was still in force, and growing your own fresh food was deemed a wonderful thing to do. Where Ma learned about the magical properties of the elephant, I don't know, but whenever she saw one relieving itself at the trough, she would rush me down with a bucket and shovel.

Elephant dung is a bit like a rabbit's, only on a much larger scale. Although it drops from a great height it retains its solid round shape, making it easy to pick up even in the hands. With the trough beside me it was easy to get clean again. If the elephant was out of sorts, it could splatter a bit, but, if you're nimble on your feet, there's no problem. On many an occasion, my mother had the longest, reddest, thickest rhubarb in the district and it was win, win for everybody because my mother got her rhubarb, I got sixpence a bucket, and it saved Hilda the work.

In this day and age, people complain about the rate of inflation, but that's nothing new. When I was about nine years of age, I was entrusted to 'go the messages' on a Saturday morning, while we were still in a state of food-rationing. Our ration-books were a sort of dirty pink in colour, the sheets scored into squares, and we had to present so many of these for whatever we were buying. A loaf of bread, the first time I bought one, cost fourpence-farthing with a quarter of a coupon. The first rise in price I remember was to fourpence-halfpenny, a full farthing, which was the lowest value of currency. Four farthings in a penny is a one seventeenth increase which, if my calculations are correct, makes that roughly a 6% rise.

I used to 'go the messages' (i.e. go shopping) on a Saturday morning to the Nicholson Street Co-op, locally known as, 'the Store', either before the New Vic Club or after it. The New Vic Club was a Saturday morning film show for the kids and was shown in the New Victoria Cinema, later to become the Odeon. We used to shout and roar encouragement at the antics of the Lone Ranger and Tonto, or Tom Mix, or Roy Rogers. The Three Stooges and Charlie Chaplin were favourites in the comedy line. I elected to go before or after depending on whether or not I was playing football for the school that day. I didn't always get to play, because I was rubbish at the game, only discovering, when I went to Boroughmuir Senior Secondary School that the ball was the wrong shape for me.

In the Store we would queue at a counter of plain, scrubbed wood, and hand our shopping list to an assistant who would scurry around the shop collecting them.

Sugar had to be scooped into brown paper bags. Bread came in plain or pan, and there was no such thing as a wrapped, sliced loaf. You put it in your shopping bag as you got it. The assistant ticked off your list and wrote down all you had received on a piece of headed paper, took your money and made a note of your membership number (in our case 77287 and God help my erse if I forgot) on your receipt, placed both inside a brass tube, twisted the tube closed, and put it inside what can best be described as a pneumatic pipe. You could listen to it rattling its way up the tube to the top of the hall and along the corner of the ceiling, finally arriving in the accounts department where it was checked and sent back with any change required.

You were then free to stuff all your goods into your message bag and head home.

I always made sure I had sixpence in my pocket because Saturday mornings were when the Newhaven Fishwife set up her stall on the corner of Nicholson Street/West Richmond Street. Her 'stall' was simply her large wicker fish basket with a tray on top. For the princely sum of sixpence I got a saucer of mussels in their own fresh brine, which I ate on the spot, my message bag balanced on the pavement between my legs, and a poke (paper bag) of buckies to eat on the way home, with a pin included in the price. With a heavy message bag strapped over one arm, the fist of that arm clutching the poke, a couple of fingers meanwhile extricating a buckie, and the hand with the pin scraping off the crust of the buckie to get at the twirled up flesh inside, sometimes I did wonder if it was worth all the effort. But, of course it was.

'Divi-Day' for us was like a holiday. As a family, we trooped to the Co-op Headquarters in Bread Street and joined the queue to find what bounty was coming our way, our dividend (percentage return) from the annual total 77287 spend, hopeful that there would be enough to afford what we kids had been told we might expect 'Fae The Divi.'

I knew the area around Bread Street very well because I used to go a lot to Reigo Street just round the corner to buy horse meat and whale meat which we ate a lot during the War.

Chapter Five

A very small, cuddly lady called Mrs Greig lived round the corner from us at 5 West Crosscauseway. Unfortunately, she spoke with a lisp, which made it difficult at times to understand what she was saying except, every now and then, she went into a trance and the lisp disappeared. Mrs Greig was a spiritualist medium and when her 'guides' took control, they spoke in their own voices which were crystal clear.

My mother met Mrs Greig as a neighbour, and it was she who persuaded Ma to go to her first spiritualist meeting. She was hooked from the word go and had been to two or three of these 'meetings' before my father found out. Immediately he did, he hit the roof. Ma persisted, and so did he, until after many months of heated rows and recriminations, it all changed.

By this time she had befriended another medium who, one day, came to visit for a cup of tea, a bite of shortbread and a blether. When my father came in from work he was his usual polite, gentlemanly self, but, knowing the friend's status as a medium, couldn't resist one of his shakes of the head, accompanied by an almost silent, 'grr'. After busying himself about the house he settled in his armchair beside the ladies, lit his pipe and proceeded to read his evening paper. After a short while he rose and made his way to the window of the living room, where the two women were sitting, and looked outside. With another shake of the head, he looked out of the other window and shook his head again. He returned to his seat and continued to smoke and read, but not for long. Again he rose and walked round the room with his ear cocked, obviously listening for something.

What he heard was a dog barking and a male voice shouting. With a look of consternation, his interest finally settled on my mother's visitor who, noticing his furrowed brow, gave a slight smile but said nothing. My mother couldn't help but ask what was wrong. On hearing my father's explanation, she asked her visitor: 'Would you mind?' With a nod from her friend, my mother directed Pop's head to the friend's abdomen and requested that he place his ear against her diaphragm. He complied and, with an exclamation of astonishment, realised that the sounds were emanating from within her body. He sat down rather heavily in his chair and looked at my mother who explained that what my father had been hearing were the sounds of the medium's guide, not only a shepherd but his dog as well.

Whatever it was that my father heard it turned a ranting, raving sceptic into a dedicated believer. Not only did he attend meetings thereafter with my mother, he also encouraged and assisted her to 'develop' into a medium in her own right. 'Developing' seems to be a state of meditation. I am not here attempting to convert anyone or try to explain what I don't understand myself, suffice to say that the ranting and raving stopped.

My mother did eventually become a medium in her own right and conducted seances, or 'meetings', as we called them, in the confines of her very own living-room, assisted and abetted by the converted sceptic, Pop.

I know that it's difficult to accept this kind of thing, and I also know that, unless you've had an experience like Pop's, you are likely to ridicule people such as my mother, my father and, yes, myself, who have all had such a revelation. During my mother's 'meetings', Ian and I were banished to the kitchen. Ian had been learning a bit of unarmed combat and, one night, was determined to teach me how to disarm any assailant coming at me with a large kitchen knife, such as the one he had in his hand. The knife was indeed a large one, with a long blade and wooden handle, and he held it in his right fist, his arm raised at head height, ready to strike.

He explained that I had to face him and raise my left open hand and grasp his right wrist, the back of my hand turned towards my face. I had then to take my right arm under his raised right arm and turn my arm under his elbow and over his forearm to grasp my own hand, thereby locking his elbow. He explained that, in such a lock, by applying force forward with my left arm and body, I could break his arm, making him release the knife and probably stopping the threat of any further violence. In a real life scenario this would all have to be done almost as one movement in order to be successful. We practised a few times in slow motion before turning up the speed.

We should have dispensed with the knife but, boys being boys, we didn't, and the inevitable happened. The knife slipped out of Ian's hand during one of the moves and sliced through the top of my index finger and the top of my middle knuckle. The scars, although faint, are still there. We tried in vain to stop the bleeding but, although we had been warned never to disturb a meeting in progress, we didn't really have any option. It was then I observed the most unusual sight of Ian receiving not just one row for stopping the spooks in their tracks, but another for instigating the battle in the first place.

By this time my father had stopped moving chocolate about the country and was now driving a van for the Container Recovery Service, the CRS, a recycling organization. The containers he collected were made from strong, thick, solid cardboard, different from the corrugated paper that boxes are made of today, and were strong enough to be used again. He would go round the shops and pick up these boxes, flattened and tied in bundles, fill the van, and deposit them in a depot at

Saughton. I often accompanied him on his rounds and, while he was unloading, would wander round an iron fence which surrounded a large grassed area containing cows and pigs that were waiting to enter the slaughterhouse.

The cows were led inside, their heads pushed into a clamp, a stun-gun discharged against their forehead and, as they collapsed, a chain was tied round one leg and they were suspended by that leg to a moving pulley. As they were moving along on the pulley, their bodies hanging upside down, their throats were slit and, as they progressed, they bled to death. The pigs, on the other hand, were electrocuted and dipped in a cauldron of scalding water to remove the fine, jaggy hairs covering their bodies. The slaughtermen were completely inured to the blood, and it was quite gruesome to see them at piece time, clad from neck to toe in blood-splattered red rubber aprons, eating their sandwiches with bare, bloody hands.

Pop had his own form of recycling. The cardboard was really pretty solid, about 5mm thick and the consistency of our modern-day MDF, and now and then he would purloin a piece and take it home to make doll's house furniture. Wardrobes and tables were no bother to him, but things like sink units presented problems. He was able to simulate dove-tail joints and, when he cut two slices halfway through the card and skilfully peeled away some of the layers, he was left with a groove into which fitted, very snugly, an end piece of the board. With a tiny touch of glue this gave perfectly strong joints. In the case of the sink unit, he would set a small tin pill-box into a pre-cut hole, and use various thicknesses of wire for taps and handles. When he wasn't making things like the doll's house furniture, he would be tinting black and white photographs, a popular pastime then, using some of his precious cardboard for the frames, and passepartout, a kind of thick sellotape, for the glass.

It was only after we moved to Buccleuch Street that I realised where my father's nimble fingers had been put to other use. As I walked out of my bedroom every morning I passed a framed watercolour portrait, a copy of *The Laughing Cavalier* by Frans Hals. This had been painted by Pop when he was much younger and it was an excellent piece of work. I wasn't fully aware of just how good it was until later, while studying the History of Art, I saw the original painting in Holland.

My father suffered all his life from lack of confidence in his own ability, in joinery, framing, tinting, or mending shoes, or any of his many skills, even with the evidence all round him. I never saw any other evidence of his painting, but he was determined to bring out the talent in me, and made sure that I kept my nose to the copying grindstone.

Witness to this was the copy in pastels he set me to make of the picture of *Christ Leading the Children* I mentioned earlier, in which Jesus is sitting in the middle of a group of youngsters with a road and landscape behind them. I had a problem with it from the very start because I was being asked to do an enlarged version, some 60×60 cm, from only a 15×10 cm postcard. It seemed a bit of a tall order at that age, but I did what my father told me, starting in late spring when the light nights and good weather were coming in, and I could hear my pals playing outside.

First thing every night I had to do my homework. Every year I found myself in contention for the dux medal, and you don't get into that position without doing homework. That done, I worked on the picture before Pop came home, because, if I hadn't made progress, he would become angry. I did the work seated at the Westcrosscauseway window in the living-room with my drawing-board supported on a pile of books on the oval table. After a few weeks the picture neared completion and an argument began over one tiny area of about one half-inch squared.

The children in the picture were tightly packed together around Christ, and the area in dispute was part of one child's clothing. My father believed it was grey, whilst I was sure it was blue, but didn't have the courage to say, 'Whose picture is it anyway? 'The result was that I became more and more agitated and upset so, when I finally completed it, my stomach was churning, I wasn't sleeping, wasn't eating and, in the end, became so out of sorts that I was off school for two weeks, suffering from what was diagnosed as, 'a bit of a nervous breakdown'.

My last visit to Pressie was to take *Christ Leading the Children* on display round every class in the school as an example of honest endeavour. I then prepared myself for graduating to Boroughmuir Senior Secondary School.

At the same time, my father enrolled me as the youngest member of the Edinburgh Sketching Club which met on a weekday evening in Cranston Street, just off the Royal Mile. Whether it was a reaction to my arguments with him over the Jesus picture, or whether it was the influence of the more senior members of the Sketching Club, I don't know, but I gave up copying and instead began to draw from life. There was always a model present at the Club sessions and in drawing him I discovered my aptitude for portraiture.

I must also have tried more imaginative drawing because Ian Scott, one of my Scoutmasters, many years later brought to a Corries' concert a drawing I had done for him as a wedding present. It was of sea horses and waves and it was gratifying to learn that he had kept it on his wall all that time.

Even at that early age I received small commissions for pencil-drawn portraits from people in the district. On one occasion, I even went into the streets to draw. I was sitting on a small, folding, camping-stool in the cobbles opposite the Assembly Church on Mound Place. With my drawing-board on my knee, I was making a pretty good attempt at drawing the Black Watch Memorial, when two *Evening News* reporters appeared behind me. They had been on assignment at the Castle, but here, the completely unusual sight of a wee eleven-year-old laddie sitting in the middle of a busy city, drawing away quite happily, presented a better story than the one they had been sent to cover.

We engaged in conversation, and after a few minutes I gave them my name and address. They promised to get in touch with my parents and I rushed home excitedly to tell Ma and Pop while, at the same time, thinking they had only been joking. A few days later they contacted us, and a photographic session was set up at our house. My niece, Norma Collie, came along and we were photographed with me as the artist and she as the model for a portrait. Pinned to my easel was a portrait I had done at the Sketching Club, and a pencil copy of my father's water colour copy of The Laughing Cavalier. A story-line of my being the youngest member of the Club, *blad-id-di-blah*, was added, and it duly appeared in the *Evening News*. I wish I could tell you that I was suddenly 'discovered' as a result and flooded with commissions, going on swiftly to rival Rembrandt but, of course, that didn't happen. The story was a nine-day wonder on Buccleuch Street before I returned to being just a schoolboy with a bit of talent, eager to get to Boroughmuir and start playing rugby.

This wasn't all I was doing of course. Not a bit of it. I had a paper round and a milk delivery round and was paid a small wage for both jobs. I used to help Ginger, our milkman, who had a horse-drawn cart, the kind with large wheels at the back and small ones at the front. One day, I jumped off the cart having finished my deliveries and, I don't know how, managed to leave the big toe of my right foot in the way of the large back wheel of the cart as Ginger started up the horse. I've been told that I have a fairly high tolerance to pain. If that is indeed true, it must have developed over the years because it wasn't obvious that day as the metal rim of the wooden wheel rolled over my toe. I think I got off lightly though, since the cart was shed of its full load.

After about a week, the toe started to discolour. We were told that there were no broken bones, but Ma decided it warranted a spiritual healing, and so we visited a local medium who specialised in them. During the healing, we were told, 'This boy isn't going to make his name from drawing, you know, but from music'.

Chapter Six

A life in music seemed highly unlikely when my only experience of singing was on Hogmanay at home and a wee bit in St Peter's. Any such notion was certainly doused when my music teacher at Boroughmuir, Mr Golan, who had been our 'visiting' musical influence at Pressie and was now in a permanent post at Boroughmuir, 'Burrie' as we called it, collared me after class and asked me to sing a few scales. When asked why, he said that although he thought he had detected a wide range in my singing voice, upon that closer attention he had discovered that it just wasn't there. Had I been able to reach the notes, he said, he would have recommended that I go for specialist operatic training. How would Pavarotti Browne have gone down in The Meedies? Hopes were finally dashed when he suggested that I enter our Inter-Schools Music Festival Competition to sing 'The Harp That Once through Tara's Halls', accompanied by himself on piano. To his huge disappointment, I sang flat throughout this performance. The verdict of the judges, and I think they were being kind, was: 'We feel that this young man's voice is about to break.'

Back in the street, we were maturing at an alarming rate. Street fitba' was now being shared with bicycle races round the block and visits to Infirmary Street Baths, where I, together with my best friend in the neighbourhood, Ian 'Robbie' Robertson, later to be my Best Man, had joined the Hibernian Swimming Club. There were girls involved as well, and the winky game (left behind in Methilhill) was now superseded by the 'Who-can-hold-their-breath-the-longest-during-a-kiss-in-the-back-stair-of-number-38-Westcrosscauseway' game.

On our trips to the baths, Robbie and I, together with Robert Duff, Jimmy Coventry and Kenny Robertson, whom I knew from the Scouts, passed a Snooker Hall which, after a lot of soul-searching, we ventured into to find not only snooker tables, but also a table tennis section. This suited Robbie and me down to the ground because we were becoming a bit jaded by the ping-pong ball hitting the hinges on our kitchen table.

Sunday afternoons were spent with hordes of other young-sters, all at a loose end, parading round the Royal Scottish Museum in Chambers Street, eying up the talent while picking up details of the life of the snow-goose or an extinct dinosaur. When the Museum closed at 5.00 pm, it was back home for tea and straight out again to the Royal Scottish Academy, eyeing up the same talent and cat-calling the soap-box orators who were speechifying in the open space between the Gallery and Princes Street Gardens. One of these orators was the early Scottish Nationalist, Wendy Wood, usually dressed in a Lovat green two-piece suit and matching bonnet with eagle feather flying. Not too many years later I would find myself sitting in her Scottish Patriots' mini-bus, driven by a young man named Colin. Later, as the Corrie Folk Trio and Paddie Bell, we would borrow this same mini-bus to take us to venues such as the Howff in Dunfermline, or Arthur Argo's Aberdeen Folk Club.

Although my life was changing significantly, things on the street progressed as normal. Ma bought a kitten whose house training included being lowered in a shopping basket into Baillie's yard where Mr Baillie would help it out and allow it to run around until it did its business.

'Browneeeeeee! That's a damn disgrace frightenin' that poor wee beast like that. I'll get the damned RSPCA tae ye.'

There was also Willie Palmer. Willie was the eldest son, in his late twenties probably, of the extended Palmer Family who occupied some of the flats at Number 2. There were three concrete steps leading from pavement to the stairhead door, where the family were in the habit, *en masse*, from grandparents to toddlers, of sitting watching the world go by. The street was usually awash with students moving between lectures in the University rooms in Buccleuch Place and George Square and the McEwan Hall. As they passed the Palmers, the toddlers and the very young of the family, a cheeky bunch at the best of times, would spit on them and lash out at their legs with fists and feet, encouraged by the adults with calls of, 'Come on then! Dae ye want tae huv a square go wi' them?'

The students were bewildered, but knew enough to scuttle off *quam celerrime*.

It was hardly surprising that Willie grew up as a local hardman, arguing and fighting and constantly in trouble with the police. I passed him one day in Westcrosscauseway, when he was holding a young uniformed constable by the collar of his tunic, pushing him against a shop-window with his right fist cocked for a punch. I should have rushed to the copper's aid, but I was only thirteen years old and had to protect my hands, because I was an artist *don't ye know*? To tell the truth, I was afraid of what Willie would have done to me once the constable was out of the way.

Willie had been quiet for a while, which meant he had been put away again. One night I was wakened from sleep to a commotion outside my window. I got up and looked through parted curtains to see him in the middle of the road, dressed in an overcoat with the right sleeve cut open and a white stookie (plaster) covering his arm all the way down over the fingers. Standing upright, arms akimbo and head thrown back, he looked up at the tenement windows, slowly circling and shouting at the top of his voice, 'Ah'm back!!!! ... Ya bastards!!!! ... Ah'm back!!!!'

The shop under my bedroom had become a twenty-four-hour taxi office. It took me a long, long time to get used to the noisy comings and goings. With the constantly ringing phone, the stopping, starting, and idling engines, the Tommy Hand band practising over my head, Tommy's mother's lavvy chain repeatedly going up an' down like a whore's knickers, and 'Brownneeeeeee . . . It's a damn disgrace!', 'Ah'm back!!!! . . . Ya bastards!!!! . . . Ah'm back!!!!' there were days I made my way to school like a zombie from lack of sleep.

Two of the girls in the Number 38 game came from outwith our district. Cathy (apologies to her for not remembering her second name), and Betty Wilson. I'll always remember Betty, partly because her mother worked alongside mine as a part-time waitress but, more especially, since out of our group involvements we grew closer. In gang visits to the pictures, we soon found that our attraction to each other had been noticed by our friends before even ourselves, and two empty seats always presented themselves so that we could sit together.

Holding hands and quiet talks followed (when nobody else was there), but any further development was cut short when we found ourselves at the end of our third and final year at school.

Working life loomed and I was in a quandary. I had the chance, through Poltis's contacts, to take up an apprenticeship in Lithographic Design at the printing firm. In this way I might join my friends in making what we all thought was real money, as opposed to the pocket-money we had been used to; however, I was one of the lucky ones. I had a choice, and the choice was left entirely to me, no pressure. I could start work, enough said, or I could continue into Fourth and Fifth years and go on to the College of Art. I would then most probably go into teaching. Art was what came easiest to me but, to remain in the top class for my first three years required a very high class average mark. Mine for Art was always in the high nineties, although I did get 100% for Geometry in third year, which kept me up there slugging.

No doubt you've already guessed the 100% was a sheer

fluke. Everybody else in the year chose one particular way to solve a theorem, which proved to be the wrong way and, by sheer chance, I chose another way, which was correct. It didn't do me all that much good because when I went into Fourth year I went into 4A, under the guidance of the head Maths teacher, Miss McAllum. On my first day in her classroom she asked me to stand up. Big things, she said, were expected of me. She only believed my explanation that the 100% was a sheer fluke, when these big things didn't transpire and I settled back into being not brilliant, but reasonably good, under her withering, disappointed gaze.

Two factors had cemented my decision to stay on at school.

As I hope I have illustrated, my father was an unfulfilled artist. The chances I had been given all my life just hadn't been open to him when he was younger. He had a nervous breakdown through shame and frustration at not having a job during the Great Depression of the 1930s, from which his lack of confidence stemmed. I had a sneaking suspicion that, if I did end up at the College of Art, it would be for him a vindication of his encouraging me to fulfil my own potential. In a sense he would be there with me. All through my first three years at Burrie, I was unable to play rugby for the school. I could only play at our Games periods at Meggetland on Wednesday afternoons, as I was holding down a job as a message boy on Saturdays, working for Cooper the Grocer's on the corner of East Crosscauseway. My transport was a typical message-bike with a large wheel on the back and a small one at the front (oh my aching toe), with a metal frame to hold the wicker basket of goods to be delivered. I kept my wages, thereby making it unnecessary for my mother to dole out pocket money. It was decided that, if I did stay on, it would make both my parents very proud, and that I should certainly have the chance to play for the school should that chance come along.

As it happened, in my first game for the school 4ths, we beat Broughton 75-9 and I scored nine tries. That's when a try was worth only three points. The following week, the whole team was made up to 2b. The disappointing thing was that my father didn't believe me when I told him.

It was then that our wee street gang started to move in different directions. As far as Betty was concerned I think I made a deliberate decision not to pursue the relationship because a schoolboy could not afford to woo a working lady, and a working lady would surely not be seen dead with a schoolboy. It worked out for the best. When I was in 5th year, and still going the odd message, I was served by Betty in our local Rankin's Fruit-shop where she had advanced, very quickly, to become Manageress. She would obviously be earning a fair amount of money, so I knew I had saved myself, and maybe Betty too, a deal of embarrassment and emotional stress.

Pop was now driving for British Road Services on long distance hauls. He would be gone for about a week at a time which precluded my going with him. I don't think he and my mother were getting on very well at this point because they had developed a peculiar habit between them. Whenever he said something that annoyed her, which seemed to be increasingly frequent, she would scowl and say in an angry voice, 'Daddy!' Pop would just squeeze his brows together, shake his head and grunt, 'Grrrr..' Maybe their bad vibes were because he was going away so much, or maybe he was going away so much because of the bad vibes, but it was obvious that he looked forward to going away. Whatever the cause of his high spirits, he would hum and whistle as his good cap, silk scarf, pressed trousers and polished shoes were packed neatly into his case.

On the road Pop's navigation came through a good, old fashioned road atlas, all the numbered pages lying loose in a box. His job was to drive south, depositing loads on the way. With an emptied van he would pick up loads on the way back, the round trip taking about a week. He'd lay out his single sheets side by side on the oval table to save the inconvenience of constantly having to flip back and forward to see where he would be bound. When he was on the road, he told me much later in life, in the evenings he would leave his digs and visit local pubs where live entertainment took place, for example, an early Danny La Rue Revue. This was long before such entertainment caught on up here in Scotland.

Sometimes the cargo he ferried back was of the human kind. This was shortly after the end of the war and many service personnel were still being demobbed, having served abroad. Many of these men found themselves on the road, trying to get home by the cheapest way possible, hitch-hiking. Pop would pick up any guy in uniform and we often found ourselves sharing a meal with a complete stranger before he started on his way again. Although this could have proved dangerous and we, as kids, had been warned not to speak to strangers, never at any time did we feel ourselves threatened. On the contrary, all we ever received was profuse thanks for the favour my father had bestowed.

The warning about strangers manifested itself to me one day when I went on my own to see a film in the Pooles Synod Hall picture-house. The Pooles was in the West End of the City, just round the corner from the Usher Hall and Lyceum Theatre and in the shadow of the volcanic rock outcrop on which is perched Edinburgh Castle. You could enter at any time and, if you found yourself in the middle of the film, be it 'Main' or 'B' feature, you just sat until it came back to where you had taken up your viewing. The cheap seats were full when I arrived, and only more expensive ones were available, so I joined the queue for the cheap seats because somebody would no doubt be out soon. I had only been standing for a few minutes when a man approached me and said, in a friendly voice, that, if I didn't have enough to pay for a better seat, he knew my father from work and would be happy to sub me the extra. He could get it back from my Dad when next he saw him.

A small doubt did appear in my mind, but I suppose selfishness won. I smiled a thank you and we went inside where he stopped and said that it was a long film and it would be a good idea to pay a visit to the toilet. Warning bells started clanging in my head, if maybe a bit too late. I felt I had no choice but to move through the toilet door in front of him, frantically thinking, 'What the fuck do I do now?' He stood beside me as we both relieved ourselves, and, as we both buttoned up, he stretched over and ran his hand up my front and remarked on what a big one I had there. (He had obviously never heard of Wumpies.) I could say nothing. I could hardly think. It's easy to say that I should have shouted to an attendant, but you'd have to wait until it happened to you before you could appreciate the mixture of churning emotions I was feeling. Instead, I walked ahead and found myself in a seat in a darkened cinema beside this strange and terrifying threat.

I took a deep breath and tried to think. Fortunately, he made no further move or sound. After about five minutes I decided I had no choice but to get out of there as quickly as possible. I told him I had to go to the toilet again and squeezed my way along the row. In the passage I looked behind to see if he was following and was relieved to see that he wasn't. It was more than relief, it was more like elation, because I knew that, if I got outside, I could outrun him.

I did start to run, bursting out of the cinema at full speed, turning towards Bread Street and what I thought was the salvation of my bus-stop. My mind was in turmoil. Should I keep on running? Should I find a policeman? Should I hide? A bus came along and I leapt aboard to safety. Even then my mind was full of irrational thoughts. Starting to feel sick, I got off the bus and ran full tilt the rest of the way home. I fumbled to get my key in the door and staggered into the kitchen where my mother was working at the sink. I stopped beside her and rested my hands on the bunker with my head pressed against the water-heater, shaking and shivering for I don't know how many minutes before I could say what was wrong.

When I finally managed to stutter it out she leapt into fighting mode, snarling that we would immediately go back to the Pooles, have the house-lights turned on and expose this piece of vermin. I panicked again. No! No! No! If I did identify him, he would surely take revenge sometime in the future. I said that I really hadn't had a good look at him and couldn't possibly remember what he looked like. After a long time she relented and made me a cup of tea, her answer to all ills. Of course I was lying, because I never forgot what he looked like.

Ian had left the Scouts and signed up for the Royal Scots Army Cadet Force. I joined him and have to admit that I met a more bullying atmosphere than in the Scouts. Everybody had to jump to orders. I suppose that's what has to happen in the Army because, let's face it, you're being trained to kill or be killed. You should ignore all those glamorous recruitment posters about seeing the world, although a glamorous recruitment poster was one of the first tasks I was asked to perform. I did a 3-foot by 2-foot pencil drawing of a fellow cadet, Garth Heskith, standing in front of a hugely enlarged Royal Scots cap badge. Framed up, it was photographed with Garth and myself in uniform, standing to attention beside it in the foyer of the Caley picture house in Clerk Street. The manager of the cinema stood beside us. The picture appeared in the Edinburgh Evening News and, lo and behold, there was that laddie Browne in the papers again.

This was when I became convinced that Pop had been in the army because he proceeded to demonstrate to us the Art of Spit and Polish. Take a pair of army boots, apply a lot of black boot polish and brush vigorously until they shine. The crowning glory comes when you start all over again, this time applying the polish only to the toe-caps, and then spit on it, rubbing the spit into the polish with a cloth wrapped round your index finger. This procedure is repeated until a skin forms which is very shiny. The more you spit and polish, the harder the skin becomes and the shinier the cap. If you're assiduous enough, you'll end up with mirrors on the ends of your feet.

When Ian and I were picked to be members of a drill squad which was to appear at the Military Tattoo during the Edinburgh Festival, Pop volunteered to spit and polish our rifle butts. Unfortunately, I never made it on stage. Having done a wee bit of boxing at St Peters, I thought it natural to join the boxing in the cadets. I shaped up well in training with the skipping, sparring and punch- bags, but soon our Commanding Officer deemed ring experience necessary. The ring in question was not of the rope and canvas variety, but was a square of wooden seats round the perimeter of one of the rooms in Headquarters. My opponent was Lance Corporal Nichol, Scottish Champion at I know not what weight. I don't think Nichol had been told to batter the living daylights out of me, he only fought that way because he always did, but that's what happened. I didn't land a punch. If this was a test of my mettle, I failed miserably, and it made me think that perhaps this boxing game was not for me. Indeed, perhaps this cadet game was not for me. I left forthwith.

The real clincher proving my father had been in the army was the sharpshooting. He bought an air-rifle for us, and a metal sheet that he stood against the wall opposite our living room door, which he wedged open. On the floor in front of the metal plate he put half-a-dozen or so plugs of plasticine, sticking a match-stick into each plug with the to-be-lit end upright. These weren't safety matches, but Bluebell or Swan Vestas, with sulphur tips. He then explained that what he wanted us to do was to fire our pellet at the match, not to knock the tip off the stick, but, to graze it and light the match, leaving it standing on fire. We thought he was joking, but, when he lay down on the floor of the living-room under the window, as far as he could comfortably get from the target, not only were the smiles wiped from our faces when we saw him perform the feat, but we suddenly gained a huge respect for this quiet man who was our father. We certainly couldn't wait to see if we could emulate him.

He didn't put us at the matches straight away. Instead we bought some paper targets with concentric circles and bull's eyes and set them up to train ourselves in the handling and aiming of the gun, to 'get our eye in' in effect. After a great deal of practice, over a great many evenings of shooting, both of us became very proficient at the match game, although Ma constantly complained about the smell of sulphur through the house.

Every year over the Festive Season a Fair was set up in the Waverley Market with Chairoplanes, Whirligigs and of course, stalls of every description. Some of these took the form of shooting galleries with an assortment of prizes. The prizes were worthless but it was to these stalls that the three of us made a beeline. Notoriously, the air-rifles chained to the counters are doctored. The sights are out of line or the barrels slightly twisted, or the triggers either too sensitive or not sensitive enough. Take a few shots at the target though, and you'll quickly learn to compensate and make yourself pretty accurate. So it proved with us.

We drew quite a crowd when word got round that we were, between the three of us, clearing the shelves. It wasn't the value of the stuff that was important. Who needs another dozen cheap glass tumblers, or Mickey Mouse egg-cups, or packets of balloons? It was the challenge that mattered. Showing off one's skills played its part and I wonder if that factor also played a part in me ending up on stage? The disgruntled stall-holder didn't do too badly either. We had had to pay for every set of shots and, after we were out of the way, our spectators were left with the feeling that this was easy and would spend their money trying to prove it.

Chapter Seven

The fact that we didn't have a bathroom didn't mean that we didn't have a bath or went filthy from one year's end to the next. We had a zinc bath that was filled using a thin rubber hose attached to the geyser gas water heater. When I say filled, I don't mean filled right up because that would have taken all night, but we had enough water to have a good scrub at least once a week.

In addition, also once a week, we Pressie pupils would run along to the pool at Sciennes School to have a swim and a shower under the supervision of Mr Jimmy McCracken, a well-known swimming instructor. Jimmy had a fool-proof method of getting you out of the shower if you lingered too long. He would take his trusty elastic band and ping you on the rear end, to gee you up. Mind you, we didn't really have much time to linger, with only about an hour to get from Pressie to Sciennes and back.

Infirmary Street baths had a high dive in the middle with springboards on either side. Facing this, at the shallow-end, stood the showers. The changing cubicles were arrayed along the sides. Upstairs on the balcony were the Turkish Baths where, for a small fee, you could luxuriate for half an hour or so. My father used to go on a weekly basis and I went along with him for my swim. When he was finished he sat for a while on the seats surrounding the pool and watched me doing lengths. He always maintained that I was better at swimming than running, jumping or throwing things. I didn't enjoy swimming as much as athletics, albeit I did well enough in competition for the Hibs Club, and certainly for Burrie, to win my school colours, joining colours for athletics and rugby.

As a cub and scout I ran in competition against other scout troops. A substitute for throwing the javelin, since as cubs we were far too young for such a dangerous pastime, was throwing the cricket-ball, for which I had an aptitude. In competition with the 144 Newington Troop I sprinted against, and usually lost to, a lad called Fraser Henderson, whose slight limp didn't prevent him from being extremely fast. Strangely, he only limped when he ran, never when he was walking. Later he and I would run and play rugby together for Boroughmuir.

Another lad I met at Burrie was Gordon Irving who was to become a close friend. In 1965 and 1966, we ran in the same sprint relay team and won silver medals in the Scottish Amateur Athletics Championships. I never once beat him in a straight race. We opposed each other many times in 100 yards handicaps and, although I was 'off' from one yard to sometimes three, and he from scratch, I never once got to the tape before him. In my own defence though, I was good enough in all the disciplines to become the junior champion of Braidburn Athletic Club, almost reaching the club sprint relay team to represent Scotland at junior level at the White City British Games in 1957. In the end, I went only as a reserve. To reach the team proper I ran for the fourth place against another friend called Mark Herbich. It was one to one and, needless to say, Mark won.

Our coach at the Braidburn Club was Tam Drever, a famous name in Scottish athletics at that time whose son, Ian Drever, became the British half-mile champion. Tam and Mrs Drever ran the club as if we were all their sons, encouraging us to visit any time we were passing. Coaching me on a Saturday morning, throwing javelins at Meadowbank Stadium, he was delighted when Pop came to assist. We had six at our disposal, and I would pick them up in turn and make my run to launch them towards the other end where my father stood. He would wait until they were all beside him, bundle them into his arms and bring them back to me, where Tam was picking up on my mistakes. Pop would trudge back for the whole process to start again. I wish I could tell you that these efforts resulted in me emulating Ian and becoming a champion but, alas, I can't. I continued to do well enough at club level, but no great honour awaited.

To become a champion at anything, you need a lot more than just talent. You need guts and determination, guts being foremost, and I knew I didn't have any. In my final year at school I was last to run in our 440 yards relay team at the Edinburgh Schools Championships at Meadowbank Stadium. We were way behind in the race when I took the baton and, when I did get off the mark, I decided to go for it, hell for leather, treating it as a sprint. I caught up on the last bend and was visualising myself going to the front and breaking the tape in glory when, on the bend, the muscles just above my knees turned to jelly. Ignominious shame awaited as I wobbled the last thirty or forty yards and it felt as though everybody had gone home by the time I reached the finishing line, coming in a sorry last. I knew that I should go straight to Tam and explain that my legs were not strong enough and I required an exercise regime of squats, bench-work and road-work over the winter months. But, you see, no guts, and not enough dedication to make the decision which was staring me in the face.

Someone I know who did have that spirit and vision was a nephew of my wife's, Peter Hoffmann. Pat and I went to the Crystal Palace to support him when he won his place in the Great Britain team over 400 metres to go to the Montreal Olympics of 1976. We had been proudly following his progress up the athletics rankings and I remember the day he explained to me that, in training, he was in the habit of running a few 400s at full speed, then running some more, until he was physically sick. He would spew his guts up, take a short break and a drink of water, and run a few more 400s until he was sick again. You know what showed the real spirit of the man? Sometimes he would put himself through this process without the presence of a coach or anybody else to force him on. I could never have done that, and there is the difference.

Two years after running in Montreal, he moved up a discipline and, on the starting line of the final of the British Indoor 800 metres at RAF Cosford, an over-zealous official objected to the type of spikes he was wearing, although they were exactly the same shoes he had worn the day before in his qualifying heat, and banned him from wearing them for the race. Peter simply took them off without argument and ran barefoot. Trailing at the back of the pack through the bell, he came with a rush to win the title in 1min 51.4sec, his fastest time indoors or out. 'My feet are in a right mess,' he quietly told a reporter after the race, and hobbled off to seek medical attention. What a man.

As I went into 4th year I began most un-schoolboy-like pastimes with my friends, Robbie, Gabby, Graham and Harry who was a wee bit older. I'm talking about going on Thursday nights to the Palais de Danse. Sounds grand, but don't conjure up visions of the bold Ronnie, damsel in arms, waltzing gracefully around a spacious floor. Spacious the floor was, certainly, but you couldn't move an inch for couples tightly clasped together, arms entwined in as close an embrace as possible while shuffling at a snails' pace in what was called 'Moon Dancing', to the strains of the Jeff Rowena Quartet. I certainly didn't wear my green-braided school blazer with the breast-pocket badges showing my school colours for Athletics on one side and Rugby on the other (the one for Swimming I had to keep in the inside pocket as I had run out of breasts), but a sort of double-breasted zoot-suit with shoulder pads to impress the girls. I wore my hair like Tony Curtis, which was all the fashion then, although my hair was not at all compatible. Remembering the ensemble now, I understand how I never once got the lumber the Moon Dance was supposed to guarantee.

On coming out late from the Palais, we had to tread carefully and with watchful eye because the dance hall was situated in Fountainbridge, the territory of the notorious Val d'Or Gang who ruled the area with an iron fist - though maybe not when they came up against Big Tam '007' Connery, who also lived there. The gang was led by Boko, with his lieutenant Wee Boydie, and a guy by the name of Jose Hepburn. Jose arrived at Preston Street School in my last year, having been expelled from nearly every other school in Edinburgh for violent behavior. I'm glad that I was never challenged by him because his violence took the form of in-close fighting, preferably in the restricted space of a back close where he would use his thumbs to gouge eyes, nostrils, ears and the inside of his opponent's cheeks, meanwhile head-butting and beating a tattoo on the enemy's balls with his knees, and all at break-neck speed.

In the safety of our own area, our wee gang would part company after having a word with my father who would, like as not, be standing at the bottom of our stair smoking his pipe. I never could make up my mind if he stationed himself there to make sure I was getting in safely, or if he was again trying to catch the man who kept peeing in our bottom-of-the-stair alcove, slipping into the stair on his way home from the pub round the corner. Pop had in the past prevented the event from happening by being there, smoking, when the phantom piddler presented himself. Surprised by Pop's presence, he stopped, leaned against the other door-jamb and engaged him in conversation. After a while he said good-night, leaving my father with a smile on his lips until he knocked the spent tobacco from his pipe on the door-post, looked down and saw where the guy had pissed down the inside of his trouser-leg, leaving his mark yet again on the stair.

A young girl called Pat Elliot spent her early days of schooling at Moray House School and came to Boroughmuir for her senior secondary education, going directly into fourth year. She didn't enjoy her stay, she told me, principally because she was in a class where everybody was two years older and she felt out of place.

Pat came to Boroughmuir at the beginning of Autumn, Septemberish, but it wasn't until the end of that term that we met. She had caught my eye in early December, and the sight was very pleasing, but I couldn't find enough courage to say hello, nor was I any good at eliciting introductions. My daughter Lauren has a friend, Helen, who spied a guy called Derek a few times while standing at the same bar. One night, Helen boldly walked up to Derek and said, 'I fancy you. What are you gonna do about it?'

They're married now of course, and with a growing family.

Mine was a more subtle approach. I followed Pat a couple of times as she walked up Viewforth to catch her tram home, just to confirm my thoughts by watching her movements and catching a few snippets of her conversation. Still apprehensive about making the final move, I discovered that she was going to Nora Simm's Christmas Party in Minto Street and wangled myself an invitation. At the party it wasn't too difficult to get into conversation with the people surrounding her, and then speak to Pat herself. One thing led to another and when I finally asked if I could see her home, she told me that another boy had asked the same, but she didn't like his hands. His hands? Later, standing at the back-door of her home at 519 Gilmerton Road, after stealing what was for the both of us a very nervous kiss, her brother, Lee, came home. As he passed us he said, simply, 'Aye, aye'.

Whether this was a straightforward greeting, or a brotherly protective warning, I didn't wait to find out, but started to make my way down the drive after asking if I could see her again. She said that she would like that, and I walked on air all the way home having missed my last bus. That was the beginning of a fifty-eight year loving relationship which ended only when Pat died at home here with us on April 22nd, 2012.

We didn't become inseparable immediately because I was still heavily into sport, training both with the school and with Braidburn Athletic Club. Visits to the Palais very quickly went by the board though, because no passing lumber could be quite good enough now I had Pat. Some evenings were still spent with Robby, playing table-tennis or just hanging about in his house or mine, but Pat and I managed to catch fleeting moments between classes. Many a time though, we would walk over Bruntsfield Links, hand-in-hand on the way to catch her tram, followed by an entourage of first-year kids making comments and sniggering.

Each year, the senior boys were encouraged to attend school camp at a hostel in the Cairngorms. This is where my singing properly started because, at the end of a strenuous day tramping over the hills, 'bonding', we would return to the hostel late and, after showering and performing the allotted tasks of dish-washing, general ablutions, etc, would be allowed leisure-time until lights-out was called. Lights-out in such an environment is rarely respected and certainly wasn't expected to be by the two masters who accompanied us, Charlie McLennan and Gary 'Tas' Taylor. Tas was the current Boroughmuir F. P. First Fifteen scrum-half who had arrived at school as Head Gym Teacher, replacing the retired 'Honk' Ronchetti.

Nicknames always have and always will be allotted to people, and it's at camp that I got mine.

Accompanying me were friends I still have: Brian Suddaby, Davie Greig, Sandy Henderson, Kenny Ross (Boroughmuir's first Scotland rugby internationalist), the late Fraser Henderson, the late Gordon Irving and the school's Head Boy, Norrie Wilson. So many, I can't list them all. We had our own private stores of goodies which we kept for our midnight bun-feasts and shared where we could. I was safe with mine because all I took was Heinz baked Beans, eaten at the stroke of midnight straight from the tin, cold, with a spoon if one was available, scooped with fingers if not. When they were all consumed, the Pavarotti came out in me, because I would launch into such classics as I had performed at the Scout and Sunday-school shows: On Top Of Old Smokie, The Ballad of Jimmie Brown, Hear my Song Violetta, and Ave Maria of course. Pedro the Fisherman seemed to be the most popular. Norrie Wilson picked up on that one and aligned it to Wednesday's games periods and me in my purple and pink shirt. He dubbed me 'Pedro', the name Suddaby, Davie and Sandy still automatically come out with.

The singing didn't always go down well with the exhausted (possibly pissed from their own midnight feast) Charlie and Tas, and shouts would ring out, albeit in a kindly tone: 'Right, Browne! That's it for tonight. Let's all get some sleep.'

Years later, after Roy Williamson died in 1990 and I was singing on my own, I did a solo concert at Pitlochry Festival Theatre where, unknown to me, Tas was in the audience. He came backstage after the show to say hello. After his pleasantries and congratulations for my having been so successful, he said, 'Well Pedro, I never thought I'd see the day when I would pay good money to hear you singing.'

The Art Department at Boroughmuir was housed on the top floor of the building where there was, on the inside of the corridor, a series of shallow alcoves with windows to the sky and a narrow seat under the window. Face the classroom wall and you would see that it was in two sections, the lower one lined with tiles, the upper with plain plaster. On the top plastered section, star pupils might be asked to paint a mural in a subject of their own choosing. The area was pretty big for a school pupil to attempt, being roughly twelve feet by five. I was so honoured.

Those who had the good fortune to experience advanced education will remember being encouraged to do quite a bit of study on their own. For us, this allowed a few more free periods in the school week than the lower school enjoyed. I took advantage of such free time to add a bit to my mural and would invariably be found balancing on my trestle in front of the wall. Pat, when her free time didn't coincide with mine, would often skip a class to sit on the window-bench where we could chat while I worked. This engendered not a few dressings-down by the Headmistress, Ma McGlashen. By comparison with a couple of expulsions caused by what I will call 'physical contact', our few words together were quite innocent and caused no real problem.

Agnes Johnstone was my art teacher in the last months at Burrie. I don't remember anything in particular about what she told me in the field of 'the Arts', but what I have never forgotten is the invocation she shared with her class every time we exited her room, 'Good afternoon, Ladies and Gentlemen, and remember - make the most of moments!'

That phrase has haunted me all my life and, hopefully, I've done you proud on it, Agnes.

Maybe it was because of the helium balloons episode, or maybe it was my Tony Curtis hair-do, but I never made Prefect. I did end my schooldays as a Monitor, which was fine by me.

It took a number of months of evenings out together, coupled with the furtively stolen back-door kisses, before I was finally invited to meet Pat's parents whom I will call Violet and Wattie. Their life together would make a book in itself. Violet had in her youth been a nurse whose skills had been of such high standards as to take her into private nursing with important clients in various parts of the country. Before their marriage, Wattie had lived in America and Canada where, one week, he ran liquor across the border, and the next could be seen in the red uniform of the Royal Canadian Mounties. He had also done a bit of stunt work in the film industry and, when he returned to Scotland, took up Speedway riding at the Marine Gardens Stadium here in Edinburgh under the name of 'Red Elliot'. I resist the temptation to elucidate further. As I said earlier in my dispute with Pop over the *Christ Leading the Children* pastel, 'Whose story is this anyway?'

Shortly after my meeting with Violet and Wattie I took Pat to meet Ma and Pop. Explaining just a bit of the Elliots' background was one thing but, when I told my folks that they had an electrical and radio shop in Dalkeith, lived in a bungalow on Gilmerton Road which had a bathroom and a garden front and back, and ran a motor-car, I was told in no uncertain fashion, 'That girl is giving you ideas away above your station.'

That was the beginning of an animosity my parents, particularly Ma, felt for Pat thereafter. As far as Ma was concerned, Pat was stealing her laddie from right under her nose.

It was then that I met Pat's sister, Margaret, for the first time. Margaret lived with her husband, Andy Ross, in a big house in Duncan Street. As I recall, the house was owned by Alasdair Erskine-Murray, Lord of Elibank. He allowed Margaret and Andy use, provided they kept a room at his disposal any time he required it. Alasdair was what you might term a perpetual student. When he finished one course of study, and achieved honours in it, he would start another, but the reason I remember him most was that he, like my father, had been involved with the Enfield rifle. He performed a feat with the weapon he owned, and kept in his flat, that amazed everybody who witnessed it. Alasdair could take the Enfield with the muzzle end in his clasped hand and extend it at arm's length until, rifle and arm in a straight line together, the butt was resting on the floor in front of him. He would then slowly raise it, still in a perfectly straight line with his arm, up to shoulder height. He could hold it in that position, seemingly for as long as he was asked to, before slowly lowering it, fully aligned, to the floor. That took a deal of strength to perform, strength that I didn't have. I know because I tried it.

Alasdair told us of the time when he needed all of that strength. He was doing military service in India when, one exceptionally hot night, he elected to sleep in the open on the flat roof of his billet, only to be awakened in the early hours by the feeling that some kind of force was pushing at him. He felt himself being driven towards the parapet and is sure that if he hadn't had the strength he did have, he would not have been able to resist, and would have gone over to what would have been his untimely death. He could never find anybody else who had had the same experience, nor any story of anything attached to the building which would have explained such a forceful presence, but the event shook him to his core.

Margaret was in the nursing profession when we first met and Andy worked in his family's business of bagpipe-makers, J&R Glen in the Lawnmarket. It was naturally to Andy I turned for the large bohdran I used on television in 1968 on the occasion that 'Flower of Scotland' was first presented to the public.

Chapter Eight

The first half of the four year course at Art College was a general one in which we took drawing and painting, certainly, but also looked at design and calligraphy and the history of art. I'll admit to feeling a bit strange at my first life class, waiting for the model to disrobe and take up her pose. Gazing at male models was no problem, as I was sharing a communal bath with fourteen naked men after rugby training and games. Why I thought that female flesh would be any different, I don't know, particularly when it just sat there and did nothing.

Soon it became second nature and when, during breaks from drawing, the models would cover-up to sit and talk with us students, I realised that we all had a common purpose. We were there to work, as was emphasised by our tutors' constant perambulations, stopping from time to time to point out that this or that line was not quite where it should be. We had evening classes, sometimes obligatory, sometimes at our own discretion, and these, coupled with my ongoing rugby and athletics training nights and, by now, Pat's accountancy night school, meant that we saw little of each other during the week. The shop in Dalkeith closed at 9.00 p.m. and both Violet and Wattie didn't get home until later, which meant that sometimes Pat would go home to an empty house. If I was free, I would jump on a bus and head for 519 to keep her company.

Weekends were different, especially after home games at Meggetland, Boroughmuir's base. After-match catering was done on a voluntary basis in those days and we relied almost entirely on the goodwill of our lady friends to prepare and serve the victuals. Pat took her turn willingly, which meant that in the evening hospitality, after the game, she was there with me. Although she didn't do much away game travelling, she did accompany me to athletics tournaments during the summer months, and there were many Saturday nights at the pictures.

I also worked nights as a barman in The Wee Windaes on the Royal Mile, and in Paddie's Bar in Rose Street. One of the first customers I served was my Maths teacher from school, Maggie McCallum, and I found it heart-warming when she recognised me immediately, stretched out her hand and said, 'Hello, young man. Now you may call me Maggie.'

It was in Paddie's Bar that I discovered my capacity for harmony singing. One of the regular barmen, Joe, would burst into song while we were washing the glasses at closing time and I would join in, never singing the melody with him, instead finding a harmony. It was often joked that he and I should 'do a turn' in the bar one evening, but that never transpired.

In 'The Wee Windaes' I worked with Davie the barman, a large kind of chap, and a charmer. He was actually a baker to trade, but worked in the bar in the evenings and, after closing-time, went off to his bakery for what he described as 'real work'. I was still fairly wet behind the ears and Davie took me under his wing. One night, a couple of ladies from the Salvation Army entered the pub to sell their evening's quota of *The War Cry*. At that time women weren't allowed into pubs, but the male clientele made an exception for 'The Salvee' and stumped up for its good cause, lightening the ladies of their load of papers. The men were charm personified while the ladies were present but when they left the premises, all hell was let loose. Opinions were voiced about how much good the Salvation Army actually does, only to be countered by others on how much harm they had caused to this or that man's family. Having seen it all before Davie signalled me down to the cellar to start tidying up. From my place of relative safety, I listened to the inebriated fists flying and saw, in my mind's eye, Davie's massive hands round first one neck and then the other as the battling perpetrators were ejected onto the High Street. When the scuffles subsided I would sheepishly emerge from my hiding place to collect my large jar of fresh mussels, three of which were delivered to the bar every week, and take them home to my eager family. Possibly they were the reason my mother arranged the job for me in the first place.

Although I received an Educational Grant when entering College, like just about every other student, it was barely enough to cover the expense of the paper, pencils, paint, books on art history and anatomy that were required for the course. Better money was made during the long summer break and at Christmas when I took jobs as a barman, in the G.P.O. parcels department until they stopped employing students, in McEwans Brewery and as a bus conductor. Thanks to these jobs I contributed to the family purse and helped eke out my board and lodging.

My first summer job was as a bus conductor. I befriended a lad called Iain McLeod who had been at Heriot's School but hadn't done as well as his parents would have liked. He failed to gain any kind of University placement but managed to get into Art College, although his heart wasn't in it. Fortunately for Iain, or perhaps not as things transpired, he learned there that he had a fantastic ability for languages. Edinburgh College of Art, like all advanced institutes of learning, attracted students from all over the world. Surrounded by many different tongues he couldn't help but drink them in, assimilate them, and spout them back. At first it was short phrases of greeting but, very soon, longer sentences of conversation. Perhaps, and I've just thought of this, that's why we were drawn to each other.

Because, if you asked me how I can achieve a portrait likeness I can't explain it. I just do it. Iain was the same with languages.

We went together to the offices of the Scottish Ministry of Transport for our basic training in ticket punching, supervised by an SMT Inspector whom I was destined to meet later in my singing career in totally different guise, and soon were out there taking fares and learning about split shift work. The seasonal intake of temporary student employees was usually allotted to the 'Miners' Run'. This was unpopular with permanent employees because it meant a very early start of sometimes 4.00 am, stopping at about 8.00 or 9.00. At that point, we had the option of going home and then coming back to complete our hours in the afternoon (the split shift), or going back to St Andrew Square to await the possibility of another run, should an employee call off sick, or increased cover was required on a busy route. This was a good way to make extra money because we were paid overtime even if we just sat for hours waiting.

My first extra run was to Blackpool, which was very lucrative in overtime and couldn't be refused, but had mixed blessings. The journey south took us up Gilmerton Road, past no. 519, and Pat and I had a pre-arranged plan in such an eventuality. If I couldn't phone her and if, as often happened, the route took me past her house, I would write a short note on one of my report sheets, to explain why I couldn't meet her that night, wrap it round a few coppers, and throw it into her garden as the bus passed. This is what I did on that first run. Unfortunately though, not being a seasoned operator, only when I had collected all the fares did I realise that I had not left a seat for myself. I spent the whole journey sitting on my upturned metal ticket-box. Some lessons you learn very quickly. I did have a seat on the return journey.

Iain McLeod enjoyed this work so much that he decided to give up his studies and become a full-time conductor. This decision ultimately proved his undoing because as a student he was exempt from National Service, and he suddenly found himself in the Air Force, stationed in Germany. Iain laughed it off and did his two years, taking advantage of his stay in

Europe to spend his leaves, not coming home to Scotland, but honing his language skills in other foreign countries. When his forces time ended he drifted into the Import-Export business in Germany, where he was successful, occupying a very nice flat in Berlin. Unfortunately, and unknown to the bold Iain, the flat had once belonged to the Baader Meinhof group and, in the continuing war between them and the German police, the flat was raided. Iain heard the police breaking down his door during the night, rose from his bed, opened his bedroom door and saw the armed men. He banged it shut again and the police opened fire, shooting him dead through the closed door. In the press furore that followed, Iain was labelled a spy, a member of MI5, even an urban guerrilla. The closest my friend Iain McLeod got to being a spy was when, after he was demobbed, he was arrested while trying to sell the Encyclopedia Britannica to half-pissed American airmen coming home from the pub.

McEwan's Brewery was located in Holyrood Road, where now stands the Scottish Parliament Building. My job was as one of a team of four: two to pass crates of newly-brewed, warm bottles of beer up to a loft, the others to receive the crates five at a time on a two-wheeled barrow and stack them at the back of the loft.

There was a cellar in the middle of the loft which stored the hops used in brewing the beer. The first time it was opened in my presence, the smell nearly knocked me off my feet and I felt as though I was going to be sick. A dash to the loft window for a breath of fresh air restored my equilibrium and I managed to continue to work. It took but a few further openings for me to become used to the smell and accept it without upset, a valuable lesson that you can get used to just about anything.

Each student was assigned to a regular worker who ensured we didn't work too quickly. When one of us was at the loft window receiving the warm beer, the other would load his barrow at the other end of the loft with crates which had been cooling for days. It would also leave him time to have a swig of cool beer before bringing his barrow to the window and putting his cold crates on rollers to make their way down to the loading bay and transfer to the delivery lorries.

The lorries made their way to the Brewery exit gate where a security man did a quick count of the crates. It wasn't his fault that there were two sizes of crate. One was slightly shorter than the other, which meant that one stack of crates was four high, and the other five. When stacked beside one another they appeared to be the same height. All of this meant that some fortunate Edinburgh publicans received a few more crates than expected, while being billed for a few less than ordered. This is a myth in the trade; I was never shown proof.

Another story that went round was that when the warm beer was being stacked, perhaps ten high at the rear of the loading-bay, small spaces would be left as *howffs* into which a loader could slip to partake of a bottle from the cooled crates. This may also be a myth; it is no myth, however, that I watched, with my own eyes, some of my temporary brewery colleagues make their first stop on their way home at one of the many pubs on the Royal Mile.

The highlight of the College year was the Summer Revel. For weeks before the end of the academic year, the college building underwent a complete transformation to a prescribed theme. Of the four Pat and I attended, the Revel I remember best had an *Alice in Wonderland* theme. A band of the keener students, using wood, cardboard, *papier-mache*, chicken-wire etc, made a rabbit-warren of tunnels and grottos and secret corners of the corridors and rooms. It was the end of the year, when we let our hair down, although Pat would never accept that we all worked terribly hard. Her belief was that most students were nothing but wasters, putting off real work for as long as possible.

She maybe had a point given that we were left to get on with free expression pretty well at our own pace, compared to someone like herself who, working in an accountancy office, had to allot every minute of her every working day to some client's books. Considering also that her working day didn't end until she had attended night-classes in book-keeping, it must have seemed deeply unfair. It was very pleasing, therefore, when her mentor within the business, Robin Finlay, gave special praise of her endeavours in letters to her. Here I will quote one which I retain in her folder of certificates.

'Dear Pat,

I have pleasure in enclosing £1 as a token of the firm's congratulations on yet another first class examination result.

I am very pleased with the way in which you have taken your evening studies seriously and am very proud of your examination achievements.

The chocolates are my own personal contribution.

Yours sincerely,

Robin Finlay.'

One pound may seem a ludicrous amount of money now, but the letter is dated December 14th, 1956. Four years later, in 1960, I would be contemplating work as a teacher at £11 a week. Viewed in that light that one pound isn't so bad.

I can't say that I retained much respect for a large number of my contemporaries when, in my fourth year, having been elected as their spokesman on the Students' Representative Council, I was forced into argument with my flock, most of whom were in receipt of Council Grants to aid their studies. Things had become over lax, even for our somewhat bohemian existence within the College, so much so that students were coming in pretty well whenever they liked. The authorities became aggrieved at this and demanded that we all arrive by 9.00 am sharp to sign a register. All hell broke out at this demand and I was instructed to take to task our inconsiderate bosses for not allowing sufficient recovery time from last night's hangover. I'm afraid I disagreed with this attitude, feeling that it really wasn't too much to ask in return for the grants doled out by the same authorities, and presented a very weak case on their behalf. So much so, that the rule remained in place. I didn't last long as the bleary-eyed brigade's rep.

At that Revel I became aware of Roy Williamson's skiffle group. They were very good, heavy on Lonnie Donegan material, he being Roy's God and, yes, there was a lot of chewing-gum left on a lot of bedposts by Roy's band in those days.

People constantly ask me when I first met Roy Williamson. The honest answer is that I don't quite know. In general terms it was certainly sometime during our first year as students at Edinburgh College of Art. Although we were in the same intake, we were in different sections of first year. I was first aware of his presence when the word went round that there was, in our midst, a guy from Gordonstoun. That news in itself made me wonder what he was doing at an art college. Weren't Gordonstoun types set for university places? When he was pointed out to me, first impressions weren't good. He looked dishevelled, his hair an untidy mess. He wore loose T-shirts and jeans and wouldn't have gained many marks for sartorial elegance, compared to my somewhat staid grey suit and Brylcreemed 'shed'. We were also different in body shape. He usually wore short sleeves revealing muscular arms, attained no doubt by his continual squeezing of a wee rubber ball. You could see that he was also heavy of thighs and calfs, which became more obvious to me during the season when we took to the field of rugby against each other on opposing wings, he for Edinburgh Wanderers and I for Boroughmuir. Although he was fairly broad of shoulder, as I was myself, there the similarity ends because he had no chest to speak of, probably due to the asthma which, I learned in later years, he had suffered all his life, and he had a long thin body with, as I have said, stocky legs. I on the other hand had a tendency towards the pigeon-chest with a short body and long, slim legs. I'm pretty sure he also always had a bit of a pot-belly.

The first words we exchanged were on the dance-floor at a college hop where he and his girl-friend Vi were flinging themselves around in a pretty wild jive. I made some comment about Vi, and Roy said, 'Watch it pal'. A somewhat inauspicious start to what became a long and close association.

During our time at college it certainly couldn't be said that we were what I would call friends, opposing each other at times on the table-tennis table in the college club, at rugby and at athletics meetings, he competing for Edinburgh Southern Harriers and myself for Braidburn Athletic Club.

Socially, as well, we were at opposite ends of the scale. I was working class and he was from a moneyed, professional background, his mother a pianist and his father a prominent attorney. Not that that seemed to bring family happiness as I learned much later in our relationship.

We did become closer when we finished art college and took up studies at Moray House Teacher Training College. There, we both played in the college rugby team mid-week and were both on the team selection committee. Such proximity led to visits to each other's homes and "Watch it pal" was banished to the past.

My own musical taste was changing as well. I had acquired a record player from Wattie and, for my first LP, acquired Ravel's *Bolero* long before Torvill and Dean danced on ice to it. Moving on to Rachmaninov and all his buddies, I made a lot of use of Casey's Record Exchange which had opened three or four doors along in Buccleuch Street. There was still not a hint of folk music, but maybe a bit of jazz creeping in.

I was studying anatomy when I first met Drew Kennedy. Anatomy classes were taken by the famous Scottish artist, Robin Phillipson. Robin threw all his energy into everything he did, and anatomy was no exception. He had a willing accomplice in Drew who was our model in learning about the structure of muscle masses because he was an acrobat, and a diver of Olympic standard, training with Scotland diver, Peter Heatly. He had also worked in circuses both here and on the continent with his wife, Sheila, as his stage assistant.

Robin would ask Drew to get into some very difficult poses to bunch muscle groups for us to observe. It's one thing to get into a hand-stand, but try to hold it for minutes at a time, and then transfer out of it into a one-handed balance and you start to feel pain, which Drew often did. It may have been my own athletics and swimming that brought us together in a shared interest but, whatever the reason, we became firm friends. When Pat and I met Sheila we became a unit which remained close until Drew died a few years ago. I still have regular lunch dates with Sheila.

By this time Pat and I were in our fifth year of courtship and still managing to keep it clean, so to speak, unlike her brother Lee and his girlfriend, Ina. When they announced Ina's pregnancy Wattie imposed a curfew on Pat, demanding that she be home every night by ten o'clock. This seemed to us pretty stupid since, as I have said, on many an occasion Pat and I were alone before her parents got home from the shop. We had all the time in the world for hanky-panky had we so desired, and make no mistake we certainly did desire, but did not indulge.

We came very close on one occasion, though, after imbibing rather heavily at one of those notorious Revels. On walking out of the College into Lauriston Place, passing the fire station at four in the morning, Pat very slyly said, 'I bet you tuppence ha'penny you wouldn't come to bed with me tonight.'

I said that I would take her up on it, and we proceeded in haste to Duncan Street where Pat was staying over at her sister Margaret's house. We rushed into Pat's room and both stripped naked and dived into a cold bed but, don't expect any *Fifty Shades of Browne* revelations. It didn't turn out like that. Instead, I couldn't stop shivering and Pat couldn't stop sniggering and the whole escapade ended in embarrassment with me donning my clothes and escaping, leaving Pat to rue the day we had ever met. I tortured myself on my way home with that thought, but when we met the next day, she took full responsibility and we kissed and made up.

Continuing our respect for each other and our parents, we complied with orders. The curfew meant that for a couple of years after it was imposed, we didn't see the end of a film or concert, having to exit cinema or concert venue in time to catch a bus to Gilmerton.

Pat and I became engaged on August 20th, 1958, my 21st birthday. Our plan was to wait until I, like Pat, was in full-time employment before we married. That was another two years away, after Teacher Training College. Pat wasn't earning enough for us to live off her wage, so I gave up swimming and athletics and worked more in bars at night to try to get a bit of money together. Then we saw a sign which made us decide to bring our marriage date forward.

A third-floor flat was for sale round the corner from my home in No. 3 at a fixed price of £350. Driven by psychological and physical desperation to finally be together, we reached the conclusion that, if we borrowed the money from Pat's father (which Pat was sure would be possible), added my summer vacation income to her wages, included my term-time casual bar work and sale of paintings (which was starting to happen), we could get married and maybe not do too badly. A date was duly fixed when I would ask Wattie for his daughter's hand in marriage.

Although I knew full well that he had been primed for the encounter, I still approached the day with trepidation, arriving on time and being shown into the 'Good Room' where Wattie was waiting in his armchair. All I could see was his legs, poking out from beneath a fully-spread copy of the *Evening News*, his fingers grasping the paper tightly on each side; obviously he was looking forward to the confrontation as much as I. Taking a deep breath I began, meandering round the fact that I had been going out with his daughter for long enough to know that we both wanted to spend the rest of our lives together. Wattie coughed and spoke in turn, meandering round the fact that he too thought that maybe it was time that we were together and that, if I was determined to take the plunge, he had no objections. I thanked him respectfully and took another deep breath, preparing myself, and him, for the $60,000 question, or more specifically, the £350 question. As if desperate to end his embarrassment, he blurted out even before I could raise the question, 'And it's all right about the money as well.'

The paper came down and we rushed to shake hands, at which the door flew open, and Pat and Violet projected themselves into the room, the sign for tears to flow and kisses to be exchanged.

Chapter Nine

Having agreed to pay back Wattie and Violet at £1 per week, we took the money and bought the flat. Painting and decorating began, coinciding with painting for my final Diploma Portfolio. Pat helped her mother make the wedding dress and arranged all the other necessities for a white wedding. It therefore came as no surprise that my Graduation Ceremony from the College of Art towards the end of June, 1959, played second fiddle to my Wedding Day on June 30th, a few days later. This might sound like sour grapes but, believe me, my wedding to Pat was the most important day of my life. It was on a Tuesday, as it had to be, that being the Elliot shop's half-day.

The ceremony went well in St Mary's, Dalkeith, and the reception followed suit. However, I did have to run along Dalkeith High Street in my bow-tie and dickie to persuade my brother, Jim, to come back to the hotel after he'd taken umbrage at something my mother had said about spiritualism, while my brother Ian was restrained because he wanted to get in on the fight. I'll admit the proceedings were marred for me slightly after Pop's third Fowler's Wee Heavy prompted him to come out with, 'Ye're far too young tae get married, ye should have been out there sowin' yer wild oats.'

It was some time before Pat and I got the chance to sow any kind of oats. On leaving the reception we made our way to Waverley Station and an overnight train to London for a four-day honeymoon. We hadn't wanted to splash out on a sleeper, so we spent the next few hours playing cards with two other impecunious, insomniac strangers, between cups of tea brewed on a tiny Primus stove one of them had smuggled onto the train.

At the end of my second year at college, together with about ten other students who had qualified for a travelling bursary, I travelled to London for a few days to study the art of etching and engraving under the tuition of Dick Fozzard at the Royal College of Art. Dick very kindly allowed us to take up residence in his flat overlooking the Royal Albert Hall. We had the use of one bedroom. The double bed was shared by three of the girls, while the rest of us slept on the floor. We all kept in touch with Dick over the next few years and, when our honeymoon was imminent, he again kindly allowed Pat and me the use of his flat.

The only bed he had available was a blow-up Lilo, but beggars can't be choosers and we certainly fulfilled the roll of beggars. The day after we arrived Jimmy Gavin, one of my friends from college, turned up and took possession of the other Lilo in the room. Needless to say, the frustration that had been building for years grew intolerable and we couldn't wait to get home to the haven of our wee flat.

Wee flat it certainly was, but it was ours, and isn't that what makes all the difference?

On the top floor of the stair at 5 Westcrosscauseway, the flat had a tiny lounge with a coal fire, one window with box-seat and one cupboard which was actually the coal-cellar. A door beside this cellar led into another tiny room which we converted into a kitchen. The window of this room overlooked my parents' kitchen windows and, of course, the dreaded Weinsteins. In the corridor was a toilet but, unlike the one I was used to, it had a wash-hand basin. Such luxury. Its main drawback was that when you sat on the loo and drew the door towards you, it hit your knees and toes. Completing our sanctuary was a small bedroom with one window and a box-room off, that I used as a studio. It's usual for an artist to paint details of his picture at arm's length and then step back a few paces to keep track of the general effect, but my space was so limited that I had to make use of a diminishing glass when pondering the developing work. I'm sure we've all used a magnifying glass to make things look bigger, so just use your imagination please.

Whatever restrictions I was under, I managed to complete at least one successful picture. After submitting to the John Moores Liverpool Exhibition, one of the most prestigious competitive shows in Britain, in which every picture on the walls was guaranteed to sell, it was accepted and hung. I have the number 80 in mind. I can't remember if that was the number of paintings on the wall, or whether I got £80. Whatever the price, it proved of immense benefit to us, burdened at the time by new expenses like the payment of rates, gas, electricity, coal, etc, all of which had been met by parents when we lived at home.

The grant I received for my impending two terms at Moray House Teacher Training College didn't even cover the purchase of text-books necessary for the course, mainly due to the grant being based on my father's income. The same basis had been used for my Art College grant but, at the time of that application, my parents had filled in the details. Now that I had left the parental home, I was responsible for my own application and had to have sight of Pop's earnings. I was surprised to find that, as a lorry-driver, he was on £1,800 a year. I knew this to be in excess of what the Elliots were drawing from their shop, and a hell of a lot more than the £11 per week I was looking forward to when I started to teach. So much for forgetting my station in life.

As important as selling at the John Moores was the prestige it afforded a budding artist. Word of my achievement got back to Art College where I was remembered by the upcoming students. Pat and I, of course, would have loved to go to Liverpool to see my work hanging in the exhibition, so we dreamed up what was the first of several entrepreneurial schemes in our years together. When I was in the Scouts, I had gone to France on a bus-trip which was the first international commercial journey undertaken by The William Hunter Bus Group. From them I asked the price of a trip to Liverpool and posted a notice on the College notice board, inviting interested parties to add their names if they would like to go: first come, first served. The response was immediate and I made arrangements. Our pricing structure was such that, after all expenses paid, Pat and I went free. The fact that it was down overnight, a day at the exhibition and back overnight, pleased everybody, since no extra expense for accommodation was necessary.

One of my friends at College, David Harding, was dabbling in not only painting, but also pottery and glass. Indeed, I still have the pair of blown-glass vases he gave us as a wedding present and I'm sure Dave would be pleased to know that there is neither a chip nor a scratch on either after all these years. One of Dave's other interests was journalism and he came to us one evening researching an article on our Liverpool escapade. Published in *The Scotsman* and the *Edinburgh Evening News*, it gave me recognition in the wider Scottish art circles. So much so that a prominent collector, David Cleghorn Thomson, began to acquire some of my smaller works. One night I was invited to his home for a meal where he had prepared a large boiled fish. That was it, just a fish. Ah-hah, thought I, so this is how the other half live. No wonder he could afford to buy paintings.

Another collector, whose name I don't remember, was a doctor living round the corner from Raeburn Place, who invited me to his home to see what company I was in on his walls, he having purchased a small pencil wash drawing of mine. When I entered his establishment, the walls were covered with paintings from floor to ceiling. Expensive rugs and carpets on the floors were covered with things like croquet sets and carvings of all sorts. After a bit of banter and teasing, because I couldn't see my drawing anywhere, I found it in a tiny toilet not unlike my own. The difference between his 'chunky' and mine was that, there on the wall beside the toilet paper holder, was my drawing. I couldn't really take offence because, hanging alongside mine, was an etching by Rembrandt.

You might have the impression that I was now rolling in money. Not so, because I wouldn't be paid from Liverpool until the exhibition closed months ahead, and what collectors tend to do is buy cheap from budding artists at the beginning of their career in the hope that they can cash in when the artist has 'made it'.

While I was dabbling in art, before I started teacher training in August, Pat was hard at work. Her mentor, Robin Finlay, had started working on his own from his home in Braid Road and she had agreed to help. As a gesture of her new-found independence Pat acquired from her sister Margaret a Pekinese puppy which she called Suzie. It was a rare wee animal you could always hear coming because her squashed up nose gave her a permanent snuffle. Pat journeyed to work by bus, and every morning would carry Suzie downstairs, round the corner and over Buccleuch Street into Buccleuch Place and the Meedies where the dog was let down on the grass between us. She would walk with us past the tennis-courts and bowling-greens until we came to Hope Park Terrace where she was picked up to continue their journey by bus to Braid Road where she hugged Pat's feet under her desk all day. I would leave them at the bus-stop and return home to paint, or go to Moray House when I started there. Our regular perambulations were duly noted by the neighbours whereupon: 'Browneeeeeee. . . . It's a bloody disgrace, makin' tha' puir wee dug climb a' they stairs on they wee short legs. Ah'm gonnae report you tae the RSPCA'.

I did eventually start at Moray House where I became more closely involved with Roy Williamson. Now sharing classes, we began to play rugby together on Wednesdays for the College team. In addition, I was working most evenings in a restaurant/ bar called The Athenian in Howe Street, in sight of the flat where he and Vi had taken up residence after marrying while still at Art College. Now and again he would come in for a chat.

When I started at The Athenian I was told that all tips would be shared equally at the end of each week between myself and Bill, the regular full-time barman. I kept a pretty close tally on what I had been throwing in to the communal jug and was somewhat surprised, at the end of the first week, to note that the silver tips appearing were all mine. Bill seemed to be tipped only in coppers. During the second week, I made a point of keeping hold of my silver and putting in only copper which I had suspected Bill had been doing. Sure enough, there was only copper at the end of the second week. We exchanged glances, knowingly, and thereafter things worked out better.

Pat would often come into the bar for a bit of company, and sit until closing-time. One evening she had taken up her usual bar-stool seat, when she was approached by an older man who engaged her in conversation. He was a shoelace salesman, which was supposed to impress her because he offered her a drink with the possibility of a meal afterwards. Pat thanked him politely but said she was afraid he was wasting his time and that her husband wouldn't like that idea. When he said that her husband needn't know, she explained that he could hardly not because that was him over there, pointing at me behind the bar. That night we lost a customer.

As we approached the Christmas and New Year period a barmaid was taken on. I had already been promised full-time employment over the holidays but was now suddenly told that would not be possible. When I explained that this was indeed a blow, and that I had been relying on the extra money, I was told, 'Sorry pal, but she's got bigger tits than you.'

When I got home that evening and told Pat, a cloud descended, but the very next evening we had a knock at our door. A lady was there with her daughter and she explained that she had read Dave's article about me in *The Scotsman*. She owned a guest house on Broughton Street and was looking for a painting to help in the redecoration of her lounge. Supporting a young local artist appealed to her and did I have anything she could look at? As it happened, I had been working on some semi-abstract paintings of the rocks of Salisbury Crags, one in particular designated to hang over my own fireplace. She liked three of them and it was decided that I should take them to her property to see which was the most suitable. I cadged a lift from a friend and arrived with the paintings at the allotted time, whereupon she chose the one I wanted for myself. The £30 she agreed to pay was pretty close to what I would have earned in The Athenian, so I had no choice but to sell.

Pat and I had been in the habit of treating ourselves once a month to High Tea at Patrick Thomson's store, to the accompaniment of music from a trio of ageing ladies on violin, cello and piano. That Christmas, we went twice.

Craig's Bar was located on the corner of West Crosscauseway/ Nicholson Street. The entrance to the public bar was the corner door. Another door, on West Crosscauseway, opened on what had become a ladies' snug. Not long before, women hadn't been allowed into pubs but this innovation proved quite popular. The walls of the public bar were festooned with watercolour and chalk portraits of local worthies who frequented the premises, all by the proprietor, Bob Craig.

I ventured in one evening over the Festive Season to ask Bob if perhaps he required the services of a part-time barman. He said he did, and I was hired on the spot. We immediately hit it off, indeed many nights we spent more time talking about art than serving. Standing behind the bar, just before opening time, I could see ahead of me the window looking out to Nicholson Street. Beneath the window was a high-backed bench and above that a row of Bob's portraits. Above that again was a frosted panel just below the window itself, where I could see in the waiting queue, some of the very heads I was looking at on the frieze. What made my short stay in Craig's so pleasant was the fact that, being a local boy, most of these customers I already knew as neighbours and friends, I had a shared interest with Bob, another of the part-time bartenders was my former scout master, Archie Keppy, and, possibly best of all, I lived but a few yards from my work.

In these ways we progressed into the spring of 1960 when, in March, study gave way to full-time teaching. I was required to teach for two probationary years before gaining what was termed a teaching 'parchment'. My probation started when I was employed by Midlothian Council to teach a couple of days a week in Dalkeith High School, and three in Musselburgh Grammar School. Pat was still working for Robin Finlay, but even with the addition of my £11 a week salary, we were increasingly becoming more aware of just how much it takes to run a home.

Our local plumber, Charlie Easton, had his workshop at No.1c. He was always very fair with his prices and it was he who converted our kitchen. Living just above Charlie were John and Ella Farquhar. John was in the building business and did stonework repairs on my window-sills, again very fairly on price. Andy Ireland, from Art College days, had been a joiner to trade before attending College and was always on hand to chisel away at our woodwork. In spite of all such assistance, there never seemed to be anything left in the pot at the end of each week. I must take the blame since I was still buying materials for painting. My justification was that I was managing to sell a few in group exhibitions.

Roy and I would commiserate with one another on our financial positions at each other's homes. One evening, Roy told me that, at one time, when they were down to their last half-crown (12 1/2p), he asked Vi to go out and blow the lot on something nice for their tea. She came back with three African spears. Of course Roy didn't know whether to laugh or cry, and the story has followed Vi all her life. I only learned the sequel recently. Vi and I were in company together at a party, reminiscing on the old days, when I told it yet again. The laughter was interrupted when Vi raised that soft lilt of a voice and said, in the accent she never has lost, 'But Ronnie, I got three shields as well'.

I quickly became disillusioned with teaching. The staff at Moray House had obviously been out of schools for some time and had forgotten the word, 'requisition'. All the talk we had been listening to about free expression, and the use of as wide a variety of mediums in drawing, painting, modelling, etc, as possible, went completely by the board when faced with the prevailing reality in the schools.

In Dalkeith, for instance, I was faced with an art department in which every pupil's work looked the same. Same drawing technique, same compositions and, what appalled me most, the same colour schemes. You could hardly distinguish whose painting was whose. I admit this could have been due to the teacher. The head of the department, Willie Watson, was a bombastic character who let you know exactly what he thought of everything. His way was the only way, and staffroom breaks were dominated by his strident opinions. Most of the staff let him rant on, except for one gentleman teacher, a Major Chambers Crabtree, who, whilst peeling his regular lunchtime orange, would voice conflicting opinions in the softest of voices. I don't think Willie liked him too much.

Quite apart from Willie's, 'My way is the only way' attitude, it was almost one brush between two pupils and one pan of colour between four. Maybe Willie was trying to curry favour with the authorities when he submitted his annual requisition form for the department, his detailed request for material for the coming academic year, by showing he could make do with little. Ian McDonald, my head of department at Musselburgh, was entirely different. It was he who taught me that you had to request at least four times as much as you needed to get even half of what you wanted.

In my youthful exuberance, I once took a piece of stone into class to demonstrate that art wasn't all about painting. With a couple of chisels I carved a simple shape, suggesting that we might have a budding Michelangelo - 'Whae's he Sir?' - in the class. Hammer and chisels could be borrowed from the technical department; the drawback was getting enough stone for the project. Saying so was a big mistake.

'We pass auld stane on the way tae school every day, Sir. We'll bring some in fur ye.'

The stone duly arrived, followed very quickly by the whine of a police siren. The little buggers had knocked down the convent wall during the night.

When it was time to decorate the Musselburgh gym for the Christmas Party, all eyes turned on this fresh, wet-behind-the-ears, energetic young thing straight out of Art College. I fell for it hook, line and sinker and took on the job of transformation. As we had a seaside location, I chose an under-water theme. Brunton's Wireworks was just along the road from the school and I begged some lengths of wire to fabricate small three-dimensional fishing boats and islands to sit on top of a huge fishing-net suspended, end-to-end, halfway up the gym walls to represent the surface of the sea. More models of wire fish and other sea-creatures were suspended from the net and, though I say it who shouldn't, the floating effect was quite impressive.

The nets were acquired by a colleague, Leonard Broom, from his fishermen friends further down the coast. The technical department constructed a huge sea monster with the wire from Brunton's. Sitting on the gym floor it reared its head through the sea surface, almost reaching the roof, with flashing light-bulb eyes staring down. From local painters and decorators I managed to sequester paint and wallpapers sufficient for the kids to truly splash colour and make paintings of landscapes of cliffs, villages and lighthouses.

You can imagine the excitement that was generated throughout the whole school with most departments lending a hand, but then the 'Headie' walked through the gym one day when the scene was nearly completed. He stopped and looked around incredulously and walked out. I was summoned to his office. Thinking I was in for praise and congratulation for showing initiative, ingenuity and organisational powers, I went in to face questions instead on where the materials had come from, when the project had been sanctioned and by whom. While giving the answers I realised that he was miffed that he hadn't been given the chance to approach Brunton's, the painters' firms, the fishing-community, etc, on behalf of the school. In effect, I had borrowed his authority without permission. I actually had a vision of getting six-of-the-best on his carpet, just like I had been given at Boroughmuir. I did manage to get out without that happening, but also with the feeling of: 'Never again, pal.'

So, this was what teaching was all about: petty bureaucracy.

I've already said how poor we were after we were married. It was so bad at one point that we visited a pawn shop not far from us, to pawn I know not what, because we had nothing. Another time, Violet agreed to lend us more money, but Pat had to go to the shop in Dalkeith to collect it. The trouble was, she didn't even have the bus-fare. She went downstairs and round the corner to see Ma and asked to borrow the fare. The answer was, 'Certainly not. You've made your bed, you'll just have to lie in it.'

This was another manifestation of how much my parents resented my wife, but think how Pat must have felt, particularly since I was the one who was mainly responsible. Consider the following synopsis of what I was up to, the information culled from a CV which I must have prepared for a job application.

Since leaving College of Art in 1959, I had spent most of my time painting. I had exhibited in the R.S.A, the S.S.A. and the R.S.W., The John Moores, various Group Shows, The Exhibition of Young Scottish Painters of Promise and, opening on March 17th, 1962, in a Group Show in the prestigious Aitken & Dott Scottish Gallery. A solo show in The 1957 Gallery had resulted in an exciting prospect.

One of the visitors to the 57 was a lecturer from the Hull Regional College of Art in Kingston-upon-Hull. He told me that a short-leet was being put together for a lecturing post, and that my work was exactly the kind of thing that would be looked on favourably. If I was interested he would recommend that I be put on the list. This was exactly the kind of opportunity Pat's long-sufferance of my continual spending on materials (probably causing the biggest hole in our bank-account), had made possible and it was agreed that I should at least try.

I was duly called to Kingston-upon-Hull for the interview. On arrival at the College, I was shown into a room where I met the other three candidates for the job. In the ensuing conversation, I came to suspect that my presence was merely to make up the numbers. Two were already in lecturing posts. After my interview, I left dejected. Phoning Pat from a boarding-house that evening, I had never felt so home-sick in my life. Eventually I was informed that I had been unsuccessful in getting the job but Pat, as always throughout our life together, encouraged me to keep trying.

In early 1961 we discovered that Pat was pregnant. I remember being a bit mystified, until I recalled a Friday afternoon in late December 1960 when, on a regular visit to the chemist shop next to the Cafe Royal in West Register, when the chemist asked the usual question, 'Something for the weekend, Sir?' I had replied, 'No, thank you.'

The baby arrived on August 11th, 1961, and we called him Gavin John. For the birth, Pat was admitted to the Simpson Memorial Pavilion where, in spite of the best possible treatment, she haemorrhaged so badly that I nearly lost her. It was close, but she was in exactly the right place for such a thing to happen and, fortunately, they saved her.

Gavin was a good baby who hardly ever cried. He slept in

a cot at the bottom of our bed and was often awake when we roused ourselves, contentedly playing with his toes, or the wee toys affixed to the rails. Pat fancied a big pram which, although fine for walking up and down the street, was too bulky to be taken up and down the stairs. There was a small 'sell-a-bit-of-everything' shop at No. 3 which was owned by Mrs Innes, who also ran a private investigation agency on the side, and she kindly allowed us to park the pram beside her flat door in the passage leading to the back-green.

There was an old Scottish custom at that time, I don't know if it exists today, it being a long time since I had babies, of greasing a newly-born baby's palm with a silver coin. Pat, having fully recovered from her near miss, and now working from home with accounts brought to her by Finlay, spent quite a bit of time parading her treasure up and down the district. Some days her collection of silver coins bore witness to the fact that he really was a treasure.

Our accommodation had become unsuitable so we started to look for something else, finally finding it at 18 Briarbank Terrace, in the Shandon district of Edinburgh. It was quite far from my work on the other side of town in Musselburgh, where I was now teaching full-time, but there was a good bus service, so we decided to go for it. As I was in a respectable full-time job and with a property to sell, it did not prove difficult to obtain a bank loan to purchase Briarbank. When we did, Ma and Pop hit the roof. Was this not the final proof that that girl was taking me 'way out of my station'? Pointing out that our repayments to the bank, for a property which we would eventually own, were actually lower than the rent they were paying for a property that would never be theirs, made no difference.

Briarbank having been bought, we made preparations to move. I don't remember the date but do remember it was a Sunday. The reason I can be so precise is that Pat, always the practical one, asked why we should spend money on a removal firm when we could have the use of a lorry, free, to move our few bits and pieces. Violet and Wattie's neighbour, Jackie Nisbet, was a vegetable wholesaler who used an open lorry to ply his wares. Sundays were still inviolate in those days and Jackie would not have dared to work on one, so the lorry stood idle in his drive. We gathered a few friends on the fateful day and, to much merriment, everything was tied down and we set off. After a few yards of the journey we passed my parents' home. Thinking I would give them a parting wave I looked to see them, one at each of the two windows looking on to Westcrosscauseway, make a very obvious show of drawing down the blinds in perfect unison, in shame.

As the curtains were drawn on one part of my life another, much more hopeful and pleasant part, was about to open up.

Chapter Ten

Through 1961 and early 1962 I sought desperately for some way of earning money other than teaching and exhibiting. We had already considered an exchange teaching scheme to Holland where salaries were much higher but, after a bit of research, discovered that so too was the cost of living. The move would have left us in pretty much the same position financially. I even went to the Leith offices of Salveson to try to arrange a two year whaling engagement. Although being away from home for that length of time would be a wrench, I would at least come back with money to show for it. It was explained to me that Salveson was about to pull out of the diminishing whaling industry, which they did in 1963. It was possibly for the best as I heard that many men fell foul of heavy gambling and came home with nothing.

Then, in the early months of 1962, fate took a hand.

Roy and I had been seeing more of each other with reciprocal home visits when, one night at Roy's house, sitting on the floor of his kitchen with our backs against a wall of wooden cupboards which he had designed and built (right down to the wooden hinges), he picked up his guitar, strummed a few chords and sang some song or other, and I joined in with a harmony. Also sitting on the floor, Vi joked to Pat, 'My goodness, they could easily be another Hall and MacGregor.'

'Hall and MacGregor' were the famous Robin Hall and

Jimmie MacGregor who had been singing topical and folk songs every evening on the popular BBC 'Tonight' programme with Cliff Michelmore as anchor man.

We all smiled at Vi's remark, promptly forgot it and carried on with life. This increasingly meant Roy and me singing more songs together, by this time including 'Macpherson's Rant' and 'My Bonnie Laddie's Lang a'Growin', the first folksongs I learned, taken from an EP by that very same 'Hall and MacGregor'. Pat and I had also been seeing a lot more of Drew Kennedy and his wife, Sheila, who commiserated with us over the mixed blessing of evening class teaching, in which I was now involved at Musselburgh Grammer. School classes finished at 3.45 pm and evening classes began at 7.00, leaving not enough time to get home and back. I spent a lot of that spare time in the school gym throwing a rugby ball at the basketball net, honing my throw-in skills, since, in those days, rugby wingers had the job of throwing in to the lineout.

In the summer of 1962, Roy joined a folk-singing trio made up of Bill Smith, who studied architecture at College during the same years as Roy and myself, Ron Cruickshank, who was a nephew of Andrew Cruickshank of 'Dr Finlay's Casebook' fame, and Paddie Bell. Dolina McLennan hosted a folk-club in the Waverley Bar, in St Mary's Street, and, in later years, she would declare that she forfeited her 2/6 fee to pay them on their first night. Drew, Sheila, Pat and I went along to encourage and they were, indeed, excellent. Unfortunately, a few weeks later, Ron Cruickshank contracted glandular fever and was no longer able to sing. The remainder of the group were very concerned for him of course, but equally concerned for themselves because they had arranged to appear for the three weeks of the Edinburgh Festival at a coffee-house called The Tryst, on the Royal Mile. Roy mentioned that we had been singing together a wee bit and that I knew a couple of songs and might be willing to help them fulfil the engagement.

I went along to Paddie Bell's Buckingham Terrace flat for a rehearsal to see if I would fit in. I had never done any public singing, since you couldn't count scout and Sunday school shows, so I was crippled with nerves. However, with Sandy Bell, Paddie's husband, standing at his drawing-board in the bay window, his pipe in his mouth, working on his architectural illustrations, helping to make the atmosphere quite relaxed, and the thought of £5 a night, a pound each and one for the taxi, I soon relaxed. The owner of The Tryst, Sandy Buchan, intended to sell his coffees first and then we were to sing for half an hour. It was presumed that, once the singing was over, people would disperse, leaving time for more coffee and another half hour from us, but no one really knew what was going to happen.

On the evening before the first night's performance the name, 'The Corrie Folk Trio and Paddie Bell', was dreamed up. A corrie is a dip in the hillside and it crops up in place names all over Scotland such as the White Corries, Black Corries, Corrieshalloch, etc. It was in such dips in the hillside that the Covenanters conducted their illicit conventicles with guards posted on the surrounding hillsides. There was also a folksinger and folk song collector called Joe Corrie. It seemed to us that the word *corrie* conjured up sights and sounds of Scotland, and so we chose it.

No advertising had gone out in the name of the group, as it wouldn't have meant anything anyway, so we went out to face eight people who had only come in for the coffee. However, they stayed for the next session, and the next, and, in fact every one that evening, in spite of the songs being the same each time. That was the birth of our fairy story, because those same eight people came back the next night, but this time with friends, and they all stayed on for our four spots.

By the end of the first week we were singing to a full house of eighty every night. We frantically rehearsed new material in whatever time we could, and by the end of the three weeks, from our dressing-room in a flat above the coffee-house, we would look down to see an amazing sight. The audience for each half hour was having to be cleared to allow a fresh lot of people in from a queue standing on the stair and running along the High Street. Many of the people who had just been asked to leave joined the queue to come back in again.

On those same nights, Rory and Alex McEwan were running a folk-show at Edinburgh Ice Rink. Amongst their guests were the legendary 'Clancy Brothers and Tommy Makem', making their first appearances in Britain, over from America where the Folk Revival was in full swing, and already big names.

One night, after our show at The Tryst, we had a late-night celebratory party in Roy's large lounge at Northumberland Street. Half-way through a song there was a commotion at the door and a crowd of people came in and settled down. We weren't worried by the crowd because we noticed that among them was a friend from College, Pete Stitt, and we assumed that these were his friends and they would be naturally welcome, although there were quite a few of them.

When we finished, there ensued a babble of conversation, but before we could find out who was who, a lone male voice from one corner sang out loud, 'When I was a little boy, so me mother told me . . .' and from the other three corners came another three male voices singing in reply, 'T'me, . . .'way, haul away, we'll haul away Joe, . . .' and from the first corner again, the lone voice, but this time on the move towards the centre of the room, 'That if I didn't kiss the girls me lips would go all mouldy, . . .' the other three voices again, also now on the move, 'T'me, . . . 'way haul away, we'll haul away Joe, . . .' and when they met up as a group, they all sang together, "Way haul away, we'll haul for better weather, T'me, . . . 'way haul away, we'll haul away Joe'.

That was how The Clancy Brothers and Tommy Makem introduced themselves for, yes indeed it was them in person, large as life, together with a crowd of New York high society camp followers who had come over for the Festival.

The end of our singing stint at The Tryst coincided with the end of our teaching summer break so Roy and I found ourselves back to the grind, still not thinking of a career in show business. Roy, funnily enough, found himself in the daily company of two of his pupils who were themselves destined for great things, never mind their teacher. Bruce Hay, at that time a pupil at Liberton High School, and heavily into football, had no thought in his mind that one day he would be one of the greatest rugby players Scotland has ever produced, playing not only countless games for his country, but also for the British Lions. Roy liked to think that he was perhaps influential in Bruce switching codes.

Another of his charges was called Davey Johnstone. Davey and Roy got on well because they were both great musicians, even though Davey was still a schoolboy. He played that famous guitar riff in Elton John's 'Candle in the Wind', and is currently Elton's musical director because, shortly after leaving school, his musical skills took him to the London music scene, where he prospered.

Davey had been in London for some time when he came home for a short holiday to visit family. I happened to see him walking along the street and stopped to say hello. He mentioned how relieved he was to see a friendly face, because he thought everyone was moving to the other side of the street at his approach, as though he had the plague. He remained confused even when I explained to him that not many people in Carricknowe wore their blonde hair down their back and huge black sunglasses atop a tight denim jacket, the whole ensemble finished off with skinny blue jeans with flapping flares at the knee, lined in canary yellow and belted with a monstrous buffalo-head buckle. The Edinburgh boy had slightly outpaced Edinburgh.

It took a while for word to percolate through the existing

Scottish folk-scene that there were new kids on the block, the Corrie Folk Trio and Paddie Bell, and I can confirm that there was no sudden rush of invitations to come and perform.

From this point you might get the impression that I have total recall. Not so. What I do have in my possession though, are my business diaries from 1963 right through to 1990 when Roy died. I also have Pat's personal diaries from 1973 onwards. These documents provide a fantastic jog to the memory when it's required.

One of the reasons I kept my diaries was because, since I didn't play any instruments except the 'moothie' (mouth organ) during the whole career of The Corrie Folk Trio and Paddie Bell, I took on the role of business manager. This meant that I was responsible for the money side of the business, which our entry into the music world quickly became. It seemed a natural role to adopt since Pat was a book-keeper. Her boss became the group's accountant.

It was obvious after our success at The Tryst that the group was offering something people wanted. We began to sing in The Gamp Club in Victoria Street, continuing on a weekly basis into January, 1963. Strangely enough, our performances took place on Monday nights and not at weekends. Tuesday, January 15th saw our biggest fee to date coming from a cabaret appearance at Gleneagles Hotel where we entertained at a Motor Trades Association Dinner. Train fares were £1.1s, taxis 7/- and we took home £3 each. Back to £1 each on the 18th for a cabaret at the architectural firm of Ove Arup & Partners and only 10/- each the next night at The Gamp.

Thursday, February 7th saw us taking the Ferry to the foreign climes of Fife at The Dunfermline Howff Folk-club. More weeklies followed at The Gamp where, on February 25th, we 'entertained' Mr Buchan, which cost us £1.11s.6d. We must have been courting Mr Buchan because on Friday, March 29th, we were back at The Tryst. That same day we received a cheque for twelve guineas for an appearance at Peebles Hydro Hotel on March 5th. Word must have been spreading more quickly through the entertainment business than the Folk Club scene because on June 7th we did another cabaret engagement at a dance in Perth for a fee of £22.

Bearing in mind that the four of us were still in full-time employment, you'll understand my constant reference to the money side of it. It's said that musicians play for love of the music. Nonsense! This musician was playing for the cash. The cash made a big difference to Pat and me and it was earned in a more pleasant way than washing glasses in the smoky atmosphere of a pub.

At 18 Briarbank Terrace, we lived on the first floor. Outside, at the back, we had a postage stamp garden but with our own ground-floor back-passageway where we could park the pram. We had a custom built kitchen off a lounge/dining-room and a real bathroom with bath, wash hand basin and toilet, which meant we had left the zinc bath behind in Westcrosscauseway along with the long rubber pipe required to fill it. Our bedroom had a smaller one off, for Gavin's cot, and a spare bedroom across the hall I used as a studio. Yes, I was still painting. To crown it all, at the front of the house, we had a 'good' room, where I took my turn hosting group practices.

I don't know how Bill could bear to come from his home in Moray Place in the New Town to an address which he called 'Railway Cuttings'. Possibly it was funny at first, but it grated after a while. I was reminded of my mother who, after being given a mild reprimand for hurting feelings, always replied, 'Oh, you know I don't mean anything by it.'

So we progressed until another event appeared on the horizon to make our life that bit more pleasant.

The month of June, 1963 brought a truly significant advance for CFT & PB. The McEwan Brothers, Alex and Rory, had appeared a few years previously on the BBC Television *Tonight* programme. Now, they had a television series of their own called *'Hootenanny'*, and on June 20th and 21st, they invited us as guests. The fee of £7.7/- each was as nothing to the £25.4/- each we received a few days later for a BBC Recording done at Springfield Road, Glasgow on June 25th. On the 29th we were recording in the studios of the Waverley label and again on July 27th before going to Ireland, an exploratory trip to take in a Folk Festival in Kilrush, County Clare.

We had to take a bus to Kilrush and, on presenting ourselves to the driver, explained that our instruments were quite valuable and we would like to keep them with us instead of packing them away in the storage compartment. He said that would be fine and we piled aboard. As we took our seats, an old Irish lady made the same request to take her case with her, but the driver refused. When she quizzed him why not, he replied, 'Well now, Ma'am, It's all in the way of askin''.

I still puzzle over that one, but when we asked how long it would take to get to Kilrush, there was no mistaking his meaning when he said, 'Ah now, that all depends on how good the music is.'

During the journey we quickly learned about the pace of life on the Emerald Isle because, at one of his village Inn stops, a football match was being shown on television and we all had to wait until it was over before we could continue.

In Kilrush I first met Barney McKenna, better known throughout Ireland as 'Banjo Barney'. The night before we had been doing the rounds of pubs and halls singing alongside The Clancy Brothers and Tommy Makem, who were in the company of Julie Felix and an Irish singer called Maureen Hurley. I rose fairly early from my bed in a tent, which was the only place I could find accommodation (Irish Folk Festivals are like that) and as I walked down to the beach, there was Barney sitting on a low wall.

'Ah now, Ronnie,' says Barney, 'I fairly enjoyed yer singin' last night. Did I ever tell ye how Cromwell took Drogheda?'

Before I could say no, he picked up a stick and proceeded to draw on the sand a map of Drogheda Castle but, before he could start in on his history lesson, the head of a tiny black kitten poked out from the fastenings of his overcoat. Without a break in his conversation, he poked the head back inside and continued to bemoan the loss of the fortress, stressing what a bastard Cromwell was.

I left Barney cursing Cromwell and continued to the pub at the end of Capa Pier, where I met another famous Irishman for the first time, Luke Kelly. Luke had, like the rest of us, been singing the night before and, by the sound of his voice, maybe all through the night as well. He was so hoarse I could hardly make out a word he was saying. After the welcoming pleasantries, he explained he would be fine once he had a drink or two. So it proved. After three or four pints of Guinness, Luke gradually became more intelligible and we had a rare chat about his friends and fellow musicians and singers, Ronnie Drew, he of the gravel voice, and Keiron Bourke, who together with Barney and himself were to become known throughout the world as The Dubliners.

While we were in County Clare we recorded at Television Erin before returning home for yet another recording session at Waverley Records on August 15th. I have a note in the diary beside this engagement stating that we were paid fourteen guineas on November 12th that year. Do you think they were waiting to see if the record was going to sell before they paid us?

All of a sudden the Edinburgh Festival was on us again. The North Berwick Harbour Pavilion Summer Show was in full swing. Stars of the show were Moira Anderson and Bill McCue, who performed week about with the Jimmy Shand Junior Scottish Country Dance Band. We took the bus down from Edinburgh when we were booked to appear August 19th to 21st and August 26th to 28th. It was hardly the most salubrious of accommodation back-stage. Moira's dressing-room was in a curtained corner of the stairs leading down from stage right. In later life she didn't like me to mention this, so I won't now.

Rory and Alex McEwan were running their late-night Festival Folk Show in The Palladium in Bread Street and kindly invited us to do a spot for them on the Wednesday of our last appearance in North Berwick. We accepted, provided we could get back to town and The Palladium by a quarter past midnight. This meant a rush to get off-stage and onto the last bus, but we made it. We seemed to go down pretty well when we walked from the back of the stage right down to the footlights in what we hoped was a dramatic entry. I had taken time that afternoon to buy something new for the occasion and felt like a real trouper in my fawn-coloured corduroy jacket, purchased from the second hand clothes store beside the stage door of The Palladium in East Fountainbridge.

With two spots at Waverley Market the week before (7.15 and 8.30), the Crown Bar on the 24th, and another appearance at Waverley Market on the 29th, we were hotting up to a busy time. Not content to wait to be invited to sing by any interested party, we hired the Goold Hall in Nicholson Square for the nights of September 2nd to 7th to present our own unofficial Festival Late Night Folk Show for what we fervently hoped would be an expectant audience. It was a huge success, but not in the way we had imagined.

The first stumbling block to present itself was 'The Brythonic Trio', three ladies on violin, cello and harp, from Wales as their name implies. They had booked the hall for their own show which would exit immediately before ours was to begin. We had decided to dress the hall up as far as possible, which meant having a couple of spotlights at the back for atmosphere. The Brythonic ladies objected to our removing some seats at the back, to take the light stands, so we bargained with them. We paid them the grand sum of £2.10s for the privilege. It was the only money they drew for the week, the Festival audiences being sublimely indifferent to their presence in town.

With £1.13/- to The Silk Shop for muslin and black cloth to dress the stage and 2/6 for chemicals in which to steep them for fire-proofing (on which the fire department had insisted before they would accept our 10/- licence fee), £1.3/4 for timber and 3/- for hooks to be forked out, leaving only Pat's expense of £1.5/- for biscuits to sell at half-time (she also took the tickets at the door), we were set to go.

None of this could have gone as smoothly as it did without help from outside the group. I'm talking about people like Wee Wattie Wright, one of Edinburgh's back green singers who, incidentally, told me that he had sung in my back green at West Crosscauseway; Geordie Hamilton, a postman working at the GPO office building at the east end of Princes Street and author of a song we sang on many an occasion, 'In Kirkintilloch There's Nae Pubs'; Lyle Borland, a student of dentistry; and Colin McKie, who was destined to borrow The Scottish Patriots' van for our use, particularly going to the Dunfermline and Kirkcaldy Clubs on the ferry and driving back over Kincardine Bridge when we were too late to catch the last ferry.

One other man who helped us out was the College friend of Roy's, Pete Stitt, with whom he had tried to set up businesses in pottery and advertising. During the week of the show, we introduced him as a famous cockney folk-singer and he sang his big hit:

'I don't know no-one who ain't got no nine inch nails
I knows the King, I knows the Queen
I knows the bleedin' Prince of Wales
Buuuuut . . . I don't know no-one who ain't got no nine
   inch nails'.

He finished at that and took his bow, bringing the house down, with everybody taking the spoof in the right spirit.

Our spot on the show shrunk night by night as people made request after request to come on board. The easiest way to describe this is to just make a list: Eleanor Leith, Joe Heany, Hamish Imlach, Gordon McCulloch, Maureen Hurley, whom we had met in Kilrush, Liam Clancy, Luke Kelly, Keiron Bourke and Banjo Barney (Ronnie Drew had not yet joined them to make up The Dubliners), Geordie Hamilton, of course, and many others I can't remember. Altogether a great week, and we even ended up making a bit of money ourselves.

On Tuesday, September 10th, we made an appearance at The Crown Bar to celebrate the issue of our first recorded music on the Waverley label: 'The Corrie Folk Trio and Paddie Bell: ELP129'.

Chapter Eleven

After finishing at the Gould Hall, we began weekend shows in The Bothy, an establishment owned by Lawrence Demarco. Lawrie ran a restaurant on George IV Bridge at ground level and converted the floor above into a cosy space for us, with coal fires at either end. We did three or four nights a week with guests such as the Joe Gordon Folk Four, well-known at the time from countless television and variety theatre performances. There were many unknown singers too, an airline pilot for one, who surprised everybody with the quality of his singing and his wide repertoire. Even Jimmie MacGregor came in one night.

One Sunday night, there were fewer than a handful of people in, so we came down from the stage and sat around the fire and did the singing from the floor. It was the fire which in the end was our undoing at The Bothy. Because the fireplace was so big, and it certainly could appear quite frightening with huge logs burning fiercely, the fire department deemed it a risk and eventually revoked Lawrie's licence for public performances.

A lady called Enid had been following our progress since the first Tryst nights. We didn't know it, but she was secretary to a man called W. Gordon Smith, a free-lance television producer and journalist-cum-playwright whose most famous play, 'Jock', became a tremendous hit. For months Enid had been slipping one of our promotional photographs under his nose and singing our praises, but it wasn't until June 1st

1963 that he gave his approval with a BBC stamp which read, 'R E C E I V E D - 1 June 1963, EDINBURGH'.

Gordon had been invited by the BBC in London to produce a couple of pilot folk shows with a view to screening a series on network television. That meant being seen and heard all over the British Isles, really big stuff. He found what he thought would be an ideal setting in 'The Place', a club in Victoria Street which certainly had a 'folksy' atmosphere with its warren of cave-like rooms and twisting, turning corridors. There was a folk-singer/manager called Roy Guest working the circuit at that time and it was he whom Gordon asked to front the shows with many of the best-known artists, like The Spinners and The Ian Campbell Folk Group, Martin Carthy, etc., taking part. Gordon finally gave in to Enid's pleas and we were invited as well.

We presented ourselves on the morning of Thursday, November 28th, 1963 at The Place, nervous new boys amongst the elite of the folk world. The shows were recorded, both on the same day and sent to London for scrutiny. Here's a strange thing: I have a note in the diary which says that, on Monday, December 2nd, 1963, days after the shows in The Place, we were due in Leith Town Hall at 5.00 pm to do a *'Hootenanny'* recording, but have no recollection of what happened there. I can hardly believe that all of the artists who had taken part in the pilots would have hung around Edinburgh for four days, but perhaps they did because a Waverley Records album, two in fact, Volume 1; ZLP 2025 and Volume 2; ZLP 2032, have us on the cover. Roy Guest, London based, and Barney McKenna from Dublin are there too, on 12" vinyl.

News came back that London was impressed by what it had seen and Gordon was commissioned to produce a series of half-hour shows at that point not headed by Roy Guest, but with this fresh, lively new bunch, the CFT and PB, as anchors. Flabbergasted is a word sometimes misused, but flabbergasted indeed we were, not to say honoured and flattered, and any other superlative you can think of. Talk about heads in the clouds, that's where ours were as we waited for Gordon to finalise his preparations.

Unfortunately, we were told that if we accepted the shows, we would have to be available on a weekday, all day, for rehearsal, with the recording in the evening. This would stretch into thirteen weeks, which was the length of series the BBC wanted. With Pat halfway through her next pregnancy, for the first day's recording I took a day off work with the excuse that a complication had arisen at home. When the first show went on the box, shortly after it was recorded, nobody twigged at school but, after the fourth, when by that time I had taken four days off, that was me stymied.

You can imagine the excitement in Musselburgh Grammar School that one of the teachers was actually appearing every week on National Television. Two and two were put together, and it didn't take the head of Maths to come up with the right answer. The 'Hootenanny Show' was a hit from the word go, and received maximum press coverage with a lot of local interest focusing on us, the new anchors. The rest of the group experienced the same problem as I did at work, and a council of war was called to discuss the pros and cons of resigning from good, safe jobs, for a *high-diddle-de-dee* future, precariously following a yellow brick road. We unanimously agreed it was either that or give up the series.

I don't know how the others managed their problem but I, cap in hand, simply went into the Headmaster's office and apologetically owned up to the fact that I had been lying for the past four weeks, and was tendering my resignation forthwith. I was surprised by his, to me, somewhat complicated attitude: that it wouldn't reflect very well on him that I felt I had to lie. However he reported my decision, I found myself out of the teaching profession. If I'm being honest, if it hadn't been singing, it would have been something else, because I had become aware that teaching wasn't really for me, and I really wasn't for teaching.

Because of their immediate popularity, the thirteen programmes were extended to another thirteen before the first came off the air. Here's a list of just a few of the artists we welcomed as guests, some of whom may be familiar, and some who may have already passed into obscurity after fifty years: Rae and Archie Fisher, Cy Grant, The Ian Campbell Folk Group, The Spinners and The Dubliners, now with Ronnie Drew. All featured more than once on the series.

It was during a break in filming when I heard another singer, Julie Felix, talking to Ronnie Drew, both of them using fluent Spanish. I interrupted and expressed surprise, not about Julie, but certainly about Ronnie; but Ronnie, as a younger man, had been a busker on the streets of Barcelona. Somehow I couldn't imagine this so Irish of Irishmen, with his deep throated Dublin accent, hob-nobbing with Antonio Gaudi.

Allow me to bring this important phase in the group's career to a close by saying that, through our weekly presence on the show, we met probably everybody who was anybody in the world of Folk, including Tom Paxton, Peggy Seeger and Ewan McColl.

On March 13th, 1964, Pat gave birth to our daughter, whom we called Lauren Anne Violet. Pat had expressed the desire to have the baby at home and a bed was set up in the lounge. That is where I sat while she gave birth with difficulty, as Lauren came out very, very slowly to greet the world. The doctor was displeased when I became very emotional with relief when it was all over.

Once again, a few days after the birth, we nearly lost Pat. I went into the bedroom with a cup of tea to find her in a pool of blood. I was amazed that she was sitting with a contented smile on her face, seemingly unaware that she was probably bleeding to death. A 999 call and flashing blue ambulance lights saved her.

Pat recovered, and the baby was fine only, unlike Gavin, never slept. I mean she *never* slept. On many an occasion in the early months, I would come home late from one of our engagements to find Pat exhausted and at her wit's end. Being a man, I would say something like, 'Never mind. Give her to me, I'll sort her out'.

I would walk up and down with her over my shoulder, talking and even singing lullabies in her ear, but to no avail. In her cot I would rock her back and forward, the rocking becoming fiercer and her head banging from side to side. I don't know how the wee mite wasn't injured. Eventually Pat would take over again, frightened for the baby's life. Lauren is fifty years old now, but I can't imagine how she survived.

As it became known that we had turned professional and could travel distances, we started to be invited to a' the airts. During 1964 and 1965, we performed solo concerts throughout the country, filling venues from the Brangwyn Hall in Swansea, to the Festival Hall in London, Birmingham Town Hall, Liverpool Philharmonic Hall, Ludlow, Hereford, Newcastle, and most of the halls and theatres in Scotland. The first time we played the Inverness Empire the manager, John Worth who, an Englishman, but a dyed-in-the-wool Scottish Variety Show enthusiast and promoter, said when we arrived as a foursome, 'But where's the cast?'

We performed for BBC, ITV, UTV, ATV and just about every other TV you could think of, but we hadn't left the Folk Club scene. Things had changed though, and we did inform club organisers that the bar had to be closed during our one hour performance. Given the amount of practice and attention we were giving to our material we objected to competition from shouted orders for drinks, the constant distraction of busy waiters, and the incessant ringing of tills. Most of the clubs objected and cancelled engagements until it was discovered that when it was announced that the bar would be closing before we went on, there was a rush of orders and, at the end, another rush to replenish what had been consumed during our performance. Rather than selling less drink, they sold more. Cancellations became fewer.

Throughout all this, Pat, as well as looking after two small children, kept an eye on the money. Together with her boss, who still gave her work to do at home, they produced accounts for the group marked, 'Period from 1st September 1962 to 30th September 1964'.

I have these accounts on my knee as I write and they show that each of the four of us had a share of Net Profit for the period of £1,294 14/ 9. Given that most of this accrued in the later months of 1963, and that I was still on a teachers' salary of about £600 per annum until the early months of 1964, I considered that we were beginning to do rather well financially, and set to do even better in 1965.

We caught the eye of Phil Solomon, an entrepreneur and theatrical manager in London. About as big as you could get, he controlled acts like The Bachelors, and had arranged tour publicity for Jimmy Shand, Kenneth McKellar, Jim Reeves, Acker Bilk, Chris Barber, Gene Pitney, Louis Armstrong and Mantovani. He had steered the huge Dubliners hit, 'Seven Drunken Nights', owned Minor Records and ran Radio Caroline. With a pedigree like that, we felt we should listen to what he had to say.

Which is what we did, along with W. Gordon Smith, at a dinner he invited us to in a swanky Edinburgh restaurant. Gordon had become interested in our television work, and was assisting us in concert work as well. It became apparent that Solomon was keenly interested in taking us under his management wing, putting an offer on the table which he thought would be impossible for us to refuse. We were invited to sign a seven year contract with his company which would require us to move to London where, for that period of time, a flat would be provided for us to stay together. We would be paid a salary of £300 a week each for the duration of the contract with generous ancillary expenses on top. There was, however, one stipulation. One of us would have to be dropped. I don't know what went through the minds of the others, but immediately into mine jumped the expression, 'Divide and Rule'.

Had the three remaining agreed to such a condition they would be putty in Mr Solomon's hands in future. I wondered if dropping Paddie would leave a sort of 'New Bachelors' line-up. Would I be the one to go because I played no instruments? So many thoughts arrived in a fraction of a second, with another following, that, in the tiniest of small print in any contract, might there be a clause prescribing a very high price to be paid should anyone wish to leave. Yet another thought followed: could I live under the same roof as Roy and Bill if, in fact, it was just the three of us? Not a chance. To crown it all, we were all married men with children. The upshot was that we didn't sign the contract, but went on our own merry way.

When we turned professional, we asked our bass player, Robin Brock, if he would join us on the rocky road to stardom but he said no. Bill was of the opinion that the group needed a double bass to drive our sound along, although everyone agreed that what did the driving was Bill's own guitar. In my opinion it was enough, but, not being an instrumentalist myself, little weight was put on what I had to say. Unfortunately, Robin wasn't always able to appear with us on stage, particularly when we travelled in the south of England or far north of Scotland, because he was a full-time student of agriculture and couldn't always get time off. This was why he elected not to join us as professionals, even when we appeared locally at, say, Waverley Records' Festival Shows of 1964 and 1965. I have notes in my diary of dates which say 'minus Robin'. At some of our shows in the south, for instance Birmingham Town Hall on February 13th, 1965, we recruited a bass-player called Mansel

Davis, whom we met when he played with a group called The Settlers. Manse appeared on some other shows but I have to say that, when we appeared minus Robin or Manse, there were no calls of dissent from the audience. No one shouted, 'Ye's are rubbish without yer bass.'

We were by now performing, more-or-less exclusively, solo two hour concerts. In such shows it was important to get the balance of songs correct, and the way we did it was to have a meaty section in the middle of each half. This meant that we pulled out all the stops on the full group material where Paddie's voice featured prominently. The four of us agreed that Paddie's voice didn't suit all of our material.

There is on YouTube a clip of us singing for Irish Television on Capa Pier, on our 1963 foray to Kilrush, the song, 'Lock the Door Lariston'. It's very much a man's war song and in the clip Paddie is seen sitting in front taking no part whatsoever, indeed looking pretty spare. We learned from that experience and, during our concerts, Paddie would sit for quite a long time on her own, back-stage in a dressing-room, which couldn't have been all that pleasant for her. We, on the other hand were becoming a bit cheesed off at having only up tempo stuff to do, setting the stage, at least in our minds, for 'the star' to appear, self-important divas that we had no doubt become. As we progressed, Paddie's appearances became more selective. Another note in my diary of 1965, on May 6th to be precise, says, 'Give Paddie cheque for Aberdeen and Palladium £35'.

This situation is further illustrated in an advertisement on the back of the programme Waverley Records produced for their 1964 Festival Show. It announces the release, on November 6th, 1964, of:-

'THE FIRST LONG-PLAYING RECORD
by
THE CORRIE FOLK TRIO and PADDIE BELL'.

Three of the titles have at the end in brackets, '(Group)', five have, '(Trio)', one has, '(Paddie)' and one has, '(Ron)'.

Was dissension already built in, that we failed to see? It would appear so.

Chapter Twelve

Ten months after Lauren was born, Pat and I were on the move again, this time to 14 Henderson Row. It was in January of 1965 when, as addition to being responsible for the group's money, I started to do the driving. From my brother-in law, Lee Elliot, I borrowed an old green Jaguar which was often seen around Edinburgh with a big square hoarding attached to the roof. Emblazoned on its four sides were photographs of The Corrie Folk Trio and Paddie Bell.

I also bought a car of my own which had been an insurance write off. Re-built, it proved to be perfectly suitable, although it prompted another of Bill's smart quips. If now and again, I made any kind of mistake while driving, as newly qualified drivers often do, from his seat in the back he would sing, 'We plough the fields and scatter the good seed on the land'.

When it became tiresome, I would mention that I didn't see him getting off his arse to learn to drive and take a turn at the wheel.

It cannot be too often repeated that you don't achieve the kind of success we seemed destined for without the help of family and friends. We admired not only the work of The Clancy Brothers and Tommy Makem, but also their theatrical image/uniform of Irish Aran sweaters. We decided we would like to mirror that on a Scottish theme, so Pat knitted the Shetland sweaters we became synonymous with, soon to be seen on television when we met Iain MacFadyen, the power behind *'The White Heather Club'*. Through him we also met Ian Sutherland, conductor of the Scottish Symphony Orchestra with whom we recorded. Another associate of MacFadyen's was John Martin, a theatrical manager and owner of a publishing company called Argyll Songs Ltd, with whom we signed a publishing deal.

We made appearances on *'The White Heather Club'*, *'Heather Mixture'*, *'Singalong'*, and any other folkie-type television shows that happened to come along. On one such we had The Seekers as guests, one of their first television engagements. During rehearsals excitement was at fever pitch, not for anything The Corries were doing, but for The Seekers whose work was interrupted every half hour or so from their management telling them about the latest sales figures of their first huge hit, 'I Know I'll Never Find Another You'.

So, we progressed through 1965, but not without some of the dissent I've mentioned.

Because Roy and Bill provided the instrumental basis for the singing, inevitably they were thrown together for rehearsal without Paddie or me being present, no more so than during the latter stages of 1964. Because we had been college friends and team-mates, Roy and I were quite close and, when he mentioned that he was having difficulties with Bill and sometimes felt like lashing out, I placated him and acted as mediator. Since we were now inter-dependent for our livelihood I urged Roy to 'keep the heid', so to speak, although I could see how difficult it was becoming, non-confrontational as he was. Consider just one incident on the stage of a full Usher Hall.

For the balance of the trio, my position was in the middle of the two instrumentalists, which is where I was the night Bill shouted across to Roy in the middle of a song, 'Remember the arrangement!' To me this was tantamount to Bill shouting that he was the boss. Not in private either, but in front of all these people. Had I been Roy, I would have felt it to be very demeaning.

On another occasion, which Bill himself describes in an internet interview on a Balladeer site, he and Roy had a stand-up fight over Roy's handling of a song called, 'Quare Bungle Rye'. To me this was another example of Bill's insistence on having his own way.

In the same interview he admits that, perhaps, he was unfair in his attitudes, but then adds, 'For reasons I fail to understand to this day we tended to avoid each other's company socially.'

The reason for Roy and me was that his behaviour had become insufferable. As well as his treatment of Roy, on a few occasions in concert he had started to jump in on some of my stage introductions before I could start speaking, obviously thinking that his own delivery would be so much better than mine. The audience wasn't aware of this, but it made me fume.

One night Pat and I were wakened from sleep by a phone call. Bill was having a gathering in his home in Moray Place and in that gathering was a singer called Gerry Cairns, just over from Ireland, whom Bill said I should definitely come across and hear. Pat and I got up and proceeded to the party where it became obvious that Bill was more interested in us performing than for me to hear Gerry. I collared Gerry at the earliest opportunity and took him into the quiet of Bill's kitchen where he sang for me. He had no strap on his guitar so I knelt on one knee, the other knee bent, on which Gerry placed his foot to support his guitar on his own bent knee. Halfway through the song the kitchen filled with Bill and a few others.

While Gerry was singing, Bill worked his way round the room until he came to the window which had a gas cooker beside it. There were pots and pans hanging on the wall above the cooker and Bill proceeded to bang them with his head, creating a distraction and spoiling my enjoyment of Gerry's song. I know I should have been a gentleman, just stood up and thanked Gerry and said that maybe one day I would hear him properly. Unfortunately, I am not that much of a gentleman and, intensely annoyed at being wakened from sleep to hear

113

what I was not now being allowed to enjoy, I rose and hit Bill in the face with a clenched fist.

Suddenly Roy's arms were wrapped round my arms to prevent any more damage. My dander being up, Roy found himself thrown over my shoulders and lying with his back on the floor, his flying feet having switched on the gas-taps, and me hissing in his ear to leave it, that my fight was not with him. His action brought me to my senses though, and I fled into another room, soon to be joined by Bill complaining bitterly that I had hit him without giving him warning of the coming blow.

In the streets where I grew up, you didn't say, 'On guard, Sir, I am about to strike you'. I did, however, say that if in the future a similar incident occurred I would place my hands behind my back and allow him first shot, and thereafter try very hard to hurt him as much as possible.

Not surprisingly, the party broke up but, among the departing guests, Roy's wife, Vi, was not to be found until outside, eventually, she was discovered sitting on the branch of a tree in the gardens of Moray Place, safe from strife.

Returning to our move to Henderson Row at the beginning of 1965, Bill and the rest of us must still have been in social contact because he designed a pair of wooden settees for Pat and me which my joiner, Bill Philp, made up for us.

On another occasion we found ourselves leading a contingent of fellow 'folkies' (including Hamish Imlach and The Ian Campbell Folk Group) to a party hosted by Rory and Alex McEwan in a very posh New Town flat owned by one of them. Everything seemed to be white: carpets, curtains, furniture, even a grand piano, if memory serves correctly.

Memory does tell me that I was thinking on that evening, 'If my mother could see me now, hobnobbing with The Gentry? Talk about ideas above my station!'

The McEwans had Larry Adler and Julian Bream as house guests. When these two decided to do a party piece, Davey

Swarbrick, The Campbell group's fiddler, asked if he could join in. Davey was known for a peculiar habit. Once he got really stuck into his music, he would stick out his tongue in concentration. Sure enough, some way into the piece, the tongue appeared as he started to improvise. Improvisation was a feature of folk-music, not so classical music, and soon Adler and Bream gave up and left Davey on his own. One up for the 'Folkies'!

On January 24th, 1965, the group lined up on the Forth Road Bridge with W. Gordon Smith and his BBC cameras to do a live insert for *Tonight* as a celebration of the opening of the new bridge. Unfortunately for us that was the day that Winston Churchill died (unfortunate for him as well, of course), and our spot was cancelled, the whole show being given over hurriedly to Winston's life.

We were luckier with another important event. The Clancy Brothers were impressed by our sound and said they could possibly have us released on disc in America. We rushed into the Craighall Road studios of Waverley Records to put down some twenty-odd tracks to send out to them, one being 'The Day We Went to Rothesay-oh'. We heard nothing from America for a long time, but when The Clancy's next album came out, it had their version of 'Rothesay-oh' on it. They had personalised it, using their own names as characters in the song, and we suspected that their kind offer was no more than a ruse to half-inch our material. We were wrong, of course, because we did eventually appear on the Electra label, EKL291, as The Corrie Folk Trio with Paddie Bell. This must have been immensely important because there's a note at the back of my 1965 diary which says:-

'U.S.A., 6 - 8 weeks
Minimum 6 performances per week
They pay fare
Folk Shows $1,000 week
Not top of the bill'

Nothing came of that, because, at roughly 1.45am on January 1st, 1966, The Corrie Folk Trio was no more.

1965 had been very busy, culminating in ringing in the New Year with the BBC Hogmanay Show live from Queen Margaret Drive in Glasgow. When the cameras were switched off, the cast became involved in a 'stage' party which Bill wanted to stay for, but Roy and I didn't. We wanted to get home to catch the end of our own family celebrations and told Bill we would wait for him in the car. On the way out of the building we offered two Glasgow City Police pipers who had also been on the show a lift to the outskirts of the city so, when Bill eventually arrived at the car, Roy was in his usual seat in the front and the two policemen were seated in the back. Bill remonstrated that there was no room for him and, when I explained that the pipers would be getting out in a short while, he jabbed his finger in my face and shouted, 'Shut up, you, and just drive!'

Sorry, folks: *red rag tae a bull*. I quietly turned off the ignition and opened my door, stepped onto the road and, opening the back door for Bill, invited him to come with me down a dark lane at the back of the BBC building.

Once hidden from view, I reminded him of the promise given on that unpleasant night in his flat and waited for him to take his first swing. When it became obvious that it wouldn't be coming, I turned and proceeded back to the car. Again we waited for him to join us but he didn't, so we left for home. Needless to say, the policemen were embarrassed, apologising for having caused trouble between us. We told them not to worry, this kind of thing happened all the time. We made our way back to Edinburgh and, as I dropped Roy, said I'd see him the next evening at the usual pick-up spot, the Trio being engaged for the Royal Jubilee Arms Hotel in the village of Cortachy, arranged by one of The White Heather Club dancers, Jackie Cooper. Since the hotel was away up in the hills of Angus and might be difficult to find in the dark, we agreed to meet Jackie in Dundee and be led.

Pat had been left on her own for many nights prior to this busy Festive Season, and wanted to come to the Jubilee Arms with us. Therefore she was in the car when, once again, Bill didn't turn up. After a while I said that we'd better get going. Since he knew of the meeting with Jackie Cooper, Bill would no doubt meet us in Dundee. However, he wasn't in Dundee; nor was he in Cortachy when we arrived. Further, there was no phone message from him. Not believing that he would let us down like this, in spite of what had happened the night before, Roy and I hurriedly cobbled together material for our two spots. We insisted that we would not accept any fee but the owner, John Duguid, the nicest of men, just said that we would all wait and see what happened.

Pat was a bag of nerves and couldn't sit in the dining-room where we were to sing. In the small cocktail bar she met two of the locals, Bert and Patsy Paton, who said they would look after her. Roy and I did the two scheduled spots and, in spite of ourselves, thought it went quite well. Audience reaction was good. Later, when we went to join Pat and the Patons, she reassured us by reporting that a couple of ladies had said after the show, 'That Hall and MacGregor were great'.

John Duguid approached us saying that, for bravery if nothing else, he was paying us the full fee of £100 and a bottle of Hundred Pipers whisky each, with the promise of further bookings to come.

On the way home in the car, Roy, Pat and myself discussed this disturbing new turn of events.

Was Bill's failure to make an appearance for the engagement because of illness, or perhaps just the result of a heavy hangover, or was it a more sinister, deliberate attempt to show to Roy and me that we were nothing without him? We gave him the benefit of the doubt and decided to await an explanation from him the next day, and acknowledged the fact that other groups experienced the same kind of, shall I say, personality clashes.

Previously, during our time in Kilrush, I learned in talking to Liam and Tom Clancy that they were constantly at each other's throats, resulting in blows being struck at times. Always though, there was a shake of the hand before their next professional appearance. They put it down to the tensions of being in the limelight, in the same way Bill and I had the year before after I punched him.

I did, however, take the chance to explain to Roy, as I had already discussed with Pat on many occasions, that, in the past year while we had been seeing less and less of Paddie, the Trio moving even closer together during that time, the closer I had gotten to Bill, the further away I wanted to be. Laughingly, Roy asked me how I thought he had felt during that time I had been exhorting him to 'keep the heid'.

The result was that upon arrival home, Roy and I arranged to meet to take our discussions forward and, next day, when no telephone call was forthcoming from Bill, we decided that he had either been trying to teach us a lesson regarding his importance, or else he just didn't want any more to do with us, and our talk moved towards the possibility of making a go of it on our own. Roy and I were rugby players, and therefore 'team' men, and you just didn't let your team down as Bill had done with us, in spite of arguments and differences of opinion, especially in this case about something as trivial as a cramped seat for a few minutes beside a couple of policemen.

Over the next few days, during which time there was still no word from Mr Bill Smith, our conversation crystallised into continuing to sing on our own. I picked up a guitar and a capo, the metal bar encased in rubber and elasticated to hold it firmly against a fret of the finger board, and I learned to play three chords. With the aid of the capo, these basic three chord shapes can be made to play in almost any key. This is a somewhat simplistic explanation of the principle but it suited me down to the ground. I made a start, a start I was practising with Roy on the day that Bill finally made an appearance at Roy's front door. I suggested that perhaps it would be better if Roy, the diplomat, answered the summons, which he did. I heard Bill enter the hall and, with a light-hearted slap and rub of the hands he enquired, smugly, 'Okay guys, what's happening?'

Harsh words passed back and forward after Roy explained our decision to carry on without him. As he slammed the front door shut behind him, Bill shouted, "Yer group's fucked."

When Roy came back into the room, all thoughts of further practice went by the board and a discussion ensued where we asked ourselves, not for the first time, whether we were being realistic about sallying forth on our own. The main factor as I saw it was, could I in fact do what I had been trying very hard to do over the last few days, to learn some chords and handle the instrument confidently. I still had nearly a full month to get the hang of things because the first possible engagement for us would be on January 30th. Let's face it, we argued, we had done very well at The Jubilee Arms with no preparation whatsoever and Roy was doing exactly as he had been doing with the trio, albeit with the added worry of what I would be doing, or not doing, as the case might be.

It wasn't a two hour concert we would be involved in, but a shorter spot in a club. We also argued that, were we to call Bill back and carry on as before, as his re-appearance suggested he wanted, it would only strengthen any conviction he might have that we could not do without him, which would make things increasingly more difficult. That was the deciding factor. Neither of us could face that possibility.

We didn't glibly say, 'What do we have to lose?' because we had everything to lose if we couldn't make it on our own, but we decided success as a duo was worth the risk and shook hands on what we saw as the birth of *The Corries*.

Chapter Thirteen

Word of the split soon got to W. Gordon Smith who was worried about an imminent show in the Lyceum. It was called, 'Folk is Singing', and it ran for a week. We honoured the engagement, and that was the last of the trio.

The very next night was our first as The Corries and Pat travelled with us to The Queen's Hotel, Elie, to hold my quivering hand. To sit in rehearsal under the sympathetic gaze of Roy for a couple of weeks, for that was all the time I had to prepare, trying to smoothly provide a basic rhythmic accompaniment to his more complex instrumental fingering, was one thing, but now I was on my way to a serious professional engagement where all eyes would be on me.

With all due respect to Roy, he was fulfilling his proven, accustomed role, but this was my first time on instruments. All I could do was rub my brass neck, take a deep breath and look at him with a huge, fake grin of confidence, and step on the stage. In the car on the way home, Roy told Pat that we had started our spot at 8.00pm, and that I first changed chord at 8.45. All I know is that, every time I was aware of making a mistake, I stopped playing and jumped down into the audience to deride somebody for not singing loudly enough and to try a bit harder. I was helped in this by having in the audience a local worthy who just couldn't stay seated but kept getting up and down and walking about, a real attention seeker who got a bit more attention than he was looking for that night. There were lots of laughs, and the performance couldn't have been nearly as bad as I feared because, as at The Jubilee Arms in Cortachy, we were asked when we could come back.

Nothing was in the diary for some time ahead, which gave Pat and me a chance to try to get our new house at Henderson Row in order. Huge compared to our first two homes, its entry was up three stone steps to a stone landing flanked by two tall, fluted stone columns supporting a stone canopy. Through the front door was an entrance hall with a double cupola, and a wood-slatted floor into which was inserted a couple of doormats, leading to a double door with glass panels opening on a huge hall. Turning right you'd see a large room with two windows looking on to Henderson Row and, next to that, a bathroom. Along the wall was an inside stairway down to the basement.

Beside the stairway was the door into a spacious kitchen, then two more rooms one of which was a single bedroom. The next was about the biggest room I had ever seen in a house. A large hall cupboard in the middle of the wall led back to the grand lounge, again with two windows looking out on to Henderson Row. Our basement was only half this size because there was another basement cheek by jowl with ours which belonged to a family called Bailey. There was no possible chance of us furnishing all of the house, so we settled in only the basement. One of the front rooms upstairs became my office and the huge room at the back became a practice room for Roy and me. Don't ask me how a full-size table-tennis table found its way in there as well.

We had two bedrooms in the basement, a bathroom and lounge with dining recess and tiny kitchen off. A window in the lounge looked out on a walled garden which, unfortunately, never got the sun, but was very handy for the kitten Pat acquired, and the Great Dane she felt she needed for security. We called the dog Dane. Not original, no, and the beast was mad from the word go.

As the front door was more pleasant and convenient for visitors compared to the basement door, we used it to greet our friends. Once inside we ushered them downstairs via the inside stairway which had a small landing halfway down, turning on itself to proceed to the ground. Dane had no problem letting people into the house, but when it came time for them to depart he would run to the landing before them, to look back at them ascending. And do you think he would stand aside to let them pass? Not he! He stood glowering, and we had a hell of a job getting him to move. I admit that I played this up and it became a source of amusement.

The small kitchen door was glass-panelled, with an optional curtain to prevent draughts. This was Dane's favourite place to lie. Everything was fine if the curtain was drawn over a shut door, but if the door was left open, and he leaned on only the curtain, he would roll straight on into the kitchen. When this happened, he would get up and shake himself with a sheepish expression as if to say, 'Ahum, ahum. Don't quite know what happened there folks'.

Our doctor, Dave Tulloch, was old school, wearing a black bowler hat, a black single breasted top coat, highly polished black shoes, and carrying the obligatory Gladstone bag. I say 'old school' because he had a habit of calling in from time to time just to say hello. When Gavin had mumps, he became very worried and came in three or four times a day to check. One day, he stood in the middle of the lounge, hat on head, coat buttoned and bag in hand, ready to leave but speaking in his usual mellifluous tone to Pat, when Dane saw the wee cat coming in from the garden and made a lunge. The cat's head disappeared into his mouth, his legs dangling in mid-air. 'Wowowoh!' shouted Dave, the mellifluence disappearing, 'the dog's just eaten the cat'.

Dane walked over to his spot at the kitchen door and laid the cat gently on the carpet, splayed his back legs behind him and stretched his front legs toward his friend, gazing into his eyes with an expression which read, 'Okay, pal, what're we gonna do next?'

Exactly opposite our ground-floor lounge windows was a corner shop which was too convenient for Pat not to use. Every time she did Dane, left on his own in the lounge, would jump at the window with his full weight, his front paws scratching on the glass as she crossed the street, whining all the while and knocking his chin between his paws. He never came to harm but we eventually sold him to a man in Fife who must have been as mad as he. One time, Pat phoned to see how the dog was progressing, only to hear strange Dane-like noises in the background, and be told that the dog's body was stuck in a service hatch with his back legs sprawling on a kitchen table and his front legs pawing thin air in the dining-room. She didn't phone again.

After our first appearance as The Corries in Elie on January 30th, 1966, Roy and I got down to serious practice (between games of table-tennis, you understand) and, after doing some engagements in clubs and hotel cabaret, we arrived at Aberdeen Music Hall to do a solo concert on March 18th, 1966. My diary shows on that page the word, 'packed', with a proud circle round it.

April saw us back at The Jubilee Arms Hotel, Cortachy, for three nights this time, and club appearances in Perth, Dundee and Alexandria. May 4th, 5th and 6th saw us in Leeds Town Hall, Sheffield City Hall and The Liverpool Philharmonic Hall. All of these built our confidence to appear on May 7th, this time in concert with Paddie Bell, at The Usher Hall, Edinburgh.

At this point, I'd like to offer thanks and gratitude to Eileen Hetterley (nee Kinnear), for giving me a scrap-book of hers which traces her whole family's interest in the developing career of The Corries.

One page in the book has stuck to it two tickets for the above Usher Hall concert. The tickets say:

'The Corries with Paddie Bell at 8 p.m.
GRAND TIER 10/6
ROW A SEAT 60 (And of course one ticket for Seat 59).
(Reserved)'.

Please let me quote her comments on the show. She says:
'This was the first concert after the split up of the trio. I think
everyone was wondering just what they would be like and I
don't think anyone could have been disappointed.

WHAT A PERFORMANCE.

WHAT A DIFFERENCE ! !

We wondered what all the instruments on stage were for. We
soon found out'.

The middle of May saw us in meetings with John Martin and
Iain Sutherland who tried to persuade us that we really should get
back together with Bill since we might not make a go of it without
him. W. Gordon Smith was after us again but soon realised that
our minds were made up, and accepted us as a duo. Soon, after
shows in Glasgow Concert Hall, Fort William Club and Paisley
Town Hall, we were back in Edinburgh at The Lyceum in a show
produced by Gordon called 'Late Folk' featuring us and a young
group Gordon had found called, The Karlins.

We recorded television shots, indoors and out, for a production he called, 'Like a Bird on The Wing', but this was interrupted by the Edinburgh Festival on which this year we had
gone for broke. We hired the Caley Cinema in Edinburgh's
Lothian Road for a late-night Folk Show we called 'Corriefolk',
to run for the three weeks of The Festival.

First week guests were The Settlers, Aviva Semadar, an Israeli
singer, Dorita y Pepe and the nightly singer on the *Tonight*
programme, Cy Grant, as the main guest. Cy was as Cy was
expected to be, but I was amazed to discover that the Dorita y
Pepe I had listened to so much on so many BBC Radio shows
when I was a boy, and associated with the Latin American Music
they purveyed, were actually dyed-in-the-wool Cockneys.

Week Two featured Marianne Faithfull, a name that was more associated with the Pop world but she had just brought out an album called 'Country Girl' which had a folksy feel to it. I phoned her management in London, inviting her to appear on our show and asked what the fee would be. When they quoted £1800, I immediately thanked them and said that that was out of the question as we couldn't afford that kind of money. When they asked what we could afford and I said £400 they, without drawing breath, said that would be fine.

I knew when I made the enquiry that I was chancing my arm, but when they said yes to the £400 I was flabbergasted, particularly when I was told this would include her backing group, Pentangle. They obviously regarded this as a promotional event for Marianne's new album. Eventually I met her off the plane at Turnhouse. She was an extremely well-known performer so, of course, the press were at the plane in numbers. When a reporter asked her how she felt coming to Edinburgh to appear with The Corries, she replied: 'I've never heard of them'. I wondered if we had done the right thing.

We did our best to present her stage spot in the most sympathetic way possible, but perhaps we shouldn't have bothered. Within that spot, she sang an unaccompanied, very moody song for which we set up a darkened stage with Marianne highlighted sitting in a single spotlight. With her band still on stage, but to one side, she launched into her big number. Halfway through the first line, one of them struck a match and lit up a cigarette, whereupon every eye in the audience switched to the glowing fag end. So much for creating atmosphere for the star.

Playing bass for Pentangle that week was a man called Danny Thomson who, to this day, can be seen playing behind people such as Aly Bain and Phil Cunningham on 'Transatlantic Sessions'. Danny was quite taken with one of our songs and we could see him listening carefully in the wings as we performed. It was by Matt McGinn and concerned the halting of the Roman Legions' advance into Scotland by a single Scotsman at the Cobbler Hill. On the last day of the show, on that Saturday afternoon, Danny was arrested by the police on Edinburgh Castle ramparts where he was singing in full voice, half-pissed, to the people of Edinburgh, the chorus of the song, which went:

'Gregally, Gregalloo, come up and fight ya cowardly crew

Ah'll huv ye for ma pot o' stew

Ye're feart tae fight wi' me'.

Even the police have a sense of humour it seems, because Danny was released in time to get to the Caley that night to help conclude Marianne's engagement.

The third week featured an Indian Sitar instrumentalist who, although completely unknown in Britain, captivated our other guests, Archie Fisher, Martin Carthy, Davey Swarbrick and The Islanders, as well as the whole audience. We were now becoming known for introducing a wide variety of music under the banner of 'Folk'.

I now found myself in a complete whirl of activity. On top of all the business arrangements, my workload was augmented with instrumental practice followed by instrumental rehearsal and material arrangement with Roy. Even Pat found herself busier, because by this time we had decided to forego the Shetland jersey image and plumped for shirts based on a sort of traditional ploughman's sark which she and Violet manufactured themselves. The first Corries 'uniform' was black trousers and shoes and a red shirt with paisley-patterned cummerbund tied at the waist.

This was our attire for the filming we did for W. Gordon's forthcoming St Andrew's Night programme, *'Like a Bird on the Wing'*. The colour of our shirts didn't matter for television because it was still only in black and white. Although the base for the film was back in The Place, where we had done the *Hootenanny* shows, he took us round Scotland, filming inserts. Many, many people persistently remind me of one of these inserts, which seems to have stuck in the collective mind. That's the walk we did through Pitlochry to Killiecrankie singing, 'The Braes o' Killiecrankie'. During the screening it was noticed by some viewers that Roy was a bit knock-kneed, and I had a bit of an outward twist to my left leg and, for a long time afterwards, we were known in folk circles as 'Randy and Bandy'. This was no bother. Had we not already weathered the storm of, 'The Currie Folk Trio and Chappatie Bell'?

Another sequence found us perched on the backs of a couple of Edinburgh City Police horses singing, 'Scots Wha Hae'. We started filming at 4.30 a.m. and progressed throughout that morning through The Royal Mile to finish, scarily overlooking the city-scape on the self-same ramparts where Danny had been arrested. When we stopped for a red light at the corner of the High Street and George IV Bridge, some workmen interrupted their toils to look up and one wag came out with a variation on a popular television commercial of the time, 'Go to work on a nag (an egg).'

Maybe our growing reputation for variety had rubbed off from Gordon who was full of innovation. Another of the scenes in this programme showed a girl called Felicity Joinson swimming in the sea surrounded by seals as we sang, 'The Great Silkie of Sule Skerrie'.

All of this is available on YouTube at the press of a button. What you won't find there is our summons to the Palace of Holyrood House to entertain King Hussein of Jordan on his state visit to Edinburgh in 1966. There had been a centuries-old feud running between the Percy Family of Newcastle and the Douglas Family of the Scottish Border region which had finally been put to rest through intermarriage, resulting in the Hamilton family. The Duke of Hamilton is the Queen's representative in Scotland and it is he who walks in front of her on State occasions, carrying the Scottish crown on a crimson cushion.

We were known for our singing of, 'The Lammas Tide', but there is also a long song called, 'Chevy Chase', which tells the story of a foray into England by the Black Douglas and his followers. As he passes through Newcastle, he challenges Lord Percy to combat, defeating him although not killing him, and continues south. On his way back he is met again by The Percy, who this time defeats The Douglas. In our version, we prefer to stop at the point of The Douglas' defeat of Percy. It was the Duke of Hamilton who was hosting Hussein's visit to The Palace and everyone was assembled in the ballroom when we took to the floor. King Hussein was seated at one end of the room and, ranged on each side, dramatically, were the descendants of what had been the feuding families. We started off, the song mentioning the names of some of the families:

'He chose The Gordons and The Grahams, The Lindsays light and gay,

But the Jardines would not wi' him ride and they rue it to this day.'

The song finished, we were presented to the King. An equerry escorted us and we began the long walk up the ballroom to where Hussein sat. As we walked, he asked us quietly what our names were. We shouldn't have, but we did, say that we were Robin Hall and Jimmie MacGregor. He started in surprise and told us that we certainly were not, because he had met them already. We kept chaffing him all the way up the hall but finally told him the truth just before he had to make the presentation. As we progressed, we were met with good-humoured boos and cat-calls from the guests and the whole episode ended in laughs and much shaking of hands.

This story has a sequel. A few weeks after the engagement, I was waiting for a flight from Turnhouse Airport when I met the Scottish Omnibuses Inspector who taught me how to operate the ticket machine I had used as a bus conductor. He explained that he had moved on from the buses to be a security advisor and it had been his job to 'screen' Roy and me for the Palace do. I was somewhat surprised to learn, reading between the lines of what he told me, that the Security

Services know more about each and every one of us than we do ourselves.

The reaction to '*Like a Bird on the Wing*' was immediate and extremely favourable, but we didn't sit around feeling complacent. In November we did a trailblazing tour of the Midlands where my nephew, Brian Collie, was a singer. Already involved in the local folk scene he arranged engagements in Walsall, Lichfield, Wolverhampton, Digbeth, Barton-under-Needwood, and elsewhere. Roy and I stayed in a small boarding-house in Walsall during this time and a note in the diary says I went home one weekend to give Pat £30.

We were also becoming more and more closely involved with Iain McFadyen of BBC's '*White Heather Club*' and Hogmanay Show and a few short months after suggesting that perhaps we might find it impossible to continue as a duo, he invited us to appear on 1966 Hogmanay Show. This was exactly a year after the two policemen had been dropped outside Glasgow.

Chapter Fourteen

On January 6th, 1967, The BBC screened 'The Corries in Concert' and, to my amazement if no one else's, here I was playing instruments on television again.

I smiled at not having taken the advice of the doctor who had set a broken bone in my hand when I was playing rugby whilst at Moray House. During the game I felt a bit of pain in my left hand, but thought no more about it and played on. By the time I got home to Pat it had swollen and, over the weekend, came to resemble an inflated balloon. I ignored her entreaties to see a doctor and showed her that I felt no pain by pushing and twisting it, even getting her to press it as hard as she could. If it wasn't that painful, I reasoned stupidly, how could there be anything wrong? By the end of the week the swelling remained and was starting to discolour. I was sent for an X-Ray which showed that the metacarpal bone of my pinky was indeed broken in two pieces. Strangely, the doctor asked if I played any instruments. I didn't at that time but asked why he wanted to know. He told me that the break was such that he could stretch and pin it in such a way that I would have an elongated wee finger which might help if I was a musician. Now that I was trying to play, I felt I could have done with all the help I could get, but struggled on with just an ordinary pinky.

January and February saw us back in the Midlands but, on March 6th, Roy found himself sitting in Edinburgh's meeting place for itinerant folk musicians, Sandy Bell's Pub in Forrest Road, beside two young Irishmen, evidently just arrived and feeling a bit lost. Roy struck up a conversation with them, bidding them welcome while noticing that one had a penny-whistle sticking out of his top jacket pocket, just as Roy had himself. He asked the lad to give him a tune, which he proceeded to do, playing a very basic reel, and not too well. When he finished, he asked Roy if he would return the compliment, which Roy was pleased to do, because he rather fancied himself on the instrument. The Irishman listened intently and, at the end, said quietly, 'Ah now, that was great, but have you heard this version?'

He launched into the tune again, playing such a complicated and intricate set of notes that Roy was completely taken aback. When he was done, he smiled wickedly, stretched out his hand and introduced himself as Finbar Furey. His brother, Eddie, sat next to him. Finbar Furey is known as Prince of the Pipers for his expertise on the Irish Pipes.

That was the start of a lifelong friendship between Finn and Roy. On October 31st, one year later, Roy was Finbar's best man when he married an Edinburgh girl, Sheila Peebles, at St Andrew's Church in Juniper Green. I was there as an usher and, at the reception following, was amazed to see that the band engaged for the occasion comprised of none other than Finbar himself, accompanied by Eddie, their father, Ted, and all his brothers, leaving the ladies to dance among themselves.

In March we supplied ideas to W. Gordon for songs to be used for a couple of television programmes he had in mind on the Jacobites and the Borders. At the same time, Pat and I were speaking to Bert and Patsy Paton, the couple Pat had befriended that fateful night at the Jubilee Arms, regarding the renting of a shepherd's howff in Glen Prosen from Patsy's father for which we were to pay a token rent of a few pence. When we first visited we spent a full day cleaning out a two-foot layer of dog

shit from under the solitary bed where the shepherd had lain.
Pat was keen to have the place as a haven from the city, and
a home which was fast becoming a doss-house for passing
singers such as Matt McGinn, who used to call in sometimes
at midnight after a gig, and Josh McRae, when he wasn't
'Messing about on the River'. The howff was a bit awkward to
reach. We had to drive up to The Royal Jubilee Arms Hotel in
Dykehead and up through Glen Prosen to the village of Prosen,
which was tiny. Just past the village shop was a corrugated iron
garage with space for one car. Past that the road turned left
and gave way to what couldn't even be called a track, simply
two ruts on the hillside with a bump between which, when the
grass was high, scraped along the underside of the car. The
hill on the right hand side of this 'track' fell away in a sheer
drop of about thirty feet to a hill-burn which, in winter, was a
cascade of water. The ruts went on up the hill for about fifty
yards to end at an iron gate, on the other side of which was a
field. Once through the gate we ran the car over just grass, no
road, until we finally came to the middle of the field and our
holiday home.

Once we got the accommodation cleaned up and 'furnished'
it was idyllic - in good weather. With rain we felt we were in the
back of beyond. On one occasion, we drove from Edinburgh
in an old taxi borrowed from Wattie. Having been a motor
mechanic, he was always tinkering with different modes of
transport in his back garden in Gilmerton. I had the family
with me and also Pat's grandfather, Willie Wight, a blacksmith,
still plying his trade and cycling to work in Dalkeith every day
despite his eighty-some years. The weather was atrocious all
the way.

After I was soaked opening the field gate, I drove slowly
towards our goal. As I started out, the gear-stick came away in
my hand, but I had the presence of mind to keep the car on the
move. It couldn't go very fast because of the sodden grass, and
the atmosphere inside wasn't eased as a clap of thunder rang out

and the rain became torrential. At the howff I switched off the ignition and pulled on the hand-brake which also came away in my hand. A bolt of lightning illuminated the apprehensive eyes of the occupants as the vehicle slowly settled into the mud.

There was a couple of minutes' silence before Willie piped up with, 'Well, ah've hud some hurls in ma time, . . . but that wis some hurl.'

I am positive that, if the children hadn't been in the car, his words would have been punctuated with a few expletives, gentleman though he was. We sent for Pat's brother Lee, who came and extricated us and the taxi.

Roy and I were very busy on the road at this time so I wasn't always able to stay with the family in Prosen during their holidays. On one occasion when I was though, I made arrangements to have Bert Paton come up on a Saturday morning to take me salmon fishing. Poaching, for that was what I knew we were about, is better done when few people are around. I was up with the lark waiting for Bert's appearance, but he didn't arrive until midday, with Patsy at his side. I was impatient to get going, but cups of tea and coffee were had before we set out. There was no evidence of fishing tackle on his person, but he carried a shot-gun. Strange, I thought. We walked further into the hills and finally came to a wide mountain stream. It wasn't terribly deep and was rock-strewn, but with an abundance of shallow pools. We hadn't walked far along its banks before Bert stopped, grabbed my arm and signalled silence as he peered at the water.

'There ye are,' he said, pointing at some rocks at the head of a pool, 'd'ye see that one?'

If you have any experience of salmon, you'll know that their disguise is perfect in the water. Since this was my first time, I couldn't see a thing and whispered to Bert, 'I can't see it.'

He shook his head and slowly raised his gun, shot off one barrel and suddenly, an enormous fish jumped into the air, dripping water.

'Dae ye see it now?' he shouted above the sound of the echoing gunshot. Indeed I did, and we walked over to retrieve the first salmon I had ever fished for.

I don't know where we found time for holidays in 1967 because we seemed to be very busy indeed. April through May and June we were a week at the Pentland Nightclub in Edinburgh where Pat was chatted up by a performer and his monkey. Then it was back down to the Midlands for more appearances in my nephew Brian's clubs, taking in television and radio programmes into the bargain. All of a sudden the Festival was on us again with 'Corriefolk '67. The Incredible String Band made a huge hit during our first week. Mike Heron and Robin Williamson, no relation whatsoever to Roy, had made their name at the Newport Folk Festival, and would go on to even greater things. We had The Fureys, Dorita and Pepe again, Archie Fisher and groups like The Grehan Sisters, The Livingstone Folk Four, The Skerries and The Tinkers. September and the first part of October were taken up with filming for W. Gordon Smith in the Highlands and The Borders.

Meantime, Iain McFadyen had come up with a series in which we starred called, *'Degrees of Folk'*. This took us filming in Universities all over the country including Dublin and Belfast. Helping us out on the series was a new eighteen-year-old singer called Bernadette.

Was McFadyen's inclusion of Bernadette a veiled hint that perhaps we could still do with a third member, or just the BBC's way of saying that a television series has a better chance of being successful if there is the pleasing sight of a pretty young girl figuring on the screen? Only two years into our still young singing partnership as The Corries, Roy and I didn't want to upset any apple-carts and we didn't argue the point, especially since it wasn't just Bernie's company we would be in, but a whole array of international artists as well. Even as I write this, I have the thought that, with two sell-out houses on the same night at The Caley Cinema on December 28th coming up and

134

Top: My big brother
Ian and me. 1938.

Bottom: The Broons,
circ. 1941.

Left: My drawing of The Black Watch Memorial, done at age 11. The Memorial stands at the top of The Mound in Edinburgh.

Below: I draw my niece, Norma Collie, for the Edinburgh Evening News reporters. Pinned to the easel is my pencil copy of my father's water-colour copy of The Laughing Cavalier by Frans Hals.

Top right: Me as a scout aged 13.

Bottom right: Boroughmuir School 1st XV, 1954 - '55. That's me, standing third from the left.

Pat and me in Paisley for the Grammar School Sevens of 1955.
No, it's not my car.

Above: I collect the Braidburn Athletic Club Junior Trophy in 1957.

Left: Graduation Day, Edinburgh College of Art, 1959.

Top right: We met at the church on time, 30/06/59.

Bottom right: Lauren and Gavin at Briarbank Terrace.

Left: Pat and my niece, May Stuart. Much later, May married Ritchie Laing. Pat and May were always good buddies.

Bottom: The Corrie Folk Trio and Paddie Bell with the BBC stamp of acceptance, 1963.

Right: The Corrie Folk Trio and Paddie Bell sing in The Hoot'nanny Show, 1963.

RECEIVED
-1 JUN 1963
EDINBURGH.

Top left: Circ. 1968.
Roy, with his first
wife, Vi, mother of his
two girls, Karen and
Sheena.

Bottom left: Circ. 1968.
With Gavin, Pat and
Lauren.

Top right: In the
seventies, (l. to r.), Jim
Wilkie, Brian Wilson
(M.P. to come), and
Dave Scott, founders
of The West Highland
Free Press.

Bottom right: 1973?
Lauren, Maurice and
Gavin in Petticoat
Lane, London.

Left: The Corries, a publicity shot.

Above: Family and friends gather round for the 1977, 'Peat Fire Flame' album cover shot.

Bottom: 'Where did that note go, Roy?'

Left: I interview Lonnie Donnegan in our 1983 award-winning STV series, 'The Corries and other Folk'.

Below: My first solo commitment as Founder Member of The Beechgrove Garden Club.

Top right: My two Grand Slam Commemorative paintings and members of the 1990 Squad.

Bottom right: The 1991 Official S.R.U. Calendar.

Overleaf: 'Ah cannae hear ye!'

Ronnie speaking to Lonnie Donnegan, one of the guests on their 1983 STV series, The Corries and Other Folk. The series won a gold award in New York.

similar successes throughout the country, could it have been possible that the BBC was trying to further Bernadette's career on the back of our increasingly strong image?

As a couple of still quite young men perhaps getting a wee bit big in the head, with an album on Fontana called 'Bonnet, Belt & Sword' already in the shops and another, also on Fontana, 'Kisimul's Galley' on the way in 1968, and now a major TV Series in the making, all on top of increasingly successful live shows, maybe we could be forgiven for giving ourselves a pat on the back to celebrate a couple of years of intensely industrious work.

Chapter Fifteen

As early as January 1968 we were hailed as the 'old masters of folk-singing' by a columnist in the *TV Times*, Hugh Gray, and were pictured in that publication, both families together in the upstairs hall of my Henderson Row house: Roy and me, Pat with our two, Gavin and Lauren, and Vi with their two, Karen and Sheena, surrounded by toys. An ornate gilt mirror and an intricately carved, cushioned chair bear testimony that we were now reaping the financial rewards of our work.

Our terrific joiner Bill Philp, purpose-built a new kitchen for us, taking out the window and replacing it with a glass panelled door opening onto a wooden stairway into the garden. He also partitioned the large room Roy and I had used for practice (gone, alas, was the table-tennis table), so we now had a double bedroom for Pat and me and a smaller room with bunk beds for the bairns (to their great joy). The rooms were linked by a small hall. My office/practice space was now the front room diagonally opposite these bedrooms.

With successful live concert performances ahead, and television shows already in the can with more promised, we had firmly put behind us the dire warnings that came with giving up our 'safe' teaching jobs a couple of years before.

February 2nd, 1968, was a hugely momentous day for Roy Williamson and The Corries, for that was the day Roy's song, 'Flower of Scotland', was heard by the public for the first time. No one foresaw that it would be heard at countless international sports events all over the world, or that it would be recorded by the Royal Scottish National Orchestra, along with the pipes, to be played as the unofficial National Anthem of Scotland at the Commonwealth Games of 2014.

Some months before we had recorded it at Ruthven Barracks, in Badenoch, for the television programme, '*Songs of The Jacobite Risings*', accompanied only by Roy's bouzouki and my bodhran. A bodhran is a small Irish hand-drum that I first heard in Ireland, but I realised that if I was going to play it on stage I would need one big enough to be seen from the back of large halls and theatres. I therefore asked my brother-in-law, the bagpipe maker Andy Ross, to make me a king size version, and he certainly did. At just under three feet in diameter it was of epic proportions. When I first produced it on stage the whole of the folk-world laughed it to scorn. It's true what they say however, about he who laughs last, because very soon drums of this size appeared in dozens of groups.

There we were, then, in front of the television cameras, attempting to give a newly-written work an authentic archaic sound. Roy sat on a grass mound under the Barracks walls and I stood behind. He sang with many pauses and instrumental breaks, a style we later changed to play more simply and in an even tempo with two guitars making it an instant hit with our audiences. So popular did it become that we couldn't get off stage without singing it at least twice.

The Jacobite theme was followed the next week by '*The Border Ballads*', and both were very popular. By the time we were seen on February 20th on '*Cairngorm Ski Night*', and on March 9th on '*Once More with Felix*' (the Felix in question being American folk singer Julie Felix), you might have thought we were taking over the airwaves. These television appearances did no harm to the February shows in Aberdeen Music Hall, Dundee Caird Hall and St Andrews Younger Hall. If anyone ever tells you that television isn't good for putting customers on seats in live shows, just refer them to me. Roy and I were grateful for it throughout our long career.

As I write, one of my grand-daughters, Jessica, is studying at St Andrews University where she sings in the University's a cappella group, the Alleycats. When I went to see her performing recently at the Younger, I was reminded of our visit there at the end of 1967 to record one of our 'Degrees of Folk' programmes. Among our guests on that particular show was a group of limbo dancers called the Stretch Cox Dancers, which highly amused Jessica. I suppose it's in the telling, or perhaps the spelling.

On June 10th the first 'Degrees of Folk' show aired with the Manhattan Brothers as main guests. These shows, pre-recorded in Universities from Edinburgh and Newcastle to Belfast and Dublin, Sussex and Strathclyde, ran for nine weeks consecutively and were a perfect build-up to our Corriefolk '68 Caley Cinema Festival late-night shows.

One of our guests on Corriefolk '68 was the young Barbara Dickson who was then making a name for herself on the folk scene. This was a long time before she discovered her 'Blood Brothers' down south, and before she started touring in her 'Caravan', and even longer before she met Elaine Paige and that man they both knew so well. Barbara has been kind enough to say that her appearance on our show speeded her career on its way.

The South African 'Manhattan Brothers' were touring and we were lucky enough to book them. Their entrance, singing their way down the aisles of the Caley Cinema, to converge at the steps to the stage, reminded me of our first encounter with the Clancy Brothers and Tommy Makem in Roy's flat. However their image, with bright coloured shirts and welly boots with tin beer top stirrups was nothing like the Clancys, nor was their singing. They were something of a revelation to Edinburgh audiences.

If nothing else our shows provided variety, both in material and appearance. A case in point was an English folk-singer who could not have been more 'earthy'. His name was John DuBarry, and the main feature of his 'appearance' was his bare feet, which would have been perfectly acceptable had they been clean. Since it had been Roy's idea to book him I suggested he have a word. Roy's way of putting it was to ask John if perhaps he could give his feet a polish.

Others in the cast were Doris Henderson, a Blues and Gospel singer, a group called Bitter Withy, a young Mike Whellans, and another group called The Skerries, but it was our two headliners whom I remember best, for different reasons.

Rog Whittaker had received a lot of television coverage, particularly on Ulster TV, with his most unusual whistling style. It fell to me to pick him up at the airport on the Monday of the first week. When I dropped him off at his hotel he said it was very nice, and thanked me for my trouble, and then asked me what I was doing before the show. When I told him I was on my way home for tea, he asked if he could come. Somewhat surprised, I said of course he could, and it was an even more surprised Pat who greeted him at the door. Pat had by now become used to such surprises and promptly set another place at the table.

During the meal it emerged that Rog was not all that fond of hotel life and suggested, hesitantly and politely that he might stay with us for the week. The arrangement was agreed, and after spending the evening with him, we finally arrived at the Caley. I took Roy aside and suggested that perhaps we had made a mistake in booking, not a star of television and theatre, but what seemed to be an overgrown, reticent student.

When it came time for Rog to take the stage, I was really worrying about our top of the bill, especially when he reached his high stool at the microphone. He walked on to thunderous applause but sat rooted to his seat and slowly looking around. Only when he went into one of those fantastic whistling pieces of his, with accompanying facial contortions, did I relax. I was in the wings to greet him after a second encore, and when he asked me if it had gone well enough, said not to be silly and just listen to that audience. Needless to say, he knew very well what he had done to them.

During his stay I came to realise that Roger Whittaker was a true star, but without the theatrical baggage normally associated with them. He spent a lot of time on the phone to his wife and friends and fitted into our family life by washing dishes and helping with other household chores, playing with the children at times. It was as though he just wasn't aware of his abilities on stage, although I learned that what he had was wrought from hard work and practice.

Rog told me that he wrote for three or four hours every day, mostly producing very little, but it had become a habit with him. We're all aware now of the hits his 'habit' produced. Rog explained to me that his somewhat casual and slow style off-stage was deliberately adopted, that it left him something in reserve for performance. I never forgot that and have tried it myself and found it to work. My method is to ask myself why I'm rushing around when I don't need to, and deliberately to relax my shoulders. It's amazing how the tension disappears.

He maintained his slow-walk, casual style on the last Saturday when I ambled with him round our district of Stockbridge. We went into a small antique shop to look round and he bought a very nice vase, I thought he was buying a souvenir of Edinburgh to take home but, when we got back to the house, he handed it to Pat as thanks for all the trouble she had taken. He had noticed exactly the right spot for it in the house during his stay, and thought that Pat might like it.

Many years later my friend, Frank Pritchard, spent a week in Rog's home refurbishing some of his antique clocks. Frank explained to me that Rog had been every bit as kind and thoughtful a host to him as he had been a guest with us. I have a lot of time for Mr Whittaker.

Our bill toppers of the second week were The Chieftains.

The piper, and leader of the group, was Paddy Maloney, who also stayed with us as house-guest, although this time it was pre-arranged. Also pre-arranged was my hotel booking for a man called Gareth Brown. The Guinness Company had interests in The Chieftains and Gareth was one of the Guinness heirs. As such, he preferred to travel incognito and the name I was to use for his booking was (wait for it!) Mr Phartinglass. What a difference that made to making sure he was incognito, to be sure, to be sure.

Unlike Rog the week before, we hardly saw Paddy, because he was pretty well confined to his room, continually practising his pipes. I sometimes wondered if maybe he was playing a tape, just to impress, and really he was sleeping all day. Anyway, we saw enough of him to learn that Gareth was a breeder of Irish Wolfhounds, an ancient breed once given as gifts to the Caesars of Rome. Since losing her pal, Dane, Pat had been hankering after another big dog and this looked like an opportunity. We eventually travelled to Gareth's estate in Ireland and chose a female we called Neve. I know that's not the Irish spelling, but it suited us.

Unfortunately, when she was old enough to be sent to us, she travelled to Glasgow by boat at a time when neither Pat nor I could go through. That task fell to Pat's brother, Lee, who found her, not in a box as might be expected, but sharing the hold with cattle, tethered to a pole by a long lead. In panic, she had wound the lead round the pole, finishing in a lying position, neck-deep in her own, and the cattle's filth. The result was that, for the rest of her life, she didn't have quite the spirit such a noble animal should possess. Nonetheless, she was a well-loved member of our family, aided and abetted by another wee cross-bred terrier called Kirrie, whom we had got from a dogs' home.

On October 21st and 22nd we recorded our first live LP for Fontana in the Lyceum Theatre in Edinburgh, soon after Finbar's wedding. Following all this, on October 31st we were in London for three days rehearsal for *The Val Doonican Show*. Tyne Tees TV appearances and more touring followed, culminating in a sell-out Usher Hall concert on December 28th. 'Sell-out' meaning every seat in the organ gallery being taken as well. I'll admit the organ gallery sell-out was a bit of a misnomer because from there all you could see was our rear ends, so we offered those seats free to nurses, taxi-drivers and policemen. There was no shortage of takers, and, with much flag-flying and banner-unfurling, they made a fantastic backdrop for the show.

In the green room later I asked my father if he had enjoyed the show. He said, 'Well son, if ye'd only open yer mouth when ye sing, ye'd maybe get on'.

At the meal I had arranged for family and friends in an Indian Restaurant opposite the Usher Hall I was seated next to Pop, whose first experience of Indian food this was. As the usual communal dishes went round, every time a platter arrived at his place he scooped the whole contents onto his plate. When I asked him later if he had enjoyed it, he said, 'Oh yes, but they give ye far too much.'

Our last engagement of 1968 was on the BBC's Hogmanay show, and the early part of 1969 was busy with concerts and television and even included a cabaret appearance at Quaglino's in London. Before we knew where we were the Easter holidays were upon us and Pat and the children took refuge in Prosen, in the Angus glens, where I had to leave them to do two television shows with Mike Whelans, The Chieftains and Jeannie Robertson, followed by a show in the Kelvin Hall on April 11th.

It seems we had earned the reputation of being multi-instrumentalists, which we certainly didn't have as The Corrie Folk Trio. I had always played the harmonica, and seemed to have an aptitude because I could pick out a tune without thinking whether it was a sook or a blaw. I was also making sounds on the guitar, the banjo and the mandolin. I choose my words carefully, because making sounds on an instrument is a far cry from claiming to be a skilled instrumentalist, as Roy was, playing guitar, mandolin, bandurria, Northumbrian pipes, concertina, whistle, flute, and more.

Carrying all these instruments became more and more awkward as Roy increased his repertoire, and so he invented a couple of instruments which combined the sounds of some we were already playing. The combolins were born.

Roy made one for himself which had a basic guitar finger-board, a bandurria fingerboard, and a set of sympathetic strings which resonated with the guitar and/or the bandurria. He also made one for me which also had a basic guitar, but also a mandolin and a set of bass strings which could be played separately in chord shapes. You might imagine my trepidation when he handed me mine. Unfortunately the theory didn't work out as planned, because the combolins became another instrument in their own right and added to, rather than replaced, what we already had.

It was about this time that Roy and Vi were divorced. He had taken a cottage in an area of Edinburgh called the Grange to use as a workshop, and entered a relationship with a lady dentist who lived in Colinton Road, not far from his cottage, making use of her drills to shape the intricate ivory carving on the combolins. Inevitably Pat and I had got to know her and she now became our family dentist.

There were plans afoot at the time between my joiner, Bill Philp, and Roy, to draw up blueprints and go into commercial combolin production, but the plans fell through and those originals remain completely unique, the only two in existence.

The completion of the combolins also marked the end of Roy's involvement with the dentist, which in turn led to something of a situation between Roy and me. Roy had a friend called John MacKinnon, who was also his business partner in a property development scheme which had nothing at all to do with either me or The Corries. One day, he arrived at my door to inform me that, since Roy was no longer seeing Anne, perhaps it would be better if I severed my family's connection with her as our dentist.

At this suggestion I'm afraid I hit the roof. In the first place I was dumbfounded that Roy didn't speak to me himself. Secondly, did he actually think that on my visits as a patient, between the numbing of my mouth and the drilling of my teeth and the collecting of debris in my throat, Anne and I would have Roy Williamson as a topic of conversation?

My mind went back to our meeting with Phil Solomon and that suspicion of 'divide and rule'. Accept it, and you'll accept anything. I sent Roy's intermediary back with the news, thinking that he would immediately get back to me. Surprisingly, at least to me, he didn't. I therefore went to see him and explained that if this was to be the end of our relationship, then so be it. However, I did give him my assurance that, if we were to continue together, I would be very careful not to become involved in any relationship he might have with any member of the fair sex in any way.

History tells you that we did continue and, in the years that followed, he did indeed have three liaisons that I know about. I'm sure that each of these ladies thought me the most unsociable male they never met.

Chapter Sixteen

May through June saw The Corries very quiet so, on July 5th, I found myself with the family for fifteen days holiday in a fishing village called Castell de Fels, a short train journey south from Barcelona. The train stops on the beach and, when you jump down from the carriage door, your feet sink into the sand. Nothing of note to report on this except to say that it was a relief to do nothing for a fortnight but relax and enjoy the sun. Life otherwise was a constant engagement with planning, printing tickets and posters, booking halls and theatres, not to mention hotels, and learning instruments and new songs.

Holidays are quickly over and suddenly we were back in Edinburgh putting the finishing touches to Corriefolk '69. The programme I prepared is before me as I write, and has photographs of the cast: Paco Pena, The Orange Blossom Sound, The Amulree Trio in week one, Derek Brimstone, The Grehan Sisters and The Other Half in week two, and Wally Whyton, Shirley and Dolly Collins and John McKinnon in week three.

All of these acts are ticked off as having been paid, but my diary also shows that on Saturday, September 13th, I paid £75.00 to The McCalmans and £30.00 to Isla St Clair. Shirley and Dolly had called off at the last minute for domestic reasons and we hastily drafted in Isla and the boys. I remembered Isla as a wee girl on my knee in an Aberdeen hotel while I sang her a birthday song in the presence of her folk singing mother. Isla,

145

of course, went on to fame in *'The Generation Game'* with Larry Grayson.

Another person I met at this time, at 9.30am precisely on September 9th, 1969, also carved a highly successful career for himself, albeit in a very different field. Brian Wilson, together with two friends from Dundee University, Dave Scott and Jim Wilkie, had a collective dream which was destined to become a reality. To this day the *West Highland Free Press* serves the islands of the west coast of Scotland from its base in Portree on the Isle of Skye.

Brian and his colleagues were interested in promoting Corries concerts in their area, with some of the profits going to financing their newspaper dream. We agreed to help them out, and the purpose of my meeting with Brian that morning was to thrash out the final details of the first of these shows in Stornoway, Islay, Dunoon and Campbeltown. We agreed to take a fee of £150.00 per show, and even allowed them sixpence on every programme sold. Who says we haven't done our bit for Scotland?

Brian's talents are many, and his energy boundless. In addition to founding the *West Highland Free Press* he went on to serve Cunninghame North from 1987 to 2005 as its Labour Party Member of Parliament, and the whole country as a Minister of State from 1997 to 2003.

After the Campbeltown show we continued with our own venues until late October when Roy went to London to discuss our next L.P. with Fontana. Our 1969 disc (for them), 'Corries in Concert', had entered the best-selling charts of the *Record Retailer*, been voted Folk LP of the month in *Melody Maker*, and Fontana were eager to strike again while the iron was hot.

An ideal opportunity presented itself when we accepted an engagement at The Savoy Hotel in London. It came, no doubt, because of the successful album, but our recent television series, *'Corriefolk'*, must also have played a part. Being committed to three weeks at The Savoy, we were able to spend our days in the recording studio.

The Savoy restaurant, incidentally, was a notoriously difficult venue for entertainers. We heard that the comedian Frankie Howerd had been received so badly on his first night that he stomped out, never to return. Bold as brass we, accustomed to performing two-hour concerts, felt we'd have no difficulty filling our twenty minute spot, even if no one was listening. For us, it would be a quick on and a quick off operation. As it turned out we did make a success of it, and were asked back the following year.

One night's success was substantially due to the late Scots actor, John Gregson who, when he saw who was on stage and recognised the song, joined in heartily. The remainder of our slot was spent accompanying John as he strolled around the tables, cajoling the other diners into singing along. On other nights John *Freeman*, our then Ambassador in Washington, found that he had a good singing voice when we squeezed it out of him, and Lord Robens surprised himself in a chorus of Johnnie Lad, where we sang verses based on what was in the newspapers that day.

During our last week at the Savoy, we heard that the Marquess of Lothian was selling the large, green American estate-car which we had seen around Edinburgh on occasion. A huge beast of a thing it had plenty of room inside for our instruments, so we made a long-range purchase. Lee picked it up for us from the Marquess's home at Monteviot, Jedburgh, and we drove home in splendour in time for our Christmas Usher Hall concert. That year we also appeared live on the BBC's Hogmanay Show with Moira Anderson and Bill Simpson.

Sometime in 1969 Diana, Pat's other nursing sister, heard of an ailing nursing-home business comprising two homes, one in Edinburgh and one in the country. The Edinburgh establishment was run by the husband of a married couple, and the one in the country by his wife, and they were trying to get rid of the lease of the country element to close down that part of the business. Situated in the Ettrick Valley in the Scottish Borderland, twenty or so miles from Selkirk and about eighteen from Hawick, only a couple from Tushielaw Inn, it nestled in the rolling border hills: West Buccleuch Farmhouse.

Although we had fun running up and down to our but-and-ben in Glen Prosen, it was tiny and, at times, inaccessible. Diana thought we might be interested in looking at this place in Ettrick and Pat was keen to do so. When I say Pat was keen, I don't imply any dissent between us. It was just that The Corries' singing business, and the contacts I was making, encroached on family life, and Pat needed some measure of respite from the pressures. With success increasing as quickly as it was, she fully accepted that pressure there would be. She was very willing to accept it, but we both recognized that she needed time and space away from it.

We went to look at the house and its surroundings, finding them at the end of a pleasant drive through the hills between Edinburgh and the Ettrick Valley. First glance showed it to be vastly bigger than Prosen, and I do mean 'vastly'. The lease included not only the large farmhouse, but also various barns and sheds set in about four acres of farmland that just cried out for Neve and Kirrie to frolic in. On the ground floor, it had three public rooms and a large kitchen with scullery off, leading to what was called a 'cold' room (harbouring a couple of deep-freezers), and another two utility rooms, together with a family bathroom.

Upstairs was another bathroom and no fewer than six bedrooms. Up more stairs was a large attic and two smaller bedrooms. A winding stair from a corner of the kitchen led to yet another wee room and, to crown it all, along with the lease came a couple of fishing permits for the river bounding the fields on the south side. The more we saw, the more an image of myself in 'coming-and-going' hat with fishing-rod on one shoulder and shotgun on the other appeared in my head.

The lease was a pittance and had only two years to run, so

what had we to lose? The nursing home was already closed and the guests moved out, leaving more than enough in the way of furnishings for us to take residence. We gave up Glen Prosen and a few days later spent our first week-end in West Buccleuch Farmhouse with what became, in the coming years, an oft used telephone number: Ettrick Valley 230.

As it transpired, it was a very good decision. In all my arrangements for Corries concerts and guaranteed engagements, I allowed for Roy and I being married men with children, not gad-about young blades hell bent on stardom and collateral opportunities. I always planned, where possible, to leave weekends and school holidays free. It was a policy that seemed to bear fruit as, when I was looking at our family photographs and videos taken through the years, I discovered that I was, without exception, the cameraman.

Starting with our move from Henderson Row to West Buccleuch in 1971 when Gavin was ten years old, they include early family holidays in Barcelona, Las Palmas and Canada, through sledging and snowballing and birthday bikes and motor-bikes, hanging Christmas decorations, salmon and trout fishing with the children, weddings, Pat blowing bubbles for the grandchildren at bath-time. They seem to testify that I was with my children more often than most nine-to-five fathers. When I mentioned to them that I have felt guilty all my life for being an absentee father, they immediately assured me otherwise. It seems to me that a topic of conversation amongst their childhood friends had been that the Browne family's father was always at home. So it must have appeared, and perhaps I wasn't such a bad old stick after all. Is that another pat on the back I feel?

In those first, leased Buccleuch months, we weren't the only ones to use the property.

My brother, Ian, left the Army after nine years of service, but didn't come home to Scotland. Instead he settled in the South of England, eventually becoming a fishing tackle salesman for a firm called Pegley Davis. As a lot of his time was spent on the road, and some of that in Scotland, we gave him a key so he could visit even when we weren't present. This he did, and spent the time in fishing.

He had all the equipment, so why not take up the hobby? I had to laugh about the equipment though. He sold things like special wee hammers for killing the fish, and 'bite indicators', a flashing light that came on when a fish took the hook. In my experience you picked up any old rock to *dunt* the fish on the *heid*, and if you weren't aware of a fish taking the bite, it wasn't worth catching.

Ian's boss at Pegley Davis heard of his escapades and decided to join him one week-end when we were also going to be there. Immediately Gavin and Lauren got home from school that Friday we left town, arriving at the house to find Ian and his boss flat out on the sofas in front of a blazing coal fire, both exhausted.

If you leave our front door and drive over the iron bridge crossing the Rankle Burn, turn left at the East Buccleuch intersection (a fancy word for where two earthen tracks merge), go up the hill to turn right onto the main Hawick road, and continue for about three-quarters of a mile, you come to Clearburn Cottage with Clearburn Loch behind it in a dip in the hills.

That had been Ian's route with his boss that morning as he obviously had success there on a previous visit. Selected from their company's fishing catalogue, they had brought an inflatable dinghy. As a herd of bemused cows looked on at the battery pumped awakening of this flattened piece of rubber, the two intrepid anglers donned (again from their catalogue) their overalls with attached hoods. To complete the assemblage they snapped on specially designed leather belts with hammers and bite-indicators attached, and various boxes of assorted flies and hooks.

Alas, what they didn't have from the catalogue was a Clearburn Loch wind-indicator, which would have been especially useful that day as it started to blow a gale. Every time they launched their craft, they were swept to the other end of the water. They persevered, however, taking advantage of any breaks in the wind, and spent the day in constant labour on and off the loch. The result was two spent human forces. To make things worse they caught nothing. They hadn't even been burnt by the sun. Naturally we sympathized.

Cruelly though, and out of sheer bravado, I asked if they would like a nice tea of freshly caught trout, making a show of putting on my fishing waistcoat and taking my rod from the cold-room. The line was already threaded with a cod-hook to which I attached a squirming bramble-worm from the Oxo tin in my fishing basket. Slinging it over my shoulder I proceeded out of the door and up towards the rock pool underneath the iron bridge, quipping merrily, 'Back in a minute!'

They laughed of course, but then a once-in-a-lifetime coincidence occurred. I steadied myself on the bank and dropped hook and line into the swirling current to immediately feel a tug. Sheer instinct drew back the rod for me to find, twisting and turning on my hook, the biggest trout I have ever caught, then or since. It was all of three pounds. As I dunted its head with a stone, I quickly re-wormed the hook and dropped it in again, but it didn't take long to realise that the big fish had been in that deep part of the pool for a long time and it would take another long time for a fish to take up residence and gorge itself to the same size. About to leave I felt a wee bite and out popped a tiny wee trout. I pulled it off the hook, scrambled up the bank, and made my way back. The whole sequence had taken only ten minutes.

Nonchalantly opening the lounge door I was met with questioning stares; so briefly had I been away it must have seemed as if I hadn't really gone out at all. I withdrew the wee fish and said, 'There ye are then.' 'Och', says Ian, 'We've been throwing

151

things like that back all day.' Drawing the big fellow from the basket I retorted, 'Aye, but I got his big brother as well.'

I have never in my life seen an exhausted human being spring so quickly back to life as my brother at that moment. He hurtled me towards the kitchen and grabbed a knife from the drawer to slit the still wriggling beast open and see what it had eaten to make it so big. He was laughing like a drain as we prepared the fish tea I had offered in jest.

Another once-in-a-lifetime coincidence occurred on a weekend when Pat and Violet went down with the children on the Friday and I joined them on the Sunday afternoon. When I arrived I made a joke of them not having my tea ready, saying they should have something special for the return of their favourite man. Violet joined in the joke by saying that they had indeed thought of a duck casserole but there was no duck in the freezer. 'No problem,' I replied, and how many ducks would she need? When she said two, as with Ian I replied, 'Okay, just give me a minute'. Again I went into the cold room, this time unlocking the gun-cupboard and taking out my shotgun.

After walking a hundred yards I arrived at an area of marshy ground just beyond our boundary fence, to find a flock of sitting ducks. As quietly as possible, I loaded both barrels. When I crept forward the flock rose and, since the birds were thickly bunched, I could hardly miss. Two birds fell to the ground which I picked up and quickly took back to the house. Approaching from the back garden I knocked on the window of the lounge and, as the ladies turned to face me, I lifted the birds and asked if these would fit the bill. Again, as with Ian's trout, I had only been away a matter of minutes and their incredulous expressions matched my own incredulity at my luck.

Only twice in my life (three if you count my hundred percent for geometry at Boroughmuir), have such fluke happenings occurred, but they are strange memories and stories worth telling.

When Roy left for London and his Fontana meetings, I

attended the wedding of my niece, May Stuart, to her fiance Ritchie Laing in Fife. Lauren was a flower girl and proud as punch. Pat and I were very selfish though, and drove to the airport immediately after for a flight to Las Palmas, leaving Gavin and Lauren in the care of Violet.

Whilst in Las Palmas, I met an American oil man called Curtis O. Walding who very kindly took me on a helicopter flight to one of his oil-rigs off the coast of Africa. It's a scary feeling stepping from the cockpit of a helicopter onto a landing pad which amounts to no more than a trampoline between you and the vast ocean. Living conditions on the rig were first class but, when I learned about the riggers' long periods away from not only their temporary home in Las Palmas, but their countries, and the unrelenting hard work, I felt lucky to be just a simple folk-singer. Compared to theirs, mine was an easy life-style.

Hold on! I hear you ask, what's all this about two foreign holidays in the year? That's easily explained. Our balance sheet for the year ending 31st May, 1969, shows that both Roy and I were then taking a salary of £4,287: 3: 10. In 1970, this went up to £4,937: 8: 8, and in 1971, further increased to £9,497: 86. Had we stayed as teachers, even allowing for an incremental scale increase, we would still be earning under £1,000: 00 per annum.

However, I'm jumping the gun by a couple of years. Let's go back to 1970.

As artists we were still not completely independent. Nor were we making large fees for every performance. I note that, on February 20th of that year, we performed a one hour spot in a two-hour concert in Tilliecoultry for a fee of £150.00. This show was promoted by Mike Hart, a banjo player with an Edinburgh jazz band and also an entertainments' agent who, in 1978, was instrumental (if you'll pardon the pun) in setting up The Edinburgh Jazz Festival. Mike is now an MBE. That night he agreed, in his capacity of agent, to let us use the venue microphones, although we had started to carry a fairly simple sound system of our own. Two nights later in Girvan he paid the same for another one hour concert spot, this time using our own sound. In turn, we paid Mike three pence per programme sold, these programmes having been printed and supplied by The Corries.

John Worth, now sadly deceased, was at the time the extremely popular manager of the Empire Theatre, Inverness. John paid us a guaranteed £600.00 or two-thirds of anything over £1,000.00 for two solo shows.

That year I brought the family back from Spain to help Roy host a BBC television show for Iain MacFadyen on July 6th. An open-air recording, it would eventually air as a celebration of the opening of the 1970 Commonwealth Games with guests Roger Whittaker (South Africa), Cy Grant (Jamaica), The Settlers (England), Lyn and Graham McCarthy (Australia), The Johnstons (Ireland), Deena Webster (Hong Kong), Mari Griffith (Wales), Aly Bain and Mike Whellans (Scotland) and The Kathakali Dance Company (India).

Our next solo concert appearances in Edinburgh were on July 24th, 25th and 26th, late night at the Odeon Cinema, and our sell-out last night performance was graced by the Games' Light Middleweight Boxing Champion, the Scotsman, Tom Imrie. You can imagine the singing of Flower of Scotland as the last item of the night after we introduced Tom as a surprise guest. He stood beside us singing every word, and the roof was lifted.

I hope I don't sound too big-headed when I say that we had become used to roofs being lifted at the end of our shows, because such popularity as we had achieved didn't go without detractors. Some people on the folk scene, club organisers and columnists, didn't entirely hold with our performances, thinking we should present a more serious blend of what they considered to be authentic, leaving the lighter and funnier material to what might be called the 'Tartan Brigade'.

By 'lighter' I mean such songs as The Lass of Fyvie, Johnnie Lad, The Wild Rover, Come O'er the Stream Charlie and all songs referring to the Bonnie Prince. They didn't seem to think that an audience should be allowed to laugh. We disagreed, however, and thought that we had found a perfect blend. Although some lighter material was certainly included, and an amount of clowning was present, we also led a very mixed audience into the world of obscure and, indeed, forgotten folk music. I'll illustrate.

Bill Hill wrote a hilarious parody of the old Frankie Laine hit, 'Ghost Riders in the Sky', changing the words to 'The Teuchter That Cam' Fae Skye'. It's not a true folk song but, my, it is funny, and it never failed to have our audience of mums and dads and children and even some folk club members (who may have sneaked in in disguise, shame on them), in stitches, clapping, foot-stamping, laughing and singing the chorus. At the end of such a song we would invariably dim the lights, quietly change the guitars for say, concertina and mandolin, and I would recite something along the lines of:-

'The unrelenting cruelties of the Duke of Cumberland
Spared neither age, sex, nor condition
And Scotland for a while realised a prophecy of Peden
Which foretold that the time was nigh
When her people might ride fifty miles through her hills
    and valleys
And never see a reekin' hoose
Nor hear a crawin' cock.'

Into the silence that would descend we would sing The Highland Widow's Lament, a true ballad from our Scottish Troubled Times which starts;

'Oh I am come tae the Low Countrie
Ochon, ochon ochree-e
Withoot a penny in my purse
Tae buy a meal tae me.'

It continues to describe the Widow's forlorn condition after her husband's demise at the hands of an invading English force.

It was certainly not material for The Palladium, but was stunningly effective and thought-provoking at just that spot in our programme. We would follow, lest the folks out there became too morose, with something a bit lighter but just as authentic, such as 'The Braes o' Killiecrankie'.

It wasn't only the audience we wanted to entertain, but ourselves as well, as we could not possibly last two hours without a laugh or, at the very least a smile or two. Against a certain amount of criticism we continued, like Frank Sinatra, doing it our way.

I also know that some people objected to the stage uniform we adopted of leather doublets with epaulets, very much in a mediaeval style, atop the ploughman's sark shirts Violet and Pat made for us but, with more and more people flocking to our shows, and more and more television offers coming our way, we had to believe that we were doing things right.

Chapter Seventeen

We wondered if we were pushing things, arranging yet another late-night show for the three weeks of the 1970 Edinburgh Festival. The Odeon Cinema had a bigger capacity than the Caley of our last few years' shows, so we hedged our bets by doing Wednesdays to Saturdays instead of the full week. The experiment was successful and we again played to full houses. This year firm favourite Paco Pena was accompanied by a troupe of Flamenco dancers who tore the place apart with their wild gyrations, Cy Grant, The McDonald Sisters, more favourites Dorita y Pepe and, for local interest, an Edinburgh group, Tyler's Acre.

In the last week we had a rather unusual combination of Canada's Bonnie Dobson and Spencer Davis. Spencer was more associated with the Spencer Davis Group he formed in 1964 but, by now, after various personnel changes, was presenting a much more gentle, melodic, acoustic rock. Finally we welcomed a former Liberton pupil of Roy's, Davey Johnstone who, together with musician/comedian Noel Murphy and former Strawbs' bass player, Ron Chesterman, made up the group known as Draught Porridge. We found it difficult to relate to Davey's nickname of 'Shaggis', coined by Noel. I'm not sure that nowadays, as Elton John's musical director, Davey would want to be reminded of it.

Of the after-show parties in my home at Henderson Row, I especially remember the night Paco brought his whole troupe along, arriving at about 3.00 am. I had taken the precaution of laying a couple of sheets of plywood on the carpet for the Flamenco dancing, which my father-in-law, Wattie, chose to call 'Knockin' fuck oot the linoleum'. I'll never understand how, through all the Festival parties we hosted at home, I never received one complaint from the neighbours. Maybe the reason was that, during the Festival, the whole city buzzed up to all hours of the night.

Manolo, one of Paco's singers, excused himself for a comfort break and, when he returned, requested that Paco accompany him in a song. A couple of bars of dazzling finger-work preceded Manolo's soulful tenor as he made his way through the piece. Flamenco singing is frequently improvised and, in this particular instance, that was the case. Although he was singing in Spanish and we couldn't understand a word, the emotion he conveyed went beyond the bounds of language and soon tears were flowing from both singer and audience. When he finished I asked Paco about the meaning of the song and was flabbergasted when he explained.

When we moved from the basement to the upper part of the house my joiner, Bill, fitted the stair landing, where Dane was wont to prevent visitors leaving, with a sunken bathroom. The bath fitted in the stairwell and Bill put in a large shower to go with the toilet. The whole room was lined with mirrors and ornate tiling and lavishly carpeted. It was into this room that Manolo had disappeared earlier and which provided the theme of his song: a paean of praise for a room such as he had never seen in his life, that expanded into the theme of wonderment at bathrooms in general. Paco didn't seem at all put out by the emotion that this had stirred but the rest of us were highly amused that, only minutes before, we had been crying at the description of a toilet.

As the dancers again sprang into action (once started, try stopping them), there was a knock at the front door. Accompanied by half of the Edinburgh City Police Pipe Band, Chic Murray, my favourite Scottish comedian, was standing at our doorstep. For my money Chic ranks alongside Billy Connolly, who is widely recognized as the funniest man in the world. Chic had been with the band at a competition and, when their celebrations had ended, invited them along to ours. Chic and The Corries were running a sort of mutual admiration society at the time and he was constantly on at us to do an album with him on his honky-tonk piano. We never got round to it, but that hadn't damaged the friendship.

Henderson Row was becoming a pretty crowded dwelling place by this time. The band gave us a very loud party-piece, after which Chic stood to his full six-foot-odd and asked for silence. Explaining that, although it was quite right to be thoroughly enjoying ourselves, it was at times like this that we should spare a thought for those less fortunate, like his friend George. Suitably chastised, we stopped what we were doing to learn how George had recently been diagnosed with a blood disorder which would prove fatal if he didn't receive a course of fresh human breast-milk. George reckoned that he was obviously doomed, but his doctor held out hope. One of his lady patients had recently given birth and was producing more milk than her baby required. She had discussed George's situation with her husband and agreed that this man should be helped, hopefully saving his life. A course of suckling was offered and gratefully accepted and three-times-daily visits were arranged to the lady's home. After three weeks she looked down at George, cradled in her arms, and told him that over the period of treatment she had become exceptionally fond of him. If there was anything more he wanted he had only to ask. George thought for a bit and, wiping his mouth with his sleeve, said, 'Now that ye come tae mention it . . . I wouldnae mind an Abernethy biscuit.'

The room erupted and Chic gave one of his characteristic nods, accompanied by his famously understated smile, and sauntered – this big man never just walked – to an empty chair.

Immediately the curtain came down on our last Odeon show we left for London and talks with EMI about our next record. Concerts organised by ourselves, all over the country, included some for Brian Wilson, others for Mike Hart and Watt Nichol, and John Martin of Argyll Songs booked us solo in the Festival Hall, London, the early show of two on the same evening.

The latter was by Joni Mitchell who, we learned afterwards, had been standing in the wings while we were on, taking particular note of the combolins. She asked us to accompany her in her show later, in a song with the combolins, but we declined. As a matter of interest, in our talks with her, we learned that she and her management made little or no money from her prestigious Festival Hall concert, treating it as a promotional engagement for a new album release. Roy and I weren't surprised since, again during our chat with her, we learned that her lighting and sound rig had been hired from The Rolling Stones. Within the rig was a wind machine which was used in only one of her songs, to fan her dress gently while she sang. Such rigs do not come cheap, especially with a Rolling Stones tag.

At one point during her performance, she had difficulty changing her guitar into an open tuning, so much so that one of her musicians came down to her microphone to do the tuning for her. The shuffling and obvious discomfort of her audience was proof, yet again, of a belief we held firm to during all of our time together, that you rarely 'lose' your audience during a song, but often in the awkward pauses between if these pauses aren't covered with a pre-arranged piece of banter or information. Stéphane Grappelli of the Hot Club told his many local backing groups that they shouldn't worry about mistakes within a piece. As long as they started and finished together, there were no worries.

We saw out 1970 with the growing belief that we might be better off doing everything on our own, as we did for our last two concerts of the year in the Odeon on December 27th and

28th. These were our 17th and 18th appearances in our home town in that one year and we deemed ourselves most fortunate that they were full.

At one of our shared shows we had met a group called Folklore, made up of the McGie sisters, Ailsa and Morag, brother John, and Morag's boyfriend, Davie Watt. As well as being a singer and concertina player, Davie was interested in the business side, promotion in particular. Our growing belief that we should do everything for ourselves was somewhat undermined when we allowed Davie to promote us and found ourselves in Hamilton and Perth on a guaranteed £300 per show.

This meant that Davie had joined our other gang of promoters: John Martin doing concerts in England, Mike Hart and Watt Nicol in some parts of Scotland, and Brian Wilson and his post graduate colleagues still taking us to the outlying districts of Islay, Campbeltown, Mallaig and Corpach.

Thinking of the West Highlands I here return to our transport. By now we were hiring a mini-bus to get around, with Lee doing the driving, the bus being lifted onto ferries bound for the outlying islands in a huge rope net, with accompanying creaking and groaning as it sailed through the air. On one occasion, during a transport strike, Jim Wilkie was waiting for us on one of the islands. It looked as if we were not going to make the show, but he displayed remarkable ingenuity by hiring a small plane. We were accompanied on the flight by two marooned businessmen whose financial contribution more or less paid for the journey.

Another promoter to compromise our wish to be independent was the Edinburgh International Festival Society, which engaged us for two weeks of the official Festival at the Lyceum Theatre. According to the *Edinburgh Post* columnist, Ken Thomson, we played to 97% audience capacity, which was excellent business, even for the Official Festival. I wonder where the other 3% were – they missed a good night out.

Maybe watching our appearance on the BBC's *'Stars from Scotland'* on September 7th was enough for them, a show that had been recorded at His Majesty's Theatre earlier in the year on June 3rd and 4th.

It was on that show we discovered that Lena Martell suffered from stage-fright. She had to have two or three goes at moving off her spot to walk towards the cameras when the curtain opened. Rooted to the spot she just couldn't respond to the intro of her big hit, 'One Step at a Time, Sweet Jesus'. Given the memory of my childhood Hogmanay 'Ave Maria', I have never understood how I managed to avoid that dreaded affliction.

We couldn't help feeling pride at finding ourselves as part of the 'Establishment' festival, and we also took pleasure in being in the same company, at His Majesty's, as some of Scotland's show business greats. Along with Lena, we stood shoulder to shoulder with Moira Anderson, Kenneth McKellar, Rikki Fulton and Jack Milroy, Jimmy Shand, Jimmy Logan, and of course, Chic Murray.

The best ever Corries performance, albeit in the name of 'The Curries', with Rikki Fulton and Gregor Fisher in brown leather doublets and orange ploughman's sarks, can also be seen on You Tube. In this skit they exhort you to join them in a chorus, the words of which read;

> 'They grabbed his heid and severed it, and then ripped oot his tongue,
> It wriggled like a jeelied eel on the grund where it was flung.
> They beat his brain tae a throbbin' mush, and hacked his guts asunder,
> They cut his heart oot wi' a dirk . . . and he died. . . .
> Nae bloody wonder.'

It's priceless and I won't spoil it further for you.

This brings me neatly to our dressing room in Falkirk Town Hall on Wednesday, October 13th, 1971. Just before curtain-up, Roy was discovered writhing on the floor in agony with, yes, his guts. There was no way I could help him, and the only thing I could think of doing was to go on stage, part the closed curtains, and ask the time-honoured theatrical question, 'Is there a doctor in the house?'

Our audiences were used to unusual openings and, thinking this was one of them, started to laugh. Minutes later I still hadn't persuaded them that Roy really was in trouble. Fortunately, a doctor was present, and, to cut a long story short, Roy found himself in an ambulance bound for Falkirk Royal Infirmary. I had no option but to announce that the show was cancelled and that refunds would be arranged from the local agent. Word would eventually appear in the local press of a substitute date. It was late into the evening before Lee and I struck the equipment, cleared the Hall, and went straight to Ward 10F at the Infirmary. Roy was in bed and in not quite so much pain, but with a diagnosis of Renal Colic – kidney stones.

On the advice of his doctors, next day I cancelled our Aberdeen concerts for that evening, Kirkcaldy on the Saturday, and Stirling on the Sunday. At times like this we were fortunate to have maintained good relations with bookers and the press, as well as an understanding public, all of whom were totally sympathetic about an awkward and painful situation. Fortunately, Roy recovered and we continued the tour with three shows in Glasgow City Hall and one in Dundee from Wednesday of the following week.

An article in the *Daily Record* of November 22nd, 1971 reveals that we had refused offers of Christmas and New Year television shows. This suggests that we were, indeed, worrying about over-exposure. The article also states that we had installed recording equipment in Roy's home where we planned to produce our own tapes for offer to the recording companies.

This was very much Roy's baby because I wasn't too interested in the technical side of recording. He, having already made a couple of guitars and the combolins, had the necessary drive and I was not one to stop him. It seemed to me that, having exercised his inventive capabilities, he was looking for another outlet for his imagination. If the venture was successful we wouldn't have to go up and down to London for recording sessions, leaving more time to sleep in our own beds at night. Or so I thought.

Chapter Eighteen

Friday, May 2nd 1969 was a red-letter day for the Browne family.

As you know, my mother was a spiritualist medium, but being a spiritualist medium does not necessarily make for a nice person. When Gavin was born, Ma didn't seem particularly interested. It was a different story with Lauren. After she was born, Ma complained that she was being left out. To appease, and build bridges, Pat decided to leave the baby with her for a night. When Pat went to collect her, my mother said that she had been 'not bad' but to bring her back when she was out of nappies. This added to the list of rebuffs she had handed to Pat since Day One.

Nonetheless, Pat continued to act the dutiful daughter-in-law and, when a bus excursion to Holland for the Dutch Bulbs Experience was advertised, she and her sister Margaret, being keen gardeners, booked passage. Ma had expressed a desire to go, so she was also booked.

On the day of departure Violet, my mother-in-law, made her way down to Henderson Row to look after me and the children for the week-end, also carrying three dozen fresh farm eggs from farming friend Bessie Calder. As she came in from Gilmerton along George IV Bridge, at the crossroads with the High Street, she drove too quickly into the sharp left-hand turn at the top of The Mound, crossed to the wrong side and ran into the front of an approaching double-decker bus. Traffic was stopped for about two hours as she was extricated from the wrecked car.

The funny thing was that she was actually found in the passenger seat with the expression of one saying, 'What, Me, officer, I wasn't driving.' Every one of the eggs was broken, covering her in a thick yellow blanket mixed with blood from a gash running between her hair-line and her eyebrows, deep and wide enough for the bone of her skull to shine through. I was informed at the earliest possible moment, with a dire warning from Violet not to stop Pat from going to Holland because of a 'wee cut'. And this is where the story gets really interesting.

Violet was taken to Edinburgh Royal Infirmary where deep stitches were placed near the bone, with further sutures on the surface to reduce the eventual scarring. Having been a nurse herself, she was fascinated by the process, at the same time as being relieved because things could have been so much worse than the cut, bodily bruising, and shock which she was suffering. At the same time she became highly emotional, slowly becoming aware that her ward was directly below the ward in which her son, Walter, had died many years before.

Walter had crashed his motor-cycle in Edinburgh and been taken to this ward where, and this gave rise to further trauma for Violet, his two nursing sisters Diana and Margaret, at that moment on their way to Holland with Pat, had been on duty. Neither of them identified the severely battered patient until they recognised his scarf. Nothing could be done and he died as they looked on.

Later in the evening, blissfully unaware of events at home, Pat, Margaret and Ma were resting in their shared hotel room in Amsterdam, recovering from their bus journey. Pat lay on one bed, slightly separated from Margaret's, and Ma lay in another across the foot of the other two. Relaxing in various stages of deshabillé, my mother in her long bloomers, elasticated below the knee, was in the act of trimming an uncomfortably long toe-nail when she suddenly looked up and said, 'Oh, there's a young boy has just rolled between your beds inside a tyre and he's stopped, and he's saying not to worry, your Mum's fine, and enjoy your holiday.'

Strange looks were exchanged as Pat and Margaret headed for the phone. I had to tell them the whole story, but was able to add that their mother was in good fettle and there was no need to rush home. When Pat eventually arrived home, I asked what the significance was of Ma's story, and only then learned that Walter, as a boy, had been in the habit, just for fun, of rolling down Gilmerton Road inside a tractor tyre.

My mother could not have known that and, even if she had, would not have offered it as consolation to Pat.

Violet fully recovered and lived until the ripe old age of 96, for the rest of her life removing tiny slivers of glass which kept forcing themselves to the surface of her brow.

Whilst I have no intention of trying to convert anyone to spiritualism, I'd like to take this opportunity to expand on the subject a little. For all the sceptics I have ever known, including my father, it has taken only some simple but personal experience to persuade them that, at the very least, some things do not quite comply with 'the normal'.

One such experience concerns Pat's father, Wattie Elliot. Unfortunately, Wattie suffered a minor stroke, which turned a normally stubborn old man into an extremely awkward person, and that's putting it mildly.

Imagine this scene: Pat sitting at the kitchen table at her parents' home, facing her father, chatting and sharing, if not the same cigarette, the same ashtray, this being in the days when many people smoked. Both have placed their lit cigarettes in the ashtray, Wattie's facing him and Pat's facing her. Suddenly Wattie stretches forward, leans over and picks up Pat's cigarette, taking a drag, and replacing it facing Pat. What could she do but attribute such an impertinent action to the effects of the stroke and say nothing?

As Wattie became increasingly strange in his ways we invited him and Violet to Buccleuch to give Violet a few days respite. By this time he had become more or less confined to a chair. First thing in the morning we would place him on the sofa in the lounge whilst we went about our domestic chores, checking from time to time that he was all right and reassuring him that he wasn't forgotten.

At meal times I would assist him to stand by taking his wrists to pull him up and steady him on a decidedly slow, shaky walk to the dining-room. Instead of trying to help me he would deliberately pull back, making a sort of see-saw fight to see who was the stronger. My dawning belief that he wasn't really as bad as he made out, and that he was maybe trying to turn his illness to his advantage was confirmed by another episode. To be clear, I believe that this 'advantage seeking' was also a result of the stroke.

Pat had taken to smoking multi-coloured Balkan Sobranie cigarettes on special occasions and had placed them, loose in a small tub, on the end of the mantelpiece in the room where Wattie sat through the day. On our frequent checks on his well-being, he would often be smoking one of these unmistakable cigarettes. Nobody in the house had been giving him the cigarettes, so the obvious answer was that he was getting up at will, unaided, to grab one.

Eventually it all became too difficult and meals were brought to him. The same became true of his toilet requirements and it was me who got him into the standing position, dropped his trousers, and held a large green bottle for him to relieve himself. Now to the crux of the story.

Not long after these events Wattie had another, more severe, stroke and died. Sometime after his death, Pat and I attended a public display by a spiritualist medium in one of the book shops on George Street in Edinburgh. Messages were passed to many people until it came to my turn. The medium looked in my direction and said to me that an old gentleman wished to make contact but all he wanted to say was, 'Remember the bottle'. It was a simple enough statement, and hardly earth shattering, but one I immediately associated with, and all of the above events came back in a flash.

Some years after Wattie's death, Violet was sitting sewing, one warm summer day, on the doorstep of her bungalow at 519, when she heard what she thought was Wattie's voice calling to her from the rear of the house. She got up and went to the kitchen to investigate. No one was there, of course, nor was there anyone in the garden, so she closed the door and went back to the front of the house to discover that the stone lintel had somehow dislodged itself and smashed into pieces on the doorstep where she had been sitting. It would surely have killed her had she still been under it when it fell.

It was when we had moved to West Buccleuch, in the spring of 1972, that a very excited Ronnie Browne took possession of his first new motor car, a mustard yellow four-wheel drive Range Rover. I noted down all of the details in my diary of that year.

It seemed to me to fill the bill admirably for someone now living more as a country gent than a townie. It was a particularly good drive at night-time since it had a high driving position which meant that on-coming headlights didn't dazzle as much as in the lower saloon car. This was important as I was now doing many more long night drives.

When we moved permanently to Buccleuch concern was expressed that being so far out of town might prove inconvenient for Roy and Lee, but I guaranteed that any such inconvenience would be entirely mine. I always left home in plenty of time for practice or for meeting them for tour starts and engagements. Even the family thought we were being a bit selfish in isolating ourselves in the back of beyond as they put it, but such doubts disappeared when they found that our new home was very convenient for short holidays, or 'Just to keep Pat company'.

Although a lot of our work was in touring, much of it was also at venues within a short drive of Edinburgh. As The Corries we had purchased a Ford Transit Mini-bus for engagements, with Lee doing the driving and keeping the vehicle at his house door in Eskbank. We adopted the practice of Roy and me making our own ways to Eskbank to join Lee, leaving him there after returning from the show. It was on my drives home that I enjoyed the 'high drive', on country roads that were full of twists and turns and ups and downs and at a time of night, usually about 1.00 am, when I could see the lights of on-coming traffic for a long distance ahead.

On these solitary runs I took to relaxing by listening on tape to the ghost stories I had read as an art teacher to my pupils before asking them to illustrate what they had just heard. It might seem strange, but I've never been much of a listener to music just for relaxing. In fact, I listened almost exclusively as research for the job. In these ways I enjoyed driving the Range Rover very much until the autumn of that year.

As a hobby Pat had begun to collect Boehm plates and pottery and had spotted a porcelain owl, with an unsupported wing-span of about four feet, in one of their catalogues. We decided to take a couple of days off to visit the Boehm factory in Malvern in England. Since such an unsupported wing-span was unusual and very delicate, it followed that it was very expensive, and Pat didn't want to buy the thing, have it delivered, and then not like it.

Lee and his wife, Maureen arrived the night before to look after Gavin and Lauren and we set off at first light to take a leisurely drive south. We found ourselves in Malvern before lunch-time, much earlier than expected, found the Boehm factory and viewed the owl. Although Pat liked it very much, we decided, because of the very high price, not to take it with us, uninsured, in the car, but work our way through the proper purchase procedures for such an expensive item. This proved wise in a way we did not foresee.

I felt quite fresh and didn't see the point of hanging about, so we set off for home in the early afternoon. The sun began to set as we approached St Mary's Loch. It was a beautiful evening and I reversed into a lay-by so we could watch it go down over the water. I don't know if it was the car, the sight of the beautiful porcelain, or the romantic sun-bedecked surroundings, but very quietly Pat said, 'You know, Ron, I'm feeling a bit fruity. How about you?' I had to admit that I was beginning to match her mood, so I started up the car and turned left onto the road for home.

I swear it wasn't over excitement that distracted me but I found myself in a skid on wet autumn leaves, unable to stop the car sliding onto the wrong side of the road. Later, on reflection, I thought maybe the rear wheel traction of the four-wheel drive might have pulled me further into the skid as I went through the normal anti-skid procedures. We mounted the grass verge and accelerated down the loch bank towards the water, in spite of my feet being glued to the brake. I didn't steer deliberately towards the tree, as far as I was concerned it just appeared, but the engine wrapped itself round the trunk and we came to a dead stop.

Although we were wearing seat-belts, we were both projected forwards, bashing our bodies on the dash-board and steering-wheel. Pat's head hit the windscreen and she bounced back into her seat almost unconscious. My first thought was that the car might catch fire so I shouted to her to get out as quickly as possible. Her door wouldn't open and, as I called for her to crawl towards my now open door, I saw that her brow bore exactly the same deep gash that her mother's had. The flesh was wide open and the bone of her forehead was exposed before my eyes.

I pulled her towards me and we scrambled clear. With injuries to my left knuckles and my chest I realised that I had not escaped entirely scot free. As the first numbing shock of impact wore off, and the pain set in, I tried to think what to do. The Rodono Hotel loomed ahead on the left side of the road so we struggled up the bank and made for the front door. It was locked but, after a few bangs, I heard a timorous voice from inside asking what was wrong. When I tried to explain, between short painful breaths, that my wife needed urgent medical assistance, the voice said, 'Oh no! Not another one.'

The owners of the hotel had taken a day off and left the children with Grannie and, earlier in the day, some other unfortunates had done as we had with a similar skid. Grannie was still recovering from the trauma of screeching ambulances when we knocked on her door.

After making the necessary phone-calls, while waiting for the ambulance to arrive, we tenderly considered our aches and pains. Pat had indeed sustained a very nasty gash running, just like Violet's, from the hair-line to the centre of her brow, and she felt a laceration on the top of her head under her hair, in the form of a flap of skin.

Although her nose had been bashed she didn't think it was broken, but her arms, shoulders and knees had suffered and even her back and rear end were sore from being recoiled back into her seat. She didn't lapse into unconsciousness, but felt definitely *no' weel*, as she put it. The knuckles of my left hand were obviously broken and I had severe pain in my breast-bone. Apart from bearable pain in my knees and elbows that seemed to be all.

After an interminable wait we found ourselves in a reception ward with a curtain between Pat's bed and mine, reflecting on how lucky we were not to be at the bottom of St Mary's Loch. The ward sister on night duty made her initial examinations and assessed Pat first. As she was doing so I mentioned Violet's similar injury and the scar-reducing deep sutures. She said that she would certainly speak to the doctor on duty but thought that, since he was young and inexperienced, he might not be able to do the job successfully. That indeed was his reaction adding that his boss, who was asleep on the premises, might not appreciate being wakened.

The young man agreed that, since Pat was still a young woman, she would not wish to go through the rest of her life with prominent scarring on her face. He bowed to our entreaties and summoned the older medic who did as I asked in sewing up the wound, not appearing in the least disgruntled as he worked. Some years later I met him again, in charge of the Blood Donor Unit in Hawick. He remembered the night of our encounter. I had been quite correct, he said, for Pat's sake, to insist on getting him out of bed. He was delighted to learn that her scars were almost invisible.

The matron wasn't very pleased, especially when I said that, because of the demands of my work, I would prefer to wait until the next day to visit a bone specialist in Edinburgh. Pat was bandaged from head to toe like an Egyptian mummy and we were taken to spend the night in regular wards. What finally put the peter on things as far as Matron was concerned was when we insisted on occupying the same ward. In high dudgeon, she said, angrily, that if we weren't satisfied with the treatment we were receiving, we should perhaps just check ourselves out and go elsewhere, and that is exactly what we did.

I telephoned Lee to come and collect us and soon we were home trying to get ourselves comfortable in bed. By now, as I'm sure you can imagine, we were both feeling very, very sore. Not surprisingly for Pat, considering the injuries she had sustained, but even I, after thinking I had got off lightly, now felt the effects of bumps and bruises which I hadn't noticed earlier. As we assisted each other down from a seated into a lying position, the pain heightening with every move, Pat said quietly, 'Well there's no' much chance of a ride now, is there Ron?'

I don't recommend laughing through pain, it's excruciating, but we just couldn't stop. Even after the loud guffaws ceased and we were finally lying down, the sniggers and the mirth continued until, I suppose, we drifted off to sleep.

I had to force myself up early next morning to call Roy and start the series of phone-calls that cancelled our two concerts of that night and the next. I didn't take cancellations any further as I assessed my injuries. It was apparent that, apart from some bumps and bruises to my body, the only real damage I had sustained was to the knuckles of my left hand and I thought that, just maybe, something could be done about that by the Sunday, when we were due to sing in Elgin Town Hall. I quickly arranged an appointment at Edinburgh Royal Infirmary for the next day where I was seen by a most understanding consultant. Although an all-encasing plaster cast was recommended, I had no great pain in my hand. He agreed to settle for a half cast which came down from the top of my arm over the knuckles, leaving my hand in a cupped position which fitted comfortably over the gear-stick of my mother-in-law's car which I borrowed to make my way to Elgin.

At the hall I met Roy who had taken the precaution of bringing John McKinnon with him to save the concert if I was unable to go on. I had been flexing my fingers constantly for the last couple of days in the plaster 'cup', so it wasn't too much of an effort to get them into the chord positions. To cut a long story short, we did the whole show without the need for John's participation and, signing autographs afterwards, I was frequently informed that I actually played the guitar better with my hand in plaster than without.

As the tour progressed, so too did I, and my bodily aches and pains gradually subsided except from my chest, which continued to give me discomfort. So much so that I became convinced something more was afoot. My concern heightened when pains began in my stomach and, I must confess, the word 'cancer' crept into my mind. The idea became so convincing that I actually started to build a Georgian doll's house for Lauren to remember me by when I was gone. Many months later, I sought medical advice and was diagnosed with severe anxiety. Thankfully, I was soon back to normal.

Pat, in the meantime, returned to full health with the scar on her forehead healing so well that it was almost invisible. She had never yet told anyone in the medical professional about the flap of skin under her hair, which also healed perfectly. What a woman!

Chapter Nineteen

From 1973 onwards, we seemed to be continually adding nights each year to venues like Aberdeen and Inverness, Glasgow and Motherwell, where the Council's Director of Entertainments, David Cunningham, did a great job. We didn't do three nights in Falkirk, but to follow our one night we had two in close by Grangemouth.

Of course, we still found time to attend Lee's Doo Night at Hardengreen Social Club to see him pick up his Pigeon Trophies, and a few nights later a Railway Social Club for the retirement party of Willie Thomson. Willie was Roy's former wife Vi's father. Although Vi and Roy had been parted for a while, Roy was still friendly with her Mum and Dad and saw them regularly. We continued to visit Brian Wilson's neck of the woods in out of the way places like Corpach, Portree and Benbecula, as well as going down south with John Martin to Swindon, Oxford and Wolverhampton.

Davie Watt and Morag were now married and staying in Jedburgh where Davie managed the local creamery as well as arranging shows for us. Pat and I and Davie and Morag had become friends, had meals together and visited on a regular basis because we lived not far apart. I think they might have been with us when I decided that Roy Williamson wasn't going to continue to hog the limelight as an instrumentalist, and I was going to learn the bagpipes. I was talking through drink, but I did pursue the matter to discover that you don't just pick up a set of pipes and start to blow. You learn the fingering on a practice chanter and graduate to a full set after many lessons . . . eventually!

Gavin continued his fiddle lessons, started when he was at Stockbridge School in Edinburgh, and was attending classes in Hawick, so I found a pipes teacher and started to coincide my lessons with Gavin's. First lesson: May 30th. There was a tiny room above our kitchen approached up a winding stairway which I used for practice. It was there I kept my chanter.

Through her connections in the WRI, Pat had become interested in social work, and we had collected a couple of youngsters from Prestonpans to give them a week's holiday in the country. James and Anne Pearson were nice kids, although they would have been much nicer with a regular bath and wash of the hair. However, they responded immediately to kindness and, after discovering that the snotters, for want of a better word, could be made to disappear with a simple blow on a paper tissue, became interested in staying clean. I must confess I thought I was going to have trouble with James.

Sitting at the bottom of my wee stairway, at the kitchen table, I was making notes for some show or other when down the stair came James, clutching my chanter. 'Can ah ha'e a sho' o' yer twumpet, Mr Bwowne?' (He still can't pronounce 'r'.)

I said no and explained that it wasn't a toy, and it wasn't a trumpet but a chanter, a valuable instrument, and could he please put it back on the table where he had found it. 'Dae you want a kickin'?' says James.

Coming from a pint-sized three-year-old built like a stick of wood, this couldn't fail to draw a smile, which I found difficult to hide, even as a stern 'no' and a firm hand on his arm gave him the message. They came back for a holiday each year until we left Buccleuch in 1978 and I still have the odd lunch with James. He's been in care for most of his life and I've met quite a few of his carers at these meals over the years.

Pat's interest in social work stemmed from our failure to

adopt a child. The idea of adoption was prompted by Pat's desire to expand our family of two children, Gavin and Lauren. I've told you that, after each of their births, Pat nearly died. In spite of those two close calls, she still had the desire for more children. I certainly had no objection to a larger family, but didn't want it at the expense of Pat's life. When we discussed the pros and cons she had joked that she only had to look at me to fall pregnant, and finally decided that the safest way to avoid any danger was to go on the pill. This started her regular visits to the Family Planning Clinic.

As Gavin and Lauren grew up, the idea of adoption grew stronger and we decided to try to find a girl, younger than Lauren, who had already displayed, even at the age of three, very motherly tendencies. We knew she would be over the moon with a wee sister to look after. It was only then that we discovered how difficult it was for someone in even our lowly branch of show-business to become an adoptive parent.

Over the next five or six years we couldn't have tried harder through the usual channels, only to be met with rebuff after rebuff. At the time of our move to Buccleuch we had all but given up until, one night in the unlikely setting of a Boston Hall social gathering, light began to dawn.

We were in the company of Margaret Anderson, our neighbour from across the Rankle Burn, when Pat noticed a frail old couple sitting beside a young coloured girl. To see any coloured people at all in the Borders was unusual in 1973, but to see this youngster with the old buddies prompted Pat to mention it to Margaret. Margaret explained that the girl was their adopted daughter. At that, Pat expressed surprise, saying how unfair it was that such an old couple were allowed to adopt when we were not.

'Och!' says Margaret, 'If it's a bairn ye want, just go intae Balcary in Hawick an' ye'll hae nae bother at a'.' Balcary, we discovered, was the local Dr Barnardo's Children's Home.

After a couple of phone calls, Mary McLeod from the Home

came to visit, no doubt to vet us. We must have passed the test, because, on Saturday, July 7th we went to meet Mr and Mrs Baron, the house mother and father, who explained that they thought one boy in particular, Maurice Stark, one of only two black boys in the district, would be an ideal candidate. Apart from many other considerations, at age eleven he was starting to succumb to unsavoury influences in the town.

No doubt Maurice was a bit startled at this sudden interest in his future, but he was not averse to the idea of coming to spend the day, breaking the ice and getting to know us better. As early as Wednesday 11th, I collected him from Balcary.

Maybe it helped that we had James and Anne with us, who, together with our own two, probably provided an atmosphere more like he was used to. Before I took him back to Hawick in the evening, he agreed to come again at the weekend. My brother Ian was visiting then and Maurice seemed to enjoy a fishing trip with him on the Sunday.

A few weeks later, on August 8th, we had another visit from Mary MacLeod who brought the necessary forms for fostering our boy but, when we explained we were only really interested in adoption, she changed tack and started to talk about arrangements with the Local Authority and Maurice's mother. Talk of his mother startled us, since she had never so much as visited him since placing him in the care of Barnardo's. We kept our mouths tightly shut lest we put a spanner in the works.

It was perhaps prophetic but, while Mary was with us, the postman arrived and in the mail was a postcard from Maurice from North Berwick where he was on a week's holiday with the Balcary children. The postcard was dated August 7th. I know this, because I'm holding it in my hand as I write.

While all of this was happening, we were besieged with visits from the very people who had chided us for moving to this remote spot. Of course we didn't mind at all, and it was even better when, after I had finished Lauren's doll's house, Pop and Ma came down to present her with a roof-top swimming pool

Pop had made from cardboard. It goes without question that it fitted perfectly, because . . . hadn't it been made by Pop?

I had recovered completely from my anxiety, which was just as well because I was never so busy on the domestic front. I had erected a small green-house against one of the side doors and Pat was making a great success of growing her tomatoes in it. We had bought her a new Volvo Estate and, although she never actually enjoyed driving, she was delighted with her role as occasional chauffeur to the children when I wasn't at home. On top of the new car, The Corries were now paying her £11 per week. How generous of us! She had been doing our book-keeping for only eleven years.

After being given a birthday present of a Spanish shot-gun I became the complete country gent and, for Christmas, received a full set of silver-mounted bagpipes.

Gavin and Lauren were looking forward to Maurice arriving, particularly after we arranged a weekend visit for them to the Home. Their impression of life in Balcary was frankly expressed when they said, 'Mum, you'll have to get him out of there.'

After many more visits from Maurice, which gradually became longer and longer, and more vetting of ourselves, and medical checks, on Saturday, March 30th, 1974 we collected him and all his belongings and brought him home with us for good. We must have been put on a year's probation, because it wasn't until March 25th, 1975 that we received the Extract of an entry in the Adopted Children Register to confirm that he was now to be known as Maurice Walter Browne, and he was our son.

Our closest neighbours lived a stone's throw from our kitchen door in the field adjoining our land. George Gowans and his wife Margaret were prime examples of the character of the Borders people: down to earth, no-nonsense individuals. Geordie was a hill shepherd, and proud of it.

One day, the Duke of Buccleuch was riding to the hunt when

he was thrown from his horse. He wasn't particularly hurt, except his feelings I suppose, but his mount bolted leaving His Grace alone on foot. The first house he came to as he trudged homewards was that of the Gowans. When Geordie answered the knock at the door, the Duke said, 'Good afternoon, do you know who I am?' Completely unabashed, and certainly unimpressed, Geordie replied, 'Och aye, an' ah kent yer faither tae!'

Jock Anderson, his wife Jean and his father Rob were of the same breed. Displayed all over their home, called Midgehope and situated up the Ettrick Valley from us, were trophies, rosettes and tickets from shows big and small, the results and rewards of a way of life that most of us would consider pretty Spartan. Getting up at first light, summer and winter to 'go to the hill', to keep close watch on the sheep and cattle in your charge, moving them from pasture to pasture and guarding them from snow, flood, tick, fox, hoodie-crow and even rustler, certainly seems to me to be hard work.

When I first moved into the Border hills and was visited by a few of my 'knowledgeable' townie friends I was advised that the first thing I should do was put a few animals in the field. After all, you just turn them out to graze and they look after themselves. Oh, dae ye think so?

Maybe it's because I had the chance to live among them and observe their way of life, to the extent of assisting at various dippings, knackerings, horn-clippings, tail-dockings and haymakings, that I accepted as final the words of the first song I heard Jock singing, 'The Lads That Were Reared Amang Heather.' I even went out beating with the locals on shoots for a stipend of 2/6, where, on eventually walking up to the butts, I was greeted by a very posh voice saying, 'I say, old chap, shouldn't you be on this side with us?'

It was in the bar of the Tushielaw Inn that Jock sang that song for me. I had been invited out for a drink by Willie Scott, better known in folk-circles as 'The Border Shepherd'. A very pleasant evening had passed with the drink flowing freely; enough, at least, to encourage the redoubtable host, Mick, to invite us to remain after closing time as his guests. The singing was soon under way.

To keep The Corries' end up, I did one of my own favourites, 'Jock o' Braidiesley', and then settled back to listen, first to Willie, who sang two of the songs which have made him famous here and in many other parts of the world, 'Piper McNeil', and 'The Kielder Hunt', the second accompanied by some eerie yodel-like foxhunt calls.

Joe Madonna, (I'm still convinced that's not the way you spell it), the uproarious Irishman from Greene's place up the valley, did his party piece, 'Goodbye Johnnie Dear', and his wife, Kath, let us hear 'The Blackboard of My Heart', but it wasn't until Jock got up to sing 'The Lads', that I wished I had secreted a tape-recorder about my person. Had I done so, though, I'm certain the songs would not have been so forthcoming.

After the usual burst of enthusiasm which accompanies such gatherings, and after favourite stories and songs had been rendered, and when tiredness and possibly even alcohol encouraged attention to wander, I managed to steer Jock into a corner for a chat. I said how much I had enjoyed his singing and it transpired that he and his family were admirers of The Corries. Jock's father, Rob, had a few songs that he thought might suit our style of singing.

Although now too frail to get out and about much, Rob evidently still managed to chant away at home. In the past he had been approached by official folk song collectors to give some of his local songs to this or that collection, but had steadfastly refused, thinking that, if preserved in this fashion, they might be lost to the general public for whom he had been in the habit of singing.

I was therefore pleasantly surprised when Jock told me that his father would be honoured to let me have some of these songs, and even more so if Roy and I would sing them at our shows. Not wishing to force the issue, I said that any time Rob felt up to it, I would gratefully welcome the opportunity to come and hear him. There followed two days of anticipation sitting by the phone, until Jock sent the message that one night the following week would be suitable.

The snow lay thick as I drove Pat and the family up to Midgehope to be met by Jock, Jean, and Rob with a multitude of farm dogs and cats. It seemed as though Jean had been baking for days as we scoffed sausage-rolls, sandwiches, scones, pancakes and cakes of all shapes and sizes.

Rob's big worry when he knew that we were coming was that he thought we might be a bit posh. Maybe it was the way we tucked into the food that set his mind at rest. 'If ah hud kent ye wir jist like us, ah'd huv kept ma baffies on,' he said.

So saying, he proceeded to remove his best, well-polished Sunday shoes, which hadn't been outside for months, in favour of his well-worn comfortable slippers, took off his suit jacket, and snuggled into his big armchair by the fire. That night, and on other occasions, I was privileged to hear the old man charm the gathering with his songs, delivered sometimes with a gap here and there where a word was forgotten, and sometimes missing a bit of power on the top register, but always with the authority and feeling of someone who loved every word and note.

Of the songs he gave me, we used, 'Sae Will We Yet', 'The M'mm Song', and one, which may have been of music hall origin, 'The Wild Man of Borneo', arguably the best audience participation tongue-twister we ever used. I think that, to a non-Corries reader, it should be explained.

It starts by teaching the audience the first verse, which reads;

'Oooooohhhhh, The wild man of Borneo has just come to town
   The wild man of Borneo has just come to town
   The wild man of Borneo has just come to town
   The wild man of Borneo has just come to town.'

Once they have caught on, comes the second verse which is;

"Ooooooohhhhh, The wife of the wild man of Borneo has just come to town, etc.", repeated four times. Then:-

The daughter of the wife of the wild man of Borneo, etc."
Then add; "The dog of the daughter of the wife of, etc.'
Then add; "The tail of the dog of the daughter of the wife, etc.

Then keep adding until you end with:-

'Ooooooohhhhh, The wind that whistles through the whiskers of the flea that sits on the hair on the end of the tail of the dog of the daughter of the wife of the wild man of Borneo has just come to town.' Repeat four times.

As it gets faster and faster, more mistakes are made by the audience, as you might imagine, but because we were pretty well word perfect on it (apart from Roy codding it up by putting his thumbs on his top set of teeth and pushing up, pretending they're false, or lifting the edge of his doublet to read the words secreted on the inside), the whole piece comes over as being very cleverly done by us.

Of course, to the purist, it's not 'folk' but, my, it's very funny and immensely entertaining, which was what our shows were all about, albeit also being educational in the sense of letting our audiences hear some very pure and genuine songs in the mix of a two-hour performance.

When Rob was brought to see one of our shows in Hawick, it was he who laughed the loudest.

Chapter Twenty

I'm about to write about the period in my life I call my disaster zone, but for you to understand the events of the next few years I have first to explain our situation, and indeed thinking, meaning Pat's and mine, at the time.

I have painted the picture of my earlier professional life as one of unbridled progress and unqualified success. Night after additional night was being added to our appearances in certain venues. If you can imagine doing a solo concert which ends in a standing ovation even after three encores you will surely feel confident, as we did, that these same people would return on your next visit, albeit many months away. If you knew that tickets for your shows sold out on the appearance of the first adverts, again, you would surely feel that it was worth taking on an extra night next time around. We did just that and were, in fact, successful.

When we first met Iain McFadyen, producer of the BBC's *White Heather Club* and Hogmanay Parties, he was adamant that the attention span of a television or radio audience was two and a half to three minutes and obliged us to cut a verse here and there from some of our songs. However, we had been allowed, especially in our solo television shows, to sing songs like 'The Great Silkie of Sule Skerrie', which was of fully ten minutes duration in our version.

With opinion resting on these experiences you'll forgive us for believing that we were doing things right and continuing on our own chosen way. With hindsight, it was not without justi-fication. Life was as sweet as a nut and as perfectly contained within its shell of performance and publicity, fame and finan-cial reward. We were, therefore, full of confidence.

Pat and I were able to buy the West Buccleuch Farmhouse outright for the unbelievable sum of £7,000. No mortgage was required, and we had no debts. I have indicated already the kind of money we were earning. We had no reason to think it would not continue, so when we sat down in the spring of 1974 to count our blessings, at the same time we asked ourselves if such good fortune could really continue. Should we try to diversify now, we asked ourselves, while we had the chance, to start some scheme rolling as a safeguard for the future?

I bought a mobile home for the paddock included in our property. We had room for at least six such vehicles and thought that holiday lets might be a good idea. Not so, and after a few months we sold the vehicle.

When the house up the valley, known as Midgehope, came on the market at a price of £50,000 the bank was not only willing to give us a mortgage but also agreed with our thoughts of converting it into a guest house. My brother Ian would take up residence and manage the place. That idea was also shelved, mainly because we were a bit afraid of borrowing that much. Pat was ever the cautious one (which is why she was book-keeping for The Corries) and I went along with her decision.

Finally, we decided that the safest thing to do was increase the value of West Buccleuch. We started by changing the kitchen.

C&J Brown's in Edinburgh had a large, although expensive, kitchen department, and it was there we went to choose. A floor plan was drawn up, but this meant that the small stairway in the corner, that of my confrontation with young James Pearson while he was carrying my 'twumpet', would have to go. Local builders were brought in and work began on demolishing the stair. After all these years I suppose that decision was the one that heralded our entry to the disaster zone. Almost immediately, complications arose.

The proposed kitchen had an estimated cost of £2,000 but we reckoned that the repayments would be affordable. In 1974 that was a lot of money to spend on a kitchen, but this was a big development with a collection of very up to date additions such as a foldaway table. This table did, literally, roll out of sight under the lower units. There was also a roll away trolley and space for fitted washing machine, fridge, freezer and dish-washer. All of the floor and wall units were in mustard yellow, floor to ceiling and, whatever wall space was left was to be covered in 18" square white tiles, some of which bore large flower designs. On one wall was a matching Aga with hot-platcs and stoves, the whole arrangement being set off by mustard coloured carpeting. All very fancy, and a far cry from our first flat in West Crosscauseway where my knees prevented the lavvy door closing.

Our problems started when we had to postpone the kitchen starting date because of the complications in getting rid of the staircase. A beam had to be installed in the ceiling, which proved not to be as simple as the builders had originally estimated for. In addition, a bricked-up opening in the wee room at the top of the stair was discovered to be not just an opening, but actually a doorway into another room we didn't know we had. This was a pleasant complication, because every householder would like an additional room, but time was wasted in further investigation. Investigation complete, the work involved in the refurbishing of this room meant a delay to the starting date for the kitchen.

When work on the kitchen finally began it didn't go smoothly because not enough tiles had been ordered. Then the Aga was found to be faulty and the replacement was delayed.

All of a sudden things weren't quite so rosy, but simple delays are only a matter of inconvenience. Our real problems began when we started to talk of an extension, an idea that presented itself because we had a table in the dining room which I thought was a great wee contraption. The wooden top consisted of four slabs which, when removed, revealed a billiard table which was good fun to play on, although on the small side.

I had thought of putting a full sized table in one of the barns, where I had already located a table tennis table. I didn't think it would stand that environment too well, and so scrapped the idea. This led me to think that we could maybe build an additional room in the form of an extension to take said table. This was very selfish male thinking, as I am fully aware, but Pat wasn't averse to the suggestion, suggesting that the room could perhaps include shelving for our expanding library. One thing led to another and, all of a sudden, a swimming pool was added to the vision.

On holiday in Las Palmas we had befriended an architect and his wife and, on our return to Scotland, regular friendly visits took place. It seemed natural to speak to him about these ideas, and he agreed to draw up plans. When completed, they showed drainage downpipes inside the pool and billiard-room. We disagreed with this, but he refused to be budged. I refused to change my mind and our collaboration ended there.

This meant yet more delay, but fortunately I found a local quantity surveyor, Stan Robertson, who agreed to do what he could to advance the plans. Stan had been a prisoner of the Japanese on the River Kwai and told us of an event which showed how the Japanese of that time were cruel not only to their prisoners, but also their own. A young Japanese soldier had been ordered to help him push a cannon up a steep bank. In the process the carriage slipped and pinned his leg, breaking it. Immediately, he was no longer in the army, and wouldn't be allowed back until his leg healed. He received no assistance whatsoever from his superiors.

Stan, while a prisoner, taught himself to be ambidextrous and it was amusing to watch him work, and without thinking, switch his pen from one hand to the other. It had become second nature to him.

When I went with Lauren to see the film, 'The Railway Man', she expressed disbelief at how skeletal the prisoners were made to look, probably with digital 'trimming'. I reminded her of the photographs Stan had shown us of himself in Liverpool after his return. In fact he was as skeletal as the prisoners in the film, if not worse.

Eventually we were up and running in terms of the plans. However, when the first estimate came to us on September 6th, 1974 for £39,000, we were daunted and put them aside. Nonetheless, we made enquiries through our lawyer, Dan Lockett of McLachlan and McKenzie, about loan facilities in London and on November 29th received an offer in principle of a £35,000 loan. Dan said that, in his experience, that amounted to a green light and that we should fire ahead.

Visits followed from Stan's builders, and the planning people, but the builders said they didn't want to start digging foundations until the pool kit arrived.

By February of 1975, we had a large excavation at the back of the house where the pool was to be sited, full of water and with a pump running constantly. With the foundations started for the billiard room and large garage (we had decided to put the pool's pump mechanism in its own room and were doubling up by making that room a garage as well), and with the kitchen still not finished, and with a half-finished radiator system cluttering up the house, (having decided to install central heating as well), our nerves were jangling more than somewhat.

When Dan informed us that we would not be getting the loan after all we began to question our sanity, having just a few months before been in seventh heaven.

A ray of light appeared on the horizon in the form of a meeting with an insurance broker about raising a loan of £35,000. I also managed to raise a bank overdraft for £7,000, £4,700 of which went to the builders for their first month's work. Darkness descended again, when no confirmation of the insurance company loan was forthcoming.

We managed to keep the builders sweet with an interim payment of £1,000 and a couple at £500 until, finally, the bank came through with a bridging loan of £35,000, thanks to my friends Mike Killey and Jack Carson, of the Eagle Star Insurance Company. They had managed to get agreement from Eagle Star to loan us £25,000 over four years upon completion of the extension. The bank threw in a loan of £10,000 over the same four years. The bridging loan started immediately. We knew that the repayments would be high but thought we would be all right.

Meanwhile, up in Edinburgh in February, it was all shoulders to the wheel at Roy's, picking and packing our latest single, 'Flower of Scotland' (backed with my own 'Roses o' Prince Charlie'). The record had sold 8,000 copies in one week, so things were continuing favourably on the business front.

In July of 1975, further complications arose. Problems with the pool room roof meant additional costs and, we learned, the heating for the pool and pool-room would now be in thousands instead of the £500 allowance set aside. I managed to lighten that burden in a meeting with the heating engineers who told me that a single large tank would take the oil for the heating at a cost of £4,000. I explained that they could rule that out since I could arrange with our local oil suppliers, Baxter & Johnstone, that, if we guaranteed to take oil from them for three years, they would supply the tanks for free.

The extension was certainly dragging its heels and it was October 1975 before we received a price to line the pool walls with mosaic tiles for a whopping £2,000.

At the same time we were offered more of the outbuildings surrounding our property. We thought this would be a wise buy, reasoning that, if somebody else bought and developed them, it might be detrimental to the value of our property. This meant finding more money, but that problem could be overcome by selling the basement flat at Henderson Row, which we still owned and had rented to my brother Ian, now working for our fledgling Pan-Audio record business. We accepted an offer for the flat of £7,500 on November 19th.

In a meeting with Stan we learned that the heating for the pool room would come in at £2,500 and extra money would be needed for the wooden slatted ceiling. The result of wanting everything of top quality is that it all costs more. The projected cost of the whole extension was now £40,000, and rising.

Thankfully, on the morning of November 28th a surveyor from Bernard Thorpe, representing Eagle Star, visited and said that he was recommending that their £25,000 be paid the following week, even though work had still to be done. Work most certainly did still have to be done; it was December 21st before the coping stones were placed around the area of the pool. On the same day Stan suggested he could get us beautiful 9" by 2" tongued and grooved hardwood parquet tiles from a derelict mill in Selkirk to line the billiard room floor.

In early New Year the plasterers were still working on the billiard room when the joiners came to measure for an extra beam which was required on the outside. All of this contributed to a favourable inspection by my friendly bank manager, Ian Meldrum from the Hawick branch of the Royal Bank of Scotland. Ostensibly coming to view the work he also looked at the outbuildings which we were now considering buying. He was enthusiastic, saying he thought they were worth at least £10,000 and we should consider their purchase.

Pat and I were becoming more and more depressed. Work went on constantly with the daily presence of plasterers, joiners, tilers, electricians and heating engineers. On top of all of that we had bought the parquet flooring Stan had found in Selkirk, but it did not come without problems, the trouble being that it was still on the floor of the mill.

On this we worked as a family. I would pick up the children from school and go to the mill where we would prise the tiles from where they had been anchored to the floor with tar.

They were filthy with years of grime but we discovered that soap and water was the simple solution, and a blow-torch took off the tar. After many visits we finally got them all back to the house and I began to lay them on the floor of the billiard-room.

Keep in mind that I was involved in meetings in town and live concerts, not to mention other activities. During the period of our Glasgow concerts I would get up very early and prepare an area of maybe a couple of yards square. Spreading it with adhesive, which I left to cook while I torched the tar off enough tiles to fill that area, I gave them a quick sanding and laid as many as possible before the adhesive hardened. The air was blue on the occasions I got my timing wrong, but I forced myself on knowing that I couldn't moan at the workmen if I wasn't showing an example. I would finish my laying as speedily as possible and rush to town for meetings.

This commitment did nothing to lessen the strain. Pat, too, was feeling stress, and though we were both sensible and understanding people and aware that developments such as ours don't come without upheaval, by now we wondered if we hadn't taken on a bit too much. Fortunately we were blessed with some light relief from time to time.

Some years after Finbar and Sheila were married, and the Furey family was expanding in Ireland, they came to Buccleuch for a short holiday. After settling them in their rooms, my family took Fin's on a tour of the house and into the surrounding garden and fields. Fin noted with interest what we called our 'Red Rock Pool' in the Rankle Burn, which ran from the hills behind the house and formed the boundary between us and our neighbours at East Buccleuch Farmhouse. The pool was just big enough to swim a few strokes in what was always very cold mountain water, but refreshing on a hot summer's day, a few of which we do sometimes enjoy in Scotland.

Fin's interest lay not in swimming, however, but in eels. As he examined the red rock structure of the sides of the pool, he asked if we did any eel fishing because he thought the terrain ideal. When I said we didn't he exclaimed in disbelief and looked around the bank for a long piece of strong reed.

Finbar raided my collection of hooks and selected the biggest one he could find. Then, after stripping to his underpants, tied a length of twine to the hook, threaded it through a bunch of worms from my Oxo tin, and pressed the tip of the hook hard into the end of the reed. He wrapped the twine round his right hand to the length of the reed and, also taking the reed into his right hand, slipped into the water. Finding what he deemed a suitable fissure in the rock, he slowly edged his rod as far into the hole as he could. As he did so, he took the reed in his left hand, tightened his grip on the twine, and waited.

He didn't wait long. We all sensed the tug because he suddenly pulled with his left hand and the reed was extricated and thrown to the side. Now with two hands on the twine, the hook end of which was still in the hole, taking a strain which was now very obvious, he planted his feet firmly on the rocks beneath him and gave a mighty heave. Unbelievably, out came the twine with, attached to it, a creature about two feet in length. A fresh-water eel.

It was at this point I learned to approach an eel, especially a freshly caught one, with great caution, because it will wriggle and squirm with massive strength and, if it wraps itself round, say, your wrist, can give you a nasty 'Chinese burn'. Finbar explained that the eel would have taken up its home in the crack in the rock when it was very young and just snapped passing grubs and small shrimps throughout its lifetime. A sobering thought to all of us was the fact that these holes in the rock were where we were in the habit of putting our fingers and toes to ease ourselves out of the pool after a swim. We didn't do that again.

The eel was cooked and sliced to reveal a solid body with nothing but the spine running the full length of it. It tasted quite mellow, I can't think of any other word to describe it, not at all fishy. The ladies weren't too keen to try though.

We spent a lazy day walking and reminiscing but, after tea, I prevailed on Fin to get out the pipes and play a couple of tunes, especially for the benefit of Gavin and Lauren. These two had been at Stockbridge Primary School when we were in Edinburgh, taking fiddle lessons on a daily basis, and Gavin had held down a place in the Edinburgh Schools Orchestra. I knew they would be interested in Fin's Irish pipes. To see this instrument on stage or on television is one thing but to have it in the same room as yourself, at only an arm's length, is an entirely different proposition.

Finbar made a show of strapping the bellows to one arm, attaching this to the bag under the other, and assembling the chanter and drones. When he was done he gave forth with a selection of jigs, reels and laments, interspersing the music with stories from his boyhood growing up in a very poor Irish family. Stories such as the Nail Soup his mother made sitting at a log fire with a cauldron of boiling water bubbling atop the flames, dropping a large nail into the water and saying that was all she had to put in the soup and it wouldn't be very tasty unless the children could maybe find, on their way home from school, a bit of potato, or a cabbage, or even a lettuce. A freshly dead rabbit or hare would be ideal if they came across one. And there was the story of Finbar's and his brothers' swimming lesson when their father, Ted, took them all to the banks of the River Liffey and threw them in, shouting, 'Now git out o' that if ye's can.'

The tunes came thick and fast until bedtime approached. The children were now at school in Selkirk, about 21 miles away, and an early school bus run was necessary in the morning with pick-ups all down the valley. Bed time was therefore strictly adhered to during the week. When Lauren and Gavin rose at about 7.00 next morning, Fin was sitting asleep on his kitchen chair, still strapped into his pipes, where we had left him the night before. As the children quietly sat down to breakfast, Pat asked Gavin, 'Well, what did you think of that last night?' and Gavin replied, 'Well Mum, I thought it was unbelievable. Finbar drank twelve pints of Guinness, and he didn't go to the toilet once'.

Something must have rubbed off because Gavin is now 53 years old, and for the past five has been assiduously learning that very instrument.

Chapter Twenty One

Early March, 1976 saw all sorts of workmen crawling over the house and extension. Four heating engineers came to stay with us for a few days to start installation of the pool's heating system, situated in the large garage which was taking shape around it. They worked alongside the joiners and plasterers who were still with us almost on a daily basis. The heating men actually paid us £4.00 per day for their board. A comment in Pat's diary says, 'Up at 7.00 am. Got the kids out, then the men's breakfasts, coffee break, lunch and afternoon break, and with dinners to come. It's murder running all day.'

On the same page she also sounds disgruntled when she mentions how it was 'extra cold because the plasterer has the bar window open all day for access to water'. To put the peter on it, she adds, 'Ronnie left for Edinburgh and Dunfermline at 1.30.'

In the nick of time for Pat, her mother Violet and sister, Diana, came to look after Buccleuch for a few days so that she and the children could make their way to Aberdeen where we were in concert at His Majesty's Theatre. I met them at the station. A visit to the cinema that evening while we were on stage and another next day to Camphill Village, self-sufficiently run by handicapped people, a rest in the hotel through the afternoon followed by the show at night, put Pat in a more relaxed mood.

At our late night, after show meal in the hotel, Pat was fascinated to meet for the first time, our guests Lord and Lady

Morrison, or Buss and Yvonne, as Roy, Lee and I knew them.

Lee, as I've told you, was a great trout and salmon fisherman and would instruct us in the ancient art of fly-fishing in whatever river we might be passing at the time. On a previous visit to His Majesty's we passed by the River Deveron, where we stopped to don the fishing gear (carried in the back of the bus at all times), and broke out the rods.

Intent on what we were about, we were suddenly interrupted from the bank by an irate English gentleman who informed us, in no uncertain manner, that we were violating his private beat and that he had paid a hefty sum to the local landlord for his licence. Lee retorted, also in no uncertain manner, that an ancient Scottish law said that the middle of a river was actually no-man's land and, since that's where we were standing at that moment, the English gentleman could stick his licence up a certain part of his body which I will not name. We carried on fishing, vacating our position long before any policemen might arrive, making our way back into town for the evening's show.

As we were signing autographs afterward, from the queue of fans came a quiet comment. 'I believe you had a slight run-in with our tenant this afternoon', and a couple introduced themselves as Buss and Yvonne, Lord and Lady Morrison. After we got over our embarrassment, we asked if they could perhaps stay until our signing was finished, when we would have the chance to become better acquainted.

In these unlikely circumstances a life-long friendship began. Buss and Yvonne were originally from Canada and Buss had served as a fighter pilot in World War Two. After the War he returned to join his wife, Yvonne, who was in the theatre business, but received word that he should come back to Scotland to take possession of his estates. This was the first he knew that he was indeed heir to the estates, as Lord Morrison.

This took some adjusting to, but eventually the couple returned to face their destiny as owners of rather large, but severely run-down estates, devastated by years of neglect by absentee landlords. Within their stewardship were villages, churches, pubs and rivers like the Deveron. They felt they had to accept their fate and pull up their sleeves to refurbish, replenish and, in the case of the river, re-stock. By the time we met them the estate's fortunes were turning around, and the Morrisons had won the respect of the many hill folk attached to their lands.

On the first night we met them they kindly said that, any time we felt like casting a few flies, we should just get on the phone and arrange to do so on their private beat, an invitation we accepted often over the coming years. The couple chose to live in a cottage known as Mountblairey, in Alvah, scorning the use of the family seat at Frendraught House, which anyway was in a ruinous state at that time. I believe it was restored in 1974 and is now occupied.

Pat hit it off in a big way with Buss, who had a collection of vintage cars stored in one of his barns and listened intently to Pat recounting tales of Wattie's escapades during Prohibition and as a speedway rider and performer on the Wall of Death. She and Yvonne also discovered their mutual love of flowers and soon afterwards seeds, saplings and cuttings were exchanged on a regular basis. At one point a packet of tomato seeds from California found its way into Pat's post-box.

On a visit to my bank in Hawick on March 22nd, I learned that our offer of £6,500 for the outbuildings had been accepted. We mustn't have been over-worried about money at this point because, six days later, Pat posted a cheque for that amount to our lawyer, Dan Lockett. I must have been simmering about something though, because another entry, two days later, on my return from shows on the west coast, suggests that I didn't seem too keen to get home.

Pat's respite was short lived but another break arrived when she accompanied us on a two-day trip to Germany for a radio programme on the German station WDR. We had been offered a radio spot consisting of a fifteen minute interview with one of their commentators, Joe Sonderhoff, followed by forty-five minutes of our singing. What we hadn't realised was that there would be an audience of eight hundred in the vast studio, most of that audience being Germans. We didn't panic, and it turned out to be one of the most successful engagements of our careers.

Joe was a fantastic interviewer, his witty translations of our replies settling the crowd and converting them into a most responsive audience. He could have been telling them anything, of course, neither Roy nor I being German speakers, but we were amazed when they joined in every chorus. We got the impression that they all had every one of our records, so much so that I made a mental note to check our royalties from Fontana and EMI when we got home.

After the show we met many people including George Penman, stationed in Germany with the RAF, who went off to arrange a tour for us of military stations throughout the country.

I finished laying the parquet before leaving to sing in Canada and Pat employed a couple of men to sand and polish it while I was away. I had said I would do it when I came home so we had words on the subject when she joined me two weeks later. Only Gavin and Lauren accompanied her though, because that's when we discovered that Maurice was afraid to fly.

We also discovered when I was away that the pool kit was leaking. Pumps had to be brought in again, and it was obviously impossible to tile it in that state. About that time we also learned that we had to dig another field drain to the river, resulting in compensation payment to the farmer for loss of hay. All this increased my feelings of anxiety.

We had embarked on the Canadian shows with a man called John McCuaig, a Scot originally from Paisley who had been Winston Churchill's batman and had settled in Canada after the War. John was also involved in organising shows in Canada for Max Bygraves, Andy Stewart and various other Scottish performers and invited us to perform in Toronto's Massey Hall and other venues from Brampton to St Catherine's and Barrie to Oshawa, and on to Vancouver's Queen Elizabeth Playhouse. A quick flight took us down to Los Angeles for business meetings but we eventually returned to Hamilton.

Travelling for these engagements squeezed into a Winnebago bus was decidedly uncomfortable. At one point, Roy had to scream to have it stopped so he could jump onto the highway to relieve the claustrophobia which had swept over him.

Otherwise, the shows went as well as could be expected. They were not all the sell-outs we had become used to in Scotland, but a couple were, and the rest gave us a reception that made it sound as though every seat was full. I was missing my family though, and by the time Pat and the children joined me in Hamilton for the final performance, I was really looking forward to seeing them.

As a family we said cheerio to Roy and Lee, who were flying home, and stayed on to visit Robbie and Lena, who was now calling herself Lee, to visit Niagara and an Indian shrine and settlement, but most of all to reminisce on old times. At the Indian settlement we were shown a smiddy with working bellows and anvils that the guide said had been in use on that spot for two hundred years. There was laughter when Pat told the assembled tourists that her grandfather, Willie Wight, was that very day using the same equipment in Scotland in his smiddy in Dalkeith.

I did find it strange that the highlight of the holiday for Gavin and Lauren was going to a cabaret performance by the Mills Brothers (the four kings of harmony) in the Royal York Hotel where we were staying. The Brothers were celebrating fifty years in show business.

Pat accompanied me to London for Corries' business meetings later in June and to Crystal Palace to see her nephew, Peter Hoffman, come second to David Jenkins in his heat of the

400 metres. The next day he qualified to run in the Montreal Olympics.

Progress at home was not so speedy or successful as Peter's. The firm who supplied the pool kit reported that we should not line it with fibreglass, as Drew had suggested, because fibreglass would stain badly and would last only about four years. Another setback, then, adding to the others mounting up around us in what was now a living nightmare. Nor was it alleviated in any way when, on July 4th, Wattie died, aged 74.

As The Corries moved into final arrangements for the forthcoming tour I wasn't coping too well. I don't know how Pat kept up her spirits because I know that she wasn't sleeping as well as she was used to, although she seemed to be doing better than I was. With mixed feelings we arranged a party for all our friends from Edinburgh, to celebrate the completion of the billiard room. All sympathised that we were still draining the swimming pool through holes in the concrete walls as they gazed at it through the glass connecting wall.

Every room in the house became a bedroom that night as Pat and I threw caution to the wind, had a few drinks, and joined in the party atmosphere. I must have had one too many when I accepted a challenge from one of Drew's old acrobat friends, Arthur Condie, to a game of snooker the next morning before their departure. I should have known something was afoot when the whole household presented themselves in the billiard-room and ranged themselves around the table. Even when Arthur entered with a towel round his neck and wearing shorts and trainers, and did a few laps round the table, finally stopping to be fanned with the towel by his American wife, Dharlene, I simply thought, 'Ach well, that's just Arthur for you.'

So the game began and, after about ten minutes, I lined up a long shot. Resting my cue between thumb and forefinger I slid it back and forth in true professional fashion, fingers spreadeagled on the green baize. I smoothly pushed the blue-chalked cue into the white cue ball which left its spot to begin a haphazard journey across the surface of the table. Twisting this way and that it doubled back on itself, jumping from the table a couple of times before starting back towards me.

I couldn't believe it, I had never seen such a duff shot, and reached forward to pick up and examine the ball, at which point the pent-up anticipation of the whole household erupted into gales of laughter. Arthur took the ball from me and replaced it on the table with the real ball. Quite beautifully, he had swapped it for his trick one just before I came forward to take my shot. Only then did I realise how perfectly I had been set up and that every single person in the house had been in on it since the night before. I joined in the laughter knowing my friends had at least tried to lessen the burden that lay on the household.

Events took an inevitable momentum over the next few months. The Corries embarked on our autumn tour, which was as successful as always until we got to our four nights in Dunfermline. On Wednesday the 6th October, our second last night, I was extremely depressed, and, after a business meeting with Roy, became convinced that something bad was going to happen. I phoned Andy Ross and asked him if he could go to Buccleuch to bring Pat and the family up to town. This was crazy behaviour, I admit, and I don't know why I did it unless it was a cry for help. I was at the Ross house before they arrived and Pat notes in her diary that I was in a terrible state.

Next morning we had a chat with Roy, which seems to have helped, and Pat made her way home. Next morning though, on October 8th, she received a call from John Gibson, the *Edinburgh Evening News* columnist, who told her that I had collapsed on stage at the beginning of the second half of the Dunfermline show. Pat told him she didn't know anything about that since I was in bed, asleep, at that moment. The night before, I had indeed blacked-out on stage.

202

As we were always trying to introduce something different in the show, for that tour I had been reciting a passage from the Robert Service poem, 'The Ballad of Sam McGee'. On that night I suddenly stopped and staggered towards the front of the stage. The show came to a halt and I just couldn't continue. We went backstage to the dressing room where I recovered enough to say that I would be all right to drive home, which I did, fearful of Pat getting a call to say that I wasn't well, especially after the nonsense of the day before.

On the way home, I seemingly missed my usual turn off the A7 to go down over the hill road to Innerleithen to the Gordon Arms, Tushielaw and home. Instead, and I have no recollection of travelling the road, I continued straight on to finally 'wake' and find myself on the Yarrow road. I could have hit hedges, sheep, deer or even human beings on my way and don't remember anything of that part of the journey. The family must all have been in bed when I got home.

Pat muttered something to Gibson about my having flu and, luckily, that was where it remained as far as the press was concerned. However, it was much more serious than that and, when Roy came down that afternoon to see what was going on, the next two nights in Dundee and Elgin were cancelled. His theory that all I needed was a walk in the hills to clear my mind didn't hold much water with Pat and, after I had a terrible night and was worse in the morning, becoming violent at one point, she sent for the doctor. He diagnosed a nervous breakdown and prescribed sleeping pills and Valium.

The first pills I was given were reckoned to be extra strong to induce sleep immediately. I swallowed them with a sense of relief, thinking that, at long last, I could find rest from the churning in my brain, but they didn't work. I lay for a while but started to become agitated again, finally getting up and going downstairs to find that Roy and Lee had arrived. Nobody was pleased to see me as I entered the room, particularly when I became violent again. However, the pills at last took effect and

I got into bed and slept for twelve hours. I was more settled the next day and slept for another twelve after which, by all appearances, I was fairly stable again. It was decided that we should continue the tour, but only under doctor's orders, and only if Pat were to accompany me to ensure that I kept taking the pills.

Pat and I travelled to Aberdeen together by train and Roy and Lee came up with the van. The first night I was drugged to the eyes and performed without incident, but everybody else was in a hell of a state, quite naturally, not knowing what was to come next. On stage, Roy became so upset he had to call for a doctor at the interval. In case I stalled again on Sam McGee I wrote out the words in my diary and it is with a strange feeling of *deja vu* that I read them again as they lie in my hands now.

We completed the tour successfully, but I never want to experience again the feelings I had then. I think I know pretty well what Stephen Fry meant when he described what he goes through on a regular basis, and I don't envy him his condition.

I came off Valium after a couple of weeks but was advised to continue taking sleeping tablets, which I did for some time as a safety measure. Pat stopped accompanying me and it was with much relief that, while I was in Germany doing the RAF bases with George Penman, I got reports from her that workmen were now coming to the house actually to take piles of rubble away, instead of creating them.

It was strange to visit places like RAF Laarbruch, RAF Wildenrath and RAF Bruggen, names that took me back to my youth and *Two Way Family Favourites* with Cliff Michelmore. My friend, Mike Killey from Eagle Star, had requested that he come with us and this proved to be a mixed blessing. He was a great Corries fan, as well as being a personal friend, and we allowed him to take on the role, more or less, of tour manager but, at least on one occasion, it might have caused us difficulty when we were stopped at the guard-house on one of these bases.

Mike got out, resplendent in his old school Watsonians blazer, complete with very ornately embroidered breast pocket badge, and entered the cubicle to present our passports for inspection. Ours were fine but, when the guards looked at his, eyebrows were raised. Mike was a great traveller and his passport was crammed full of visas from behind the Iron Curtain. The guards looked at each other as one of them picked up a telephone and pressed a button to be put through to his commanding officer. 'Sorry to disturb you, sir, but I think you should get down here.'

The incident was quickly sorted and we went on our way to do the show, receiving a fantastic reception from all the squaddies. We came home with fond memories, in spite of Mike, to close the tour in Dundee and Elgin, the shows we had cancelled due to my problems. Later, on the 18th and 25th of November, we recorded two solo concerts for BBC Television.

On Hogmanay Pat and I again invited all our friends for a celebratory Hogmanay party because, during December, the pool had, at long last, been completed and they could now actually swim in it.

Chapter Twenty Two

While installing recording equipment in Roy's home in late 1971, we also set up a remote control system in our sound booth. We were The Corries, after all, and felt we could do anything. Except that we couldn't. As we soon discovered, we had bitten off more than we could chew, and were exceptionally fortunate to obtain the services of a friend of Roy's, Allan Spence, as sound technician. Allan had worked for the BBC but now worked at Heriot Watt University. When we had previously recorded at Craighall Studios, under the banner of Waverley Records, Allan had known the owner, Bryce Laing, from their time at the BBC in Glasgow. When we and W. Gordon Smith became linked to the Waverley label, it was probably inevitable that we should meet up and become associated in the recording business.

Allan agreed to take control of recording and the master tapes were eventually sent down to EMI for scrutiny. It is to Allan's great credit that they were of such high standard as to be accepted by the company and eventually reach the market as an LP called 'Sound the Pibroch' on the EMI Columbia label.

It is also to Allan's credit that, many years later, he re-mastered The Corries' live albums to remove the coughs and other extraneous noises that inevitably accompany a live recording. He was aided at times in this endeavour by Davie Sinton. Davie was another of Roy's friends who, as well as assisting with recording, and being a musician himself, helped look after Roy's fishing-boat once he had built it, and it was fitting that Davie eventually inherited the Combolins after Roy died.

EMI followed 'Sound the Pibroch' in 1973 with another LP called 'A Little of What You Fancy', again from our own recorded masters, and we started to sell these, and other albums, on our continuing tours. We produced posters in excess of what was required for advertising and these were sold as souvenirs along with the concert programmes. Eventually, we added things like Corries' T-shirts, but carrying sufficient stock of different sizes proved to be too difficult.

Part of our appeal was that, after every show, we made ourselves available for signing autographs and meeting our audience even if they hadn't bought a shirt or a poster. I don't think anyone was ever made to feel that we were hurrying them along, no matter how late it got. There was a tremendously good, warm feeling between us and our fans.

A few years ago, I went on holiday to America with my daughter, Lauren, and Pat. New York, Washington, Las Vegas, the Grand Canyon were all included in the itinerary, as was Graceland. I must admit I was never a great fan of Elvis and couldn't really understand why both Pat and Lauren were. I wasn't looking forward to going to his home, thinking that I would find a Mecca of cheap and tatty American trash with jostling crowds of loud and glitzy fans. I couldn't have been more mistaken and more pleasantly surprised.

From the moment we stepped through the large iron gates to approach the house, we experienced an atmosphere of quiet dignity and orderly behaviour. What surprised me most was that, in every room, we were met by an attendant who quietly told us that there was no hurry whatsoever and that we should take as much time as we wished. This extended to the Garden of Remembrance, surely the holy of holies for devoted fans, where Elvis and his family are buried. You could sit all day in respectful silence and, I might add, with no blaring music as a disturbance. Gold discs, stage costumes and photographs of his many house parties were all on display. This place was not a big, tourist honeypot, as I had feared. We felt we were visiting the home of a generous and devoted family man.

I'm certainly not comparing The Corries to the great Elvis Presley, but I do believe that in our career, on stage and off, we engendered the same feeling of warmth and friendship in our fans as I felt for the man on leaving Graceland.

Using our own recording facility certainly did allow what I had been looking forward to: more time at home. It was so nice to spend a day recording in the studio, leave at whatever time of the day or night, and make my way home to Buccleuch and my own bed.

Meanwhile, back at the fort, Pat hadn't been sitting twiddling her thumbs. She had joined the WRI, the Women's Rural Institute, taking part in all of the activities of the branch and eventually becoming Treasurer. Her developing gardening skills bore fruit in many a competition and her baking and cooking expertise was evident in the baskets of scones, doughnuts and sandwiches which were passed round the perspiring dancers at the Boston Hall. The Hall truly epitomised for me the words of one of our best loved songs:-

'For a dance in the barn's worth ten in the hall
Wi' the lads that were reared amang heather.'

The Corries were doing quite nicely now financially speaking. Our year ending May 1972 'take' of £10,531.30 each, rose in 1973 to £15,352.68 each, and in 1974 to £20,215.32 each. These annual increases, with money still in the pot (at Pat's and her boss Robin Finlay's insistence), were not to be sneezed at, and I, for one, was delighted that Pat could now enjoy a few rewards following my leaving the safety of a teaching job ten years or so before.

One came in the form of visits to the Dominion Fur Company

in the Churchill district of Edinburgh. This was before real fur garments became frowned upon, which incidentally I rather agree with. One of her purchases was a red fox fitted jacket and hat to match, which she wore one night to the Ettrickshaws Hotel (the Shaws).

Most evenings there was some form of live music in the bar of the Shaws and I had heard that one of the local musicians was a one-armed accordion player. I don't know if this story was just a come-on for the townie newcomer because I never ever saw him play, but evidently he had the bass side strapped to his leg to work the bellows and played the melody keyboard with his right hand. Plied with drink, by the end of the evening he had slid from his stool to floor level, still playing. You might think this impossible, but I have seen it done.

One New Year's night Aly Bain came to visit, sitting on the high fender beside the marble fireplace in the house we bought on our return to Edinburgh in 1978. Relaxing after a long year of professional engagements in many parts of the world he didn't take much persuading to partake of a drink or two, imbibing between tunes. Finally he slid to the floor, still playing. When he reached the recumbent position, he put aside his fiddle and asked for another. 'Because this one is rubbish,' he said.

There are indeed some phenomenal musicians in Scotland, who perform phenomenal feats. Roy and I once accompanied Iain MacFadyen of the White Heather Club to Shetland to conduct a series of auditions for guests for one of our own shows. One of the auditionees was a fiddler who played some amazing stuff. None of us could understand how he managed to play so many notes in any one tune until we discovered that he had learned to play by ear. He had listened to fiddle music from an old 78 vinyl without realising that he was actually listening to a duet.

That night at the Shaws there were no musicians playing. There was, however, a shepherd in the bar who had brought his dog with him. Unfortunately for Pat, the dog caught sight of her fox, and attacked her. We couldn't get out quickly enough to make our way to the dance at the Boston Hall. Imagine my surprise to see the Jim Johnstone Scottish Country Dance Band setting up, with whom we had shared the stage but a few nights before at the BBC in Glasgow. The Boston was a favourite venue of this brilliant band and we danced the night away to their music. To see the tiny tots from the local families linking arms in the Lancers with the mums and dads and grannies and grandpas was quite touching.

It was also our first experience of the baskets coming out at the interval, first with cups and plates, then with sandwiches, then topped with more baskets of scones and cakes. It was volunteers to arms for collecting afterwards and washing up in the tiny kitchen. Then, on with the dance. After this Pat realised that she had been a wee bit over dressed for the occasion. Mind you, none of the ladies who tried on the fox offered any objection.

We also had spring and autumn tours in 1972, including that night at the Albert Hall in London when Lee was waiting for the lions.

In the year 1974, 'Flower of Scotland' caught on with the wider public. More and more we would catch glimpses of it in television dramas, usually as some drunken Scotsman leaving a bar and singing, 'Oh Flower of Scotland, Na Nya Na Nyaaaaa, Na Nya Na Nyaaaaa.' They had learned the first line, but hadn't quite got the hang of the second. Not so in rugby circles.

1974 saw the British Lions in South Africa for their most successful tour ever. I have it from Scotland's greatest player, Andy Irvine that this was largely due to 'Flower of Scotland.'

One of Roy's pupils when he taught at Liberton High School was Bruce Hay, who was to become another of Scotland's rugby greats. Bruce won the respect of every rugby man he played against, and I mean all over the world. The result was that, when he was facing death in 2007, after a long illness, he had visitors from all of these countries, men who had made special journeys just to spend a few last minutes with him. Towards the end of his life, he lapsed into something of a coma, from time to time rousing to troubled wakefulness. Some of us, to assist his family, set up what can only be described as a vigil, so that, when he did waken, it would be to see friendly faces beside him.

As Andy and I were sitting beside Bruce, the subject of the Lions 1974 Tour came up. Willie John McBride, the Irish captain, was something of a singer and, to foster a close unit for the games, requested songs from the team that they could sing together.

The Irish are known as singers, as are the Welsh. The English could swing quite low themselves at times in their chariot, but the Scots aren't renowned for it, in spite of having a wealth of songs from our history. However, Billy Steele, the Scottish winger in the party was a Corries' fan, or maybe just a lover of 'Flower of Scotland', and he piped up with that as his contribution. When Willie John heard it, his ears pricked up. This was the song he had been looking for, and the team adopted it to unite them as Willie John desired. It succeeded to the extent that, at the television awards at the end of the year, when the Lions were voted in as Team of the Year, they actually sang it at the awards' ceremony. As Andy said to me, it was the most bizarre turn of events to have a group of English, Irish, Welsh and Scottish players all singing what is a most Scottish of Scottish songs.

There had been much talk of this in the media between the end of the Lions tour and their appearance on the Awards Show. So, do you suppose it was mere coincidence that we released our single of 'Flower of Scotland' just a couple of months later in February 1975, at the same time as an album called, 'The Corries, Live From Scotland, Vol. 1'? If you object to the coughs and rustles and movements in the background of this live album and those which followed, you can blame me entirely. I didn't like the studio recording process and argued with Roy that, if we had been singing a song night after night throughout a whole tour of perhaps fifty venues, it would surely be as good as it could by then, so why not record it live at the end of the tour. Roy wasn't so keen, but he went along with me.

Our desire to be masters of our own destiny only grew stronger. Understanding that we might be getting into much bigger things than our career, we thought back ten years to when we were still wet behind the ears and signed a publishing deal with John Martin's company, Argyll Music. John agreed to sell back our titles and some of our more popular arrangements of traditional music. This cost us the amount these titles had earned for Argyll over the previous seven years.

Like Pat and me, Roy had been thinking of hedging his bets for the future, but his thoughts took him down a different path. He had long harboured a dream of owning a fishing boat. Unable to find a suitable boat for sale he set plans in motion to build one, largely to his own design.

He also mentioned that it might be advantageous, for tax reasons, to set up a limited company for us both. This seemed a bit cockeyed to me but I had no objection and so we created our company, The Corries (Music) Ltd, hereinafter referred to as CML. Roy and I were equal shareholders, and I must make it very clear that I never at any time had anything whatsoever to do with the *Sheena Margaret*, which was what he called the vessel on completion. It was never at any time a CML asset.

The titles we bought from Argyll were registered with the Mechanical Copyright Protection Society (MCPS), and the Performing Rights Society (PRS), as being owned by CML, and that is where they remain. This move was made in line with our policy that everything we earned from our work singing together, either cash at the concert door, or royalty payments, would be split down the middle.

A limited company requires auditors to scrutinise its financial workings and an international company, Whinney, Murray & Co., agreed to take us under their wing. This, it transpired, was not such a good idea, because Whinney, Murray proved to be too big for us, and CML proved to be not big enough for them.

In January of 1975 Ailsa McGie of 'Folklore', whom we had sung with in concert in earlier years, joined us in Roy's studios in his home in Zetland Place, setting herself up in a small room to supervise the collection, packing, and distribution of the FoS single and the album. She was aided and abetted by a youngster called Philip Thorpe, the son of our neighbours, Barry and Doreen, when we had been at Henderson Row, and he took delight in rushing around Edinburgh on his bike on CML business.

In March 1975, Ailsa married Forbes Fordyce. Forbes had been working in accountancy with a firm called Strutt & Parker and, when Roy and I asked him to join our merry band to take care of the CML side of things, he was reticent to do so. (This music business could be a bit 'fly by night', after all.) He did, however, agree to remain an independent helper and, when The Corries eventually produced and marketed our own albums, the stock ended up being stored in the garage of Forbes and Ailsa's homes in, first, Penicuik and then in Broughton. The stock soon outgrew them and was transferred to the loft of Scott's The Flower Shop, in Penicuik, where it ended its days. From this early business arrangement between Ailsa and Forbes and myself, a friendship evolved which remains one that we treasure, since, in all that time, never a harsh word has passed between us. You can't say that about many people, and I love the pair of them dearly.

As well as our wish, Pat's, mine and Roy's, to hedge our bets against the future, we had begun to think that perhaps The Corries should do the same, and decided to buy property in Edinburgh. We also set up a company called Pan Audio Ltd to specialise in recording, not just The Corries, but also other artists. The company would also branch into what is described in a Pan Audio pamphlet as 'Commercial Communication'.

The pamphlet lists, under the heading, 'Some of our facilities', sixty, yes sixty, different topics including: Advertisement Production, Educational Cassettes, Music Arranging, Tape Duplication, Photographic Processing, the list goes on and on. Ambitious aims? Very ambitious, some would say, 'over-ambitious'. And so it proved.

Property was purchased at 4 Forth Street, just along from Radio Forth, and work done on office and reception space. Recording studios were created downstairs and filled with equipment brought from Zetland Place. Roy's friend, John McKinnon, was set the task of controlling the business from behind a large desk in his office.

A few weeks after our doors were opened, Pat and I paid a visit, but I made myself unpopular when viewing a new-fangled electronic machine called a 'photocopier'. I remarked that at least one of the bosses (me) was still using two sheets of carbon paper to make copies of his letters. Of course, photocopiers are now almost redundant in most offices.

In John's office Pat was confronted with two large potted plants, and said she would love to have something like those in mine. No doubt prompted by the idea of me languishing in an office, Roy then suggested that, instead of my spending hours placing ads for the tours, I should perhaps spend more time on the instruments. Since John was here in the office why not hand that task over to him? I thought maybe he had a point.

We weren't many days into our first tour using these methods when I couldn't help reverting to the 'tested and tried' and phoned ahead to check how ticket sales were progressing. When I felt that we could do with a couple of additional ads in the press, I phoned John to request that some more be placed. His reply was that he would phone the agency to see what they could do. Agency? You can guess my reaction! I was soon back with the hands-on approach which had brought The Corries, at least the singing part of their activities, to where they now were.

No new business is likely to thrive from the minute it opens its door. I had been around Pat and her work as a book-keeper long enough to know that a period of about three years was usually allotted a fledgling company before it was expected to show profit, but after our first year I still didn't see any sign of progress.

Obviously I didn't do a good job of hiding my money worries from her because, at the end of 1976, Pat announced that we were going to do Bed and Breakfast in 1977. We now had fantastic facilities to offer guests: the pool and billiard table in the extension, a full-sized trampoline in the garden and table-tennis in the barn. We were already thinking of a skittle alley in the extra outbuildings and there was no problem with parking.

Although initially offering only breakfast in the deal, we had ample supply of venison, trout and salmon from local game-keepers and Pat's kitchen garden responded very well to her tender loving care, providing all the fresh vegetables she might need if she branched into dinners. We had what we called 'a cold room' which contained three massive freezer cabinets in case of emergencies.

If we and the children moved our sleeping quarters into the large and small attic rooms, six bedrooms would become available for guests. I welcomed her suggestion with open arms. We placed ads in December and almost immediately had a good response. In February our first customers arrived when we let three rooms for four nights from February 18th.

From the word go, we sensed it would work. During that first week our guests asked very politely if Pat could supply dinners as well as breakfasts. She could hardly refuse, thinking of the extra money this would bring. After dinner on the first evening, when the guests had retired to their lounge, which was the lounge that used to be ours, we heard a knock on the door of the wee room across the hall, which we had converted into our snug, and were asked if we would join them all for a drink. When their initial telephone enquiries came in we had explained that we weren't licensed, so they had brought their booze with them. That was the start of a four-day party. As a matter of fact, it seemed like the start of a whole season of partying.

In the last years, all of our friends and family who had been keeping the house busy at weekends and summer holidays, continued to come down to see us, but, knowing our situation, came as paying guests.

We felt from the whole experience the same sense of the fairy story start of the Corrie Folk Trio and Paddie Bell.

My favourite guests were a retired couple, Mr and Mrs Doull from the west coast, who came for a couple of nights early in the season and, before leaving, booked another few later in the summer. They were very quiet, but Mrs Doull had some questions for Pat before she left. We had on display a collection of dolls of Pat's, a cabinet full of my ivory and wooden carvings, walls lined with Pat's porcelain and frames of stamps which I had become interested in. Books and bits and pieces were spread around the shelves of the library in the billiard-room. The question she asked was: had anything ever been pilfered? Pat answered no, and Mrs Doull took her aside to say that she and Mr Doull were also collectors of antique furniture, and jewellery just like Pat wore, but she never had the chance to admire her own collection.

Mr Doull was retired from the building trade, and had built their retirement home on the side of a hill including a 'secret' room with a concealed door to store their treasures for safe keeping. The only time she ever saw any of them was on the day it was bought. She thanked Pat for having ours on display and cast a last, thoughtful, look round as she went through the front door.

When they next arrived she was wearing some beautiful jewellery which she took delight in showing to Pat, and we

216

admired photographs of some of their prized furniture. Mr Doull had brought it out from hiding for them to use on a daily basis. Every evening after dinner they took up a seated position in the billiard room and just looked around. The seats they commandeered were Orkney rockers with huge hoods we had brought from Kirkwall and which usually stood facing each other from opposite corners of the room.

They booked for another week at the end of the season, coinciding with a repeat visit from James and Anne Pearson. It was the first time they had seen a swimming-pool as such, never mind that it was in somebody's house, but there was nothing I could do to persuade them to go in the water. They wouldn't even sit on the Roman steps that were such a feature of the shallow end.

On the first day, through the glass wall the Doulls watched from their Orkney chairs my efforts at teaching James to swim. Next day Mrs Doull took James aside to explain that she had been a swimmer when she was younger but hadn't been in the water for many years. She asked him if he would mind standing at the steps while she tentatively eased herself in, just in case she got into difficulties. I don't know exactly how she did it, but by the end of James's week with us, he was swimming like a fish, and couldn't be kept out of the water.

Chapter Twenty Three

That year of B&B, although successful, was extremely hard work, more so for Pat than me. With all my meetings in town and continued involvement with touring, I had many breaks from housekeeping, cooking and serving, hoovering of the pool with attendant refilling, constant problems with the water filtration unit and adjustments to chemical levels. For Pat it was much more difficult, having taken on the roles of business manager, head cook and bottle washer, laundry maid and housemaid, as well as devoted mother. It was all with no help, because, where we lived, you couldn't get a daily help. She relied mostly on family to visit and take over for a few days, but not entirely. She did have someone to ease the burden in some of the summer months.

Christine Loudon was a student at Hamilton College. As a schoolgirl living directly opposite us in Briarbank Terrace she baby-sat for us many times. It was she who came to our aid all those years ago on the night Bill Smith got us out of bed to come to his ill-fated party. She spent student summer breaks with us over the years, just helping Pat out with the children, but eased into a more professional role when the B&B started.

Whether from our advertising, or recommendations, or passing trade, we had a constant stream of guests whom Pat was unwilling to turn away. However busy she was or how tired she became because of it, she smiled with satisfaction on October 24th, 1977, when she paid £500 into the loan account and increased the extension repayments to £450 per month. She received a £2,600 bonus from CML from which she paid £2,000 into a Building Society account of her own.

More money was forthcoming from a different source. Not ours, but CML money from Canada, when John McCuaig paid us a visit bearing cash from sales of the records and programmes we had left. He also bore the news that the feedback from our short tour was so good that he could offer us a return visit towards the end of 1978.

We also had an offer to visit Australia at about the same time, so naturally thought of working our way across Canada to Vancouver, then going straight to Australia. Ambitious maybe, but it seemed sensible. To make the whole scheme workable though, we would have to be away for many weeks and, since I would not contemplate leaving Pat so long she became excited at the thought of coming with us.

Dates had been agreed with the Australian promoter when the whole scheme came unstuck. We discovered that Musicians Union rules in Australia stated that concerts by visiting acts like ourselves must include at least 25% indigenous musicians.

Earlier in our career, we had performed at a combined concert in England, under the banner of Argyll Songs, with a folk-singer called Roy Harper. Nobody was happy with it, neither us, nor Roy, nor Argyll, and certainly not the audience because, when we were on, Roy's fans drifted to the bar and, when Roy was on, our fans did the same. We could imagine the same thing happening in Australia under such rules, and so the idea was scotched and we ended up not going. In England it was easy enough to crawl back home to lick our wounds. Across the vast expanses of Australia it would be quite another matter, especially feeling the same failure night after night. The audiences down under might have reacted differently, but we didn't take the risk.

Not long after John McCuaig left, November floods heralded the end of the B&B season. River levels rose ten feet higher than normal, moving the stone bridge supports at Deloraine, and we were left once again to ponder what the future held.

Many of our first guests had already made tentative bookings for 1978, even knowing that we would increase our prices should we decide to continue, so we were confident that another successful season was on the way. With that in mind, we presented our health and safety plans to the fire department. This was perhaps just as well because we discovered that we had been the victims of industrial espionage, as one of our guests had come only to case the joint. A Health and Safety Inspector called on a surprise visit after receiving an anonymous letter complaining that a local B&B was trading without the correct safety equipment. There weren't many other guest houses anywhere near us, and only one had an indoor heated swimming pool. So, we had our own ideas of who had shopped us. However, when we showed him our plans, he explained that we would have a period of five years to install everything necessary, so we could continue to trade at full capacity.

I sometimes wonder what might have happened in the event of a fire, but I didn't wonder for long because we decided not to open again for business. Our decision wasn't based only on the disruption that installation of fire doors, escape ladders, extinguishers and so on, at a cost of £5000, would cause, probably spoiling the very amenities which were part of our appeal. Other, possibly more important factors were involved.

Knowing our own ambitious natures, we didn't think that we would be content to continue only in B&B. With the space around us and the extra barns and outbuildings at our disposal we would inevitably expand into a hotel. Staffing costs loomed, as did the prospect of being made to improve the entrance roadway and strengthen the wee iron bridge with even more borrowing. In the end, we didn't think we had the energy for all that. It had taken fully two years to get the present extension completed and, although we now lived in a truly beautiful place, we were suffering the adverse effects of creating it.

The children, too, had to be considered. All over the Borders traditional mills were closing, affecting businesses of all kinds and making job prospects in the area a real concern. Even if we were to create a successful hotel, it would have been unfair to conscript these youngsters as the nucleus of our staff as would no doubt have happened.

To move back to Edinburgh was our final decision. When we made it known, every one of the people who complained when we 'buried' ourselves in this back-water, but who had spent nearly every weekend and large parts of their summer holidays visiting us, complained again, incredulous that we could even contemplate leaving such a wonderful haven.

Nonetheless we metaphorically turned our backs on West Buccleuch and turned our eyes towards the city. Gavin was approaching his final year at Selkirk High School with Highers impending. Maurice was about to leave anyway; by his own admission he was no scholar. Give him a rugby ball and he was happy. Lauren, at the time, didn't know what she wanted to do, but was starting to think of marriage and children and perhaps a job in teaching and the long holidays that go with it.

It was decided that, when we moved, Lauren and Maurice would accompany us to town, and Gavin would stay on in Selkirk for a year in the home of his good friend Murray McKie to complete his studies before rejoining us.

On December 1st, we instructed our Estate Agents, to prepare to sell the house. They came to inspect, and recommended a price of £70,000. We said we were looking for a lot more than that, but then, who wouldn't? On December 20th, they sent their photographers to take shots for the glossy brochure that they thought the property warranted. It looked as though we could see light at the end of this particular tunnel, and I wish I could say the same about the tunnel at Forth Street.

This was a depressing time for all concerned and I will condense what is all bad news into as short an account as possible, in the hope that it doesn't depress my readers as much as it did us at the time.

Since we bought the Forth Street property in 1975 and studios and office space had been fabricated, and in spite of no profit arising from the activities of Pan Audio for the next two years, we had extended by buying the property behind. A monastery in its time, it was now derelict. More borrowing had been required, and surviving documents show that Roy, John McKinnon, Allan Spence and I had signed as guarantors for bank loans to cover re-wiring, re-plumbing, etc. Coming events determined that we would not be able to actually use this space.

The ambitions of the Pan Audio pamphlet just hadn't borne fruit and John McKinnon now suggested that we ditch the unsuccessful ventures, most of which had been in the field of 'voice-overs'. The company had produced a couple of albums, 'The Cavendish Dance Band', and one of Bill Hill's called 'Miscellaneous Dross', a humourous look at Scotland, and our first two live albums which went out under the Pan Audio label. None of this made any great profit.

John's idea now was to forget all that and concentrate the company effort on two things: music and advertising on buses. The problem with this idea was that a great many more small sound booths would be required in the monastery, with attendant extra sound equipment. That meant further borrowing, which would require further guarantees from us as directors to the tune of £20,000. I don't mind admitting that I was first with my hand up saying that this was not possible given the borrowing burden I already laboured under. Nor did I think the bank would look at it.

So what was to be done? Roy's friend Fran Burgess was a financial adviser, and he called her in to have a look at our situation.

I won't name names in her damning report but the impression she had gained was that everybody was 'playing at offices', to put it bluntly. She said: 'A crude purchase book has been initiated'; 'a positive sales approach is imperative'; 'the studio still smells dreadfully and it amazes me that this is tolerated. Regular servicing is not maintained, nor is training given to cover general maintenance'. I won't go on.

Since this whole studio expansion had been instigated by Roy and me, we had to hold ourselves responsible, but a great deal of our troubles, in hindsight, arose from the fact that we hadn't received any up to date accounts from Whinney Murray. We were a tiny company on their books, and it felt as if our pleas for attention had not been heeded.

My friend, Arthur Condie, or 'Art', as his wife called him, although always full of tom-foolery, was certainly no fool as a businessman. I described our situation to him and he introduced me to his own accountant, Stewart Hamilton, who agreed to take us on. In his CML Report and Accounts for the eleven months to 5th September, 1978, Stewart states that Whinney, Murray & Co resigned and he was appointed in their stead. He further shows that CML had sustained a trading loss for the period of £11,820, a situation which couldn't be allowed to continue. Up to now, Roy and I as The Corries had been on a roll, and the concerts were as successful as ever. I found it hard though, to persuade Roy that the records side of our enterprise, and the property expansion, weren't making as much as he thought. I therefore requested Stewart to split his report into two sections: 'Contribution from Tours,' which showed the sum of £98,299, and 'Contribution from Record Distribution,' which showed £26,357.

A further report on Pan-Audio prepared from independent management consultants suggested that three options were open to us;

(i) liquidation,

(ii) arrange a take-over,

(iii) continuation on present basis.

A letter on Pan Audio headed paper to Corries (Music) Ltd states: 'It is agreed that Corries (Music) Ltd be allowed to continue to use the two record labels Pan Audio and Dara until one or either of the two companies decide otherwise.'

On 14th December, 1979, I wrote to Bernard Thorpe and Partners requesting that they sell 4, Forth Street for a price in excess of £50,000. In fact, we finally let it go for £35,000, a sum exactly matching the company's debt as on display at Companies House. When the buyer visited Roy and me in the Forth Street premises he must have known he was on firm ground, and I had no problem, with a simple nod of the head, in getting Roy's agreement to rid ourselves of the burden.

So ended a five year nightmare.

On February 1st, 1985, Roy and I signed a Contract of Co-Partnership and so traded until his death in 1990. The company, The Corries (Music) Ltd remained, as it still does, although in a non-trading capacity, as a clearing-house for royalties earned from the copyright works of The Corries.

As you can see, Pat and I were past masters at moving house. When you've had that kind of experience and go to view a prospective new property, you can usually make up your mind quickly about whether you can live in it, or whether you can't get out soon enough. From property ads at our disposal, we spent day after day travelling from Buccleuch to view houses. I don't remember how many of the ads gave us hope, but nothing raised the hairs on the back of the neck until, suddenly, one day, there it was: one we had to have, come what may.

In case you think it was all my fault that we had moved so many times, let me tell you in Pat's words how excited she was about this new discovery at 6, Wester Coates Gardens.

'It is incredible. Original as it was built in 1906. Fabulous panelled hall, lounge, dining-room, office or morning-room, kitchen etc. on the main floor. Upstairs 6 bedrooms, 2 bathrooms (one with marble bath) & w.c. & attic above.

Downstairs. Super panelled billiard-room & lovely square hall with cocktail bar. 3 bedrooms, laundry, bathroom & w.c. off billiard room. All with original fireplaces in the halls too. The whole thing is unbelieveable. The garden is one and a half acres but has been sold for executive houses and will leave a very nice garden. It also has a flat of bedroom, lounge, kitchen and bathroom. Upset £45,000.'

I was every bit as excited as Pat. We returned the keys, and when we got home to Buccleuch sat all night talking about it. The antiquated kitchen would have to be re-built, the house completely re-wired and a central heating system installed but, if we got it, we would be halving our present commitments and we could easily afford to do all that was necessary within the next year or two (these are Pat's words again).

Next day, Ian Meldrum at the bank assured us that they would bridge a loan and get a £25,000 mortgage, no bother. Even Eagle Star said they would lend on such a property. All of this on top of us sending bits and pieces for appraisal for selling. Bits and pieces constituted my ivories and wooden carvings, together with sets of stamps I had started to collect, Pat's jewellery, porcelain, doll and coin collections. I had sent two samurai swords to Sotheby's, having bought them for the carved ivory scabbards, but Sotheby's reported that one of these blades was very valuable, much more so than the scabbard. Apparently it had been forged in a special way, folded again and again, to give it immense strength.

When we declared our interest through Dan Lockett, our lawyer, we were informed that there were now another two people interested, and not to build up hopes anyway. His enquiries suggested that no building society would touch us since I was an entertainer.

Things started to become confusing again when, two days later, Dan phoned to say that the Nationwide would lend £25,000, quickly followed by a call from Eagle Star saying they would transfer their loan from Buccleuch to Wester Coates depending on the valuation. This arrived next day at £47,500, qualified by the statement that, 'the sky's the limit once the improvements have been effected'.

On Tuesday, January 31st, we told Dan that we would like to offer £51,500. Offers closed at noon on Monday, February 6th, which was unfortunate because we were leaving on holiday with Drew and Sheila for Italy on Saturday 4th. With false bravado, we said we had every confidence in Dan, we were sure he would get it for us and that we would keep in touch.

On the morning of the 6th, the four of us were standing beside the Trevi Fountain in Rome, where it's said that if you close your eyes and wish a wish, it will be granted. I have on film a clip of Drew and Sheila standing, eyes closed and in a tight embrace, making their wishes. As eyes opened, Drew, very disappointed, said that it didn't work because Sheila was still standing beside him. Although she well knew from experience Drew's wicked sense of humour, she never forgave him for that one.

In the hotel we endured a long wait through the afternoon before finally hearing from Dan that we had succeeded in buying our house, but that we had to pay £51,826 for it. By some strange premonition, or possibly from insider knowledge, at the last minute, Dan had upped our bid by the extra £326. Soon, on our way to Pisa by train to spend a few days before catching the plane home, by way of celebration we broke open a couple of bottles. When we reached Pisa and visited the Leaning Tower, we noticed that, by some miracle, it was standing straight up. I wonder why?

Immediately we got home, Pat phoned the doctor. She was suffering from nagging pains in her stomach which she thought was food poisoning. Sharing Drew's cruel sense of humour, we both blamed the drink in the train, but the smile soon left my face when the doctor asked for two specimens, one to test for infection, and the other to be sent to Peel Hospital for a pregnancy test. Another thing which took the smiles away was the news from Pat that we had but £20 left in our current account, and that she had only enough cash in her purse to last the month.

The results of both tests were negative, but it was decided that Pat had been on the pill for long enough, and sterilisation for her or vasectomy for me was recommended. Debate followed whether it should be me for the chop, or Pat. I obviously didn't argue strongly enough that it should be me, and I have to live with that, because at 11.45 am on February 22nd, Pat was sterilised.

The Corries still had Forth Street and Pat and Violet went in one day to spend three hours with Ailsa, sleeving singles, at the same time as I was trying to persuade a tradesman that it wasn't convenient to start the damp course at Wester Coates and he'd have to wait until May. This was because the job was priced at £2300, and we were hoping every day that a buyer was going to walk in the door at Buccleuch. Good news arrived though, from Drew's friend Dougie Bald, a heating engineer, who said that he would start on both the central heating and the rewiring and be happy to wait for payment.

Ads went into the press in mid-April for the sale of Buccleuch, at the same time as the floorboards came up all over the new house for the central heating installation. The place was a mess as the telephone engineers and gas men were also at work and we feared a repeat of the Buccleuch experience.

At the end of the spring tour I reviewed my position. Months lay ahead before I would meet Roy again for rehearsals for the autumn tour. I was always busy with preparations for the next singing, but this was done in my own time, and I could easily arrange that to suit myself.

I decided to see what I could do with my other talent, painting, but not to paint just any-old-thing and hope it would sell. The alternative was actually staring me in the face, so to speak: portrait commissions. To reassure myself that I could still get a likeness, I started on self-portrait drawings, then portraits of the children and of Pat. I moved into water colour and, very soon realised that the ability was still there. I was confident I could make a real go of it.

Money started to come in from our bits and pieces sales. For instance, a Japanese vase, bought for £30, but valued at about £700, eventually went for £450. My Japanese sword went for £350.

Although still resident in West Buccleuch, we spent more and more time getting Wester Coates cleaned up until finally moving house in July, when work was still being done. We left Gavin in the Borders where he had started work for the summer at Tilhill Forestry, and Maurice, who had earlier started work at the Commonwealth Pool and had been staying with Violet in Gilmerton, moved back home with us.

On June 8th, when we paid the damp course man his £2,100, he and his wife asked to have portraits done of them, and of their two daughters. Commissions increased quickly. For some I accepted money, for example from our local fish man and from a family friend, Jim Donald, a Sheriff's Officer (and therefore a man to keep well in with). I got a good likeness of him. Another man I accepted money from was Ed Baxter, the manager of the Usher Hall, who commissioned me to paint Stéphane Grappelli.

My portraits of Drew and his daughter Lynne were used as practice, as were my brother-in-law, Andy Ross and his son David. David's portrait was accepted for show at the forthcoming Royal Scottish Society of Water Colour Painters. In the middle of all this painting activity, a surveyor attached to our continuing work at Forth Street, Alastair Dickson, bought Pat's Volvo and also my shotgun and ammunition.

We had plans drawn up for the conversion of the basement of our new property into two flats for possible sale. A man called Gordon Drever was very interested in buying the existing flat if we decided to sell. His father was my former coach at

Braidburn Athletic Club, Big Tam Drever, and he proposed to lend Gordon money for the purchase, a possible £25,000.

We had two or three viewings of Buccleuch and two or three promises to view who didn't turn up. When Dougie Bald offered to buy my Range Rover, I accepted and bought a new Jaguar. This was following the news that the conversion of downstairs would cost only £990, with a customer sitting waiting. Between all this and more painting commissions coming my way, I didn't think it was too big a risk to buy a new motor.

What Pat had neglected to say in her somewhat breathless first description of the property was that, immediately to the left of the entrance hall door was a stone circular stairway leading down to the billiard room, and another stairway leading down right opposite this beside the main floor toilet. All we had to do to separate the main floor from the basement was block off these two stairways, and separate the electricity, water and gas. Hence, the cheapness of the conversion. It would have been silly, given our questionable current financial position, not to go ahead and do it. We did, and sold for £25,000.

On November 25th, the Sotheby's sale of my ivories fetched £6,555 and at the same time my stamps went for £1,960. This was topped up with £1,055 for some dolls of Pat's.

In December, a local man in the Ettrick Valley, Joe Newcombe, sent relations of his to view Buccleuch twice, and on January 12th, 1979, we accepted £52,000 for the property. All of this came in the nick of time, because, at a meeting with Roy in Edinburgh on January 31st, we discovered that the bank wouldn't let the CML account go into the red and we had to agree to take no salaries for the next three months.

Chapter Twenty Four

On March 17th we held a birthday party in the new house for Lauren, now at Broughton High School here in Edinburgh. A large number of guests were invited, but unfortunately word also went out on the school grapevine. Masses of young gate-crashers arrived, and booze was smuggled in resulting in a lot of sickness over the carpets and walls, to a degree you wouldn't believe. One boy had to be assisted over the hall carpet when he didn't know whether he wanted to pee or shit, or be sick. In the end, everything came out at once. Probably it was our own fault for trying over-hard to provide a memorable night for Lauren. It most certainly did, but in the wrong fashion.

By contrast, three days later, in the rather staid atmosphere of the opening of the Royal Scottish Academy on the Mound, I had my portrait of our doctor Dave Tulloch's wife, Etive, accepted. To make the day doubly pleasant when we got home, we received a letter stating that two automaton dolls of Pat's had sold for £520.

A few months before, when John McCuaig visited with his brother Charlie, I introduced them to the comedian, Hector Nicol, whom John wanted to take out to Canada. On that visit, John noticed my painting and suggested my coming to Canada to do some commissions, since he knew many of his associates might 'want to be done'. On a later visit he announced that twelve of these people could be available for sittings in the month of July. It was so arranged.

Ronnie Browne

The 75th Rolls Royce Anniversary took place at a party in the Rossleigh Showrooms on Glasgow Road at Corstorphine in Edinburgh on June 1st, 1979. To make it an occasion the manager arranged a fashion parade, an exhibition of jewellery and an appearance of an in-close magician. I don't know if you've seen any of these guys at work, but the good ones are amazing, as this one was. He also asked me to bring some portraits to adorn the walls, and to bring the sitters if I could, not exactly to stand next to their images, but to mingle and possibly be asked questions about their involvement.

Drew and his daughter, Lynne, were there, as were Pat and a few others whose portraits I had managed to get hold of. One in particular stirred some interest, that of Mike Gerber. Mike was an advocate who had a very down to earth approach with his clients, particularly when defending villains. He could speak to them in their own language, blue as it might become. He had been introduced to me by Drew as a regular visitor to Drew's Trampoline Centre in Portobello, and he had given me a commission.

The reason for such interest in his image was that, in the painting, it wasn't just his face I had depicted. I had dressed him in his robes and wig and seated him in an ornate chair as though he was at work in his chambers. In one hand he clasped a sheaf of legal papers and, at the beginning of the sittings, the other hand lay at rest on the arm of the chair. To show that he was an Edinburgh lawyer, I painted him in front of an open French window looking onto the Lion's Head of Arthur's Seat in Holyrood Park.

I didn't need Mike to sit through the painting of the background, but when I explained my plans to do it this way he told me that, centuries ago, a double gallows stood beneath the Lion's Head, about where the Commonwealth Pool stands now. Pretty well marking the entrance to the city from the south, the gallows stood as a warning to travellers to be on their best behaviour on their visit to Auld Reekie.

This fascinated me, so I decided to include a double gallows on the grassland, at the same time changing the aspect of Mike's left hand from one of repose to the clenched fist of a 'Hanging Judge'. Mike liked the idea and on the night took pleasure in recounting the story.

Back at Rossleigh's, on the night of the celebration, I asked the manager if his efforts in making a most memorable occasion had borne fruit in the form of sales of the new Rolls Royce. His answer was yes, but he qualified it by saying that, although he had taken cheques as deposits on three vehicles, he knew that two of these would be cancelled the next day, because the men who had signed them had only done so to impress the young ladies clinging to their arms.

I'm reminded of the occasion when Eddie Ramsay, another friend of Drew's, arrived at my doorstep one Sunday morning at Wester Coates to show me his latest acquisition, a brand new Rolls. He asked me what I was doing that morning, and when I told him I was about to go out for our breakfast rolls said, 'Well, why not go for the rolls in the Rolls?' which, needless to say, I proceeded to do.

Pat and I left for Canada for my portrait tour on Friday, June 29th and stayed in a flat in 2837 Yonge Street, Toronto, until we returned on July 27th. 'Tour' though, is a misnomer as the sitters all came to me at the flat. It had been explained that, because of time restrictions, the portraits would be done in a mixture of sittings and photographs. There were no arguments, as I'm pretty sure they were intrigued by this unusual exercise, more than expectant of possessing a mini Rembrandt at the end. That said, I know that most were pleasantly surprised at the quality of what they eventually received.

I was surprised myself, because I was exhausted at the end of a month that had started off with a portrait of Max Bygraves for John McCuaig, who organised Bygraves' appearances in Canada, and a pencil drawing of the actor John Cairney in the guise of Robert Burns, again for John who was writing a book on Burns. McCuaig became a well-known Burns Supper speaker in years to come.

As well as actually painting, I spent time purchasing water-colour paper and mounting board. Making sure I kept ahead with the prepared paper, most of the time I worked late into the night to produce the nineteen works. An artists' materials shop was situated just below the flat and the proprietor did the framing for me after I had cut the mounts.

During a radio interview for Denis Snowden, whose programme was listened to by an avid following of mainly expat Scots, he and I commiserated with each other at being soaked to the skin in Toronto. Every week the heat built up from day to day until eventually there was an almighty thunderstorm with heavy downpours over a few hours. Then it would clear and become cool for maybe a day and a half before boiling up again.

There was nothing I could do but work through this heat, which really only presented problems when I placed a finished painting on the floor to measure for mounting. I had to be very careful of sweat dripping from my armpits onto either the surface of the board or the image. If some of the recipients of these paintings look very carefully at the detail, they might detect a mark that looks suspiciously like a drop of water when I wasn't able to get the blotting paper out in time.

Because of the time factor nearly all the pictures were simply of the head of the sitter with a plain background, but with Tony Cunningham's I strayed into the adventuresome. Tony was an ardent member of the Scottish National Party, which always seemed strange to me, since he was so far from where he might have any influence on the fate of his country. As with Mike Gerber, I painted a background which would 'locate' him in Scotland. I chose a view of St Kilda, which I thought was quite poetic.

By the end of the month's visit, I had completed nineteen portraits, and most of the sitters came to a farewell party in the flat before we left. Yes, it was crowded, especially as friends of the sitters came as well. One of these friends approached me. Pat and I were used to well-meaning admirers coming in close to grab my hand but, this time, the guy walked past me and straight to her. Looking quite sad, he introduced himself as having been to school with her at Gilmerton, and said, 'Pat, it's so nice to see you again, but seeing you has just reminded me that I'll never see Gilmerton again.' 'Oh,' said Pat, 'How long have you been away?' Through floods of tears he said, 'Two weeks.'

We did see Gilmerton again, more quickly than we expected, because the day after we got home, Violet phoned to say that she had finished The Corries' new stage shirts and they were ready for collection.

On August 10th, we received the £25,000 for the downstairs flat, subsequently paying off all the bills, the car-loan and the bridging-loan. After paying money towards the bank loan, we were left with only £8,000 of debt outstanding, which we hoped to pay off over the following year.

By now the house was busy with a gaggle of teenagers. Gavin started a new job as a lab technician at Heriot Watt University while Murray was still staying with us, joined now by Bill Smith's daughter, Corrie, who was starting school at Fettes College. We had agreed this with her mother, Etive, to see how she would settle in. Lauren was still at Broughton, but she, and all the others, encouraged their friends to visit more or less at will. Perhaps because of the domestic bustle Pat now joined the Samaritans and took up shift work with them. From time to time, a gang of the boys' school friends would come up for a couple of days. Thank goodness I was still touring, and for the relative tranquillity of full-house theatres.

I must have saturated myself with painting in Canada as I did nothing more until December when I painted the Walker family, three girls and their brother, a family called Henderson and, at the end of the year Mike Gerber's two girls; and Pat's and the kids' faces (with me on Pat's ear as an earring).

Over the next two or three years, I was very busy on all fronts. I was constantly cutting what seemed like acres of grass with a Flymo that kept breaking down, and the slope didn't make my job any easier. I cut down four hawthorn trees to be taken away in a skip, but the skip didn't turn up until five days later. I was running Pat up and down to her Samaritans commitments, worrying about the nightshifts after learning she had been trained never to open the office door without a lighted cigarette in her hand. I was running youngsters to rugby, concerts and parties, in fact, living the life of an ordinary family man and not that of a supposed star of stage and television.

Between the lives of family man and concert star, I was again fitting in more portraits. Pat and I went to stay with a family called Henderson in Brora where we were given the use of their granny flat for two weeks whilst I painted the grannie, Mr and Mrs Henderson, and their three children. I never found out where the grannie went at night. I also painted a local businessman's family: his wife and their wee boy. I've just looked at a photograph of it in my album of commissions and can't remember a thing about it.

On October 29th, 1980 I received a letter from Max Bygraves which reads;

'Dear Ronnie Browne,

I have been presented with the portrait you did of myself and I would like to express the admiration passed on by friends and associates.

One rarely likes this sort of flattery but I had to write and say what an admirable job you did on it. I am most "chuffed" by it.

Most sincerely,
Max Bygraves.'

I was pretty 'chuffed' too.

During these same years, Drew Kennedy became the after-lunch-talk organiser for his local Portobello Rotary Club and asked if I would oblige him by being their speaker one after-noon. Knowing that when his Rotarians saw my name on their lunch menu, they would be expecting me to speak about The Corries, I decided to do what we were wont to do in the shows, spring a surprise. I spoke about the portraits, taking along a few examples, including the one I had done of Drew. They were more surprised than I thought they would be, indeed they seemed amazed.

One man who was present that day was Mike Keohane, who eventually commissioned a portrait. Mike wanted one of his wife, Maggie, and meetings ensued at their home in Lundin Links, on the banks of the Firth of Forth, for discussions on content, where I explained that I had adopted the habit of painting, not just a head, but a 'picture' of aspects of the sitter's life. In other words, making it hard for myself.

I posed Maggie on a grassy knoll in front of their house. Although actually impossible to see from their garden, the Forth Bridge miraculously appears in the picture in the distance, just behind the left shoulder of their English sheepdog, which dwarfs Maggie because of its massive size. At the time of painting, argument was raging about the Council cutting down trees near their land, so a wood-cutter appeared on the fore-shore with his chain-saw in front of a pile of burning wood. At the time Maggie and Mike were considering adoption, so Maggie sits with a photograph album in her hands. When viewed by members of their family, it would immediately be associated with their plans as it contained, as they all knew, pictures of the child.

The reason I go into so much detail in describing Maggie's portrait is because I suspect it led to a major commission. I had known he was with the Royal Bank of Scotland, but hadn't realised that he had special duties as liaison officer with the Scottish Rugby Union, Scottish Rugby being sponsored by the Bank. It was late spring, 1984, the year that Scotland won the Grand Slam for only the second time in our history. A *Scotsman* newspaper photographer, Jack Crombie, had taken a photograph of Jim Calder touching the ball down to score a try, with Jim looking jubilantly at the referee who stood with his whistle in his right hand and his left arm stretched aloft. Above them both, in the far distance at the other end of the stadium, could be seen the score board bearing the logo of the Royal Bank of Scotland, the time 16.23, and the score still standing at 12-12, this latest try not yet having been added. The try proved to be the turning point in the match and Scotland went on to beat France and win the Grand Slam. Final score: 23-12.

Mike had seen this black and white photograph and, I like to think, suggested to his superiors that here was a perfect subject for a celebratory painting – and he knew just the man to do it. He asked me to visit him at the Bank's headquarters in St Andrew's Square where I was asked if I would be able to copy the photograph, enlarging it and adding colour. I said that would be no bother but, since I was in essence a portrait painter, and not a mere copyist, why not use the photograph as a centrepiece to portraits of the winning squad and officials. In other words, making it hard for myself again.

Eyes lit up round the table as I found myself surrounded by a large group of money men, enthused about what I was proposing and who, I'm sure, were not in the habit of showing so much excitement in the middle of a business meeting. The merriment subsided when I told them how much such an ambitious project would cost, but they stumped up. Not only did they agree a fee, but they decided to make prints of the finished work for exhibition in their branches and sale to the public with a royalty per print paid to me. The deal was struck and I went home a happy man, thinking, 'There you are Ron, in the right place at the right time again!'

Back home though, with time to think, I pondered on what I had let myself in for. I had promised the bank that I could deliver what was to be a very complicated picture with nearly twenty portrait heads, all to be good likenesses, together with the centre piece copied photograph. The picture would be done in my usual watercolour, a medium in which you're lucky to get any second chances. What would happen if I got to the last head and made a complete hash of it? I'd have to start the whole thing again. Choosing not to think such negative thoughts I polished up my brass neck and set to. It was August before the picture was finished and, at a ceremony at Head Office, presented to the Chairman of The Royal Bank of Scotland.

The Scotsman Group had the prints made, finally presenting them to the public. It sold very well, and everybody was happy apart from the teams who were beaten on Scotland's march to winning the trophy.

It looks as though we got a fright with Forth Street because, in the spring and autumn tours of 1982, we seem to have been guarding against over exposure in our strongholds of Edinburgh, Glasgow and Aberdeen. Our tour schedules remind me that we dropped a couple of nights in each of these cities. It could also be that we were still strong on television shows, because these take a lot of studio time to produce.

Attention to detail paid dividends in 1983 when we did a series for Scottish Television which won us a prestigious gold award in New York. Maybe it wasn't down to us alone though, because the series was called 'The Corries and Other Folk', and some of the other folk on the show were the world renowned flamenco guitarist, Paco de Lucia; our old friends The Clancy Brothers and Tommy Makem; an exciting group from Holland called Flairk; and, to crown everything, Lonnie Donegan, Roy's hero from college skiffle group days. I could never understand why I was allotted the task of doing the interview with Lonnie, given that Roy admired his work so much. Could it have been that he was over-awed? I wouldn't have thought Roy would be over-awed by anyone, but, maybe I didn't know him as well as I thought.

It was in the spring of 1983 that we went to visit Elvis, taking in Bryce Canyon, with its fierce red, yellow and ochre rock formations, the Grand Canyon and all points west to Las Vegas and Los Angeles. Then, in the company of our friends Mike Troup and his wife Carole, who came down from the north to pick us up, Pat, Lauren and I travelled in their big van to stay with them in their home in Washington State. This extended visit was possible only because The Corries had that year dropped the spring tour and extended the autumn effort to some fifty one venues.

One of these, the Dominion Cinema in London, organised by John Martin of Argyll Songs, gave rise to an amusing encounter with old friends.

The day after a solo show we returned in the afternoon to collect our gear. When we arrived at the car park, where we had left our mini-van, we found that we were blocked in by three huge lorries. Inside, as we walked towards our dressing-rooms of the night before, we passed on the stage a massive orchestra in the process of tuning up. Sitting at the front, to our surprise, were Finbar and Eddie Furey. With them were their other brothers, together now called simply The Fureys.

Fin and Eddie had signed with Phil Solomon, the man whose advances we had spurned all those years ago, and it was he who had produced their massive hit single 'Sweet Sixteen'. Now they were on tour because of its success, with full orchestral accompaniment. After some banter in front of their bewildered backing musicians, we managed to get Finbar to organise the release of our van to let us on our, what must now have seemed to them, solitary way.

When The Fureys had been guests earlier in the year on our 'Corries and Other Folk' show they arrived at STV with an entourage of managers, secretaries and publicists. At first they sat down beside us in the canteen, but soon moved further up the room, except for Eddie. In spite of having travelled the world with his music, Eddie never lost his Dublin accent. As we sat conversing, Fin shouted from the other end of the room, 'I hope ye's can oonderstaand him . . . 'cos we caan't.'

This is indicative of what sometimes happens when we become successful. The only time you see people who were old friends is in waving to each other in passing aeroplanes. However, my abiding memory of Finbar Furey will always be him sitting asleep, still strapped into his pipes, on a chair in the kitchen at West Buccleuch.

In the early spring of 1984, I was again busy with portraits. One of the sitters was folk singer Owen Hand, a great banjo-player, and we agreed that there would be no fee. Instead, after each sitting, Owen would simply pick up his banjo, which featured in the painting, and give me a lesson on the instrument. Strangely enough Owen's portrait, of all those I undertook, presented me with the most difficulty, and took many, many sittings before it was completed to my satisfaction. I did manage to learn quite a few riffs in the time he was with me though.

A painting of Lauren was accepted for exhibition at the Royal Society of Watercolourists show, marked 'Not For Sale', in spite of which I received three offers. I wasn't surprised, because it was very attractive with the masses of bright, primary colours of her clothing.

This was how Lauren went to school. As well as outlandish colour statements in her clothing she also had tints in her hair. To indicate her sense of humour, I painted her lying on her back on a grassy knoll smelling a flower. This was not a fragrant rose, but a dandelion. I told the three gentlemen who had expressed a desire to buy it that I had painted the picture for Lauren, and it would be more than my life was worth to sell it. However, I could paint something similar for them and, better still, or so I thought, personalise it to their satisfaction. I thought this would appeal to one of them in particular who wanted to purchase Lauren's portrait for his fiancé, but none took up my offer. Two things of note arose from the tour of '84. Suddenly we were doing three nights on the trot in St Andrews, at the Adam Smith Hall. They say that music goes round in twenty five year cycles. This year was only the twenty first since we started, but a new flush of students who hadn't been aware of us in their young lives were now filling this particular hall.

Secondly, during this tour, we reviewed our running order. We were still doing our usual mix of songs, but had begun to notice that the second half didn't go quite as well as the first. We always started off with 'Johnnie Lad', a song which most folk aficionados would describe as 'trite', but it was great for settling an audience.

At any show of whatever description, you'll always get latecomers who will unsettle the rest. Invariably they are positioned right in the middle of a row, and getting there causes the squeaking of uplifted seats, mutterings when a coat or a handbag is displaced, or interruption of a whispered conversation between two ladies who have just met after a long absence. There is no point in presenting what we might call one of our 'meatier' numbers in the face of such disturbance. So, give them something inconsequential to settle in with and Johnnie Lad is ideal. Singing the first three or four traditional verses, no one would worry if I even walked up the aisle to usher any real latecomers to their seats. It was all part of the fun of 'leading' an audience where you want it to go.

Having encouraged them to clap their hands, stamp their feet, 'jump up and doon on yer wee bums', and make as much noise as possible, I would suddenly shout, 'Shut up, . . . for the intellectual bit!' Whereupon we would sing verses we had written of topical content, from what was in the papers that day, or the latest political nonsense. Over applause, we then launched into one of our standards such as 'Killiecrankie', with a good, solid beat. A few words of greeting led to another standard, after which we would stop to take breath and give a more formal greeting.

To follow, we usually introduced a completely new song, with a description of why we had chosen to learn and sing it for them. In complete contrast, we would then do a 'funny', something like 'The Portree Kid', which is hilarious and never failed to get them laughing uproariously.

Now it was time for the real 'meat' of the first half where we would bring the chairs forward and take time to rearrange the mikes, with one of us talking intimately to a whole gang of people whom we had by now, we hoped, welded into one unit. This was when, probably, the combolins would come in with something like 'The Great Silkie of Sule Skerrie', lasting about ten minutes.

Following this: a real weepie like 'Green Fields of France', but one which was new to them, then maybe a sweet love song to bring them out of the sombre mood they had fallen into. All of a sudden we were on our feet again and straight into a 'funny', another couple of standards and, before they know it, it's half-time.

A look at their watch tells them they've just sat through fifty minutes of entertainment . . . but where did the time go?

If we had done our job properly, there would be no shifting about and hoping for the lights to go up so that they could get to the bar, but the interval was all the more welcome because of it. All of that was great for the first half and it was with shock that we discovered where we had been going wrong in the second.

For years we had been using the same pattern for the second half, and only now realised that it wasn't really for the best. What was wrong was that, after the interval, they had been in the theatre for more than ninety minutes, and the meaty stuff was too close to the end of their evening, when thoughts of buses started to enter their heads. 'Can't leave the baby-sitter too long with the kids', or, 'you know what happened the last time . . . we missed the ferry'. So, we brought the 'good' part of the second half closer by two or three songs to the beginning, just before these thoughts began to surface.

In giving them a longer second part to their second half, we assaulted them with the standards and the funnies, the clapping and stamping now filling their consciousness instead of more serious and sombre 'thinking' which we had been encouraging them to do. It didn't matter to us on stage if a few in the audience started to fiddle with car-keys, or coats, or looked in handbags to check bus and ferry times. This realisation of this and its implementation gave us a new lease of life, and the audience benefited too.

In January 1987, we went into the BBC studios for a week of recording, followed by the last two weeks in January and first in February on outside broadcasts all over Scotland, miming to our recorded work. We were filmed on fishing-boats in the most inclement of weather, which might have suited the old sea dog, Roy, but not me. On his own in a rowing-boat Roy made his way over Loch Tay, rowing to the strains of the Loch Tay Boat Song. In freezing fog in a farmyard near Elgin I tried to whistle Bogie's Bonnie Bell. One of the studio shots pictured me singing The Green Fields of France against inset shots of old film from the First World War, to telling effect. This new way of presenting us on the box seemed to find favour with a new television audience.

Our continuing successful tours of '85 - '88 saw extra nights again appearing in the cities. St Andrews gave us four nights in '87 and '88. In the autumn of 1989, those four in St Andrews became six. Back up to three nights each in Edinburgh, Glasgow and Aberdeen, we embarked on the most successful tour of our career, numbering sixty-three venues.

It's a crying shame that it proved to be our last.

Chapter Twenty Five

In 1984, we were burgled.

It was Saturday, the twenty-first day of a very hot July, and we had opened all the windows in the house while working inside and outside in the garden. Later in the evening Pat and I prepared to go out for a meal at our favourite Italian restaurant on West Preston Street, Pinnochio's, a tiny wee place run by Angelo and Isobelle.

I risk shattering the vision you might have of a television and concert star forever dining in large, plush, expensive joints, making a point of being seen and photographed for the gossip columns. That wasn't for us. Risking another hammer blow I must tell you that we went on to meet another three couples at the Conservative Club in Portobello, a far cry from Las Vegas. There we gathered in the bar and exchanged notes on each other's movements through the week. After a couple of drinks, Bill, Eric, Drew and I adjourned to the snooker table, leaving Margaret, Isobelle and Sheila to talk about us with Pat. Two or three games of snooker and another couple of drinks with the ladies, and we would leave the club and go on to, on this occasion, the Langhams' house.

That night of the twenty-first was no different to many others in that we arrived home at about three-thirty in the morning and went straight to bed. About four o'clock, I was wakened by the sound of our bedroom door opening. Not thinking too much of it in the first split second of awareness, I assumed it must be Gavin coming in a bit late after a pint of Guinness and mistaking our room for his. When I called out, the door slammed shut and footsteps clattered along the hall.

In the second split second, I was out of bed and on the run myself. Even though I sleep naked, no third second of awareness reminded me of that fact, and I continued my headlong chase down our main stairs, through the hall and into the lounge after a figure in grey tracksuit and trainers. The trainers disappeared through a half open window in one of the bays and it was only when I got to the window, and was about to clamber through, that I came to my senses. On his way out the villain had picked up a heavy brass candlestick, one of a pair which sat on either side of the windowsill, and was therefore armed. Also, I at last realised that I was barefoot and naked, a guise hardly suitable for haring through the respectable district of Wester Coates Gardens, particularly when the thief had outrun me and I had to return home through the streets.

Upon reflection, I'm amazed at how many seconds were split in the passing of just a few.

Pat's anguished call from upstairs brought me back from the window. She had been awakened by the commotion, and didn't know if it was me moving about downstairs, or if I was lying injured at the feet of a stranger. I gave a reassuring call, and proceeded to check through the house, to be met with the strange scenes of the burglar's botched efforts.

In the middle of the lounge floor was a small pile of valuables: a silver cigarette-lighter, two small silver vases from the mantelpiece, and other items which had taken his fancy. Pat's handbag lay open with its contents strewn around. We later discovered that he had taken the precaution of pocketing her bank and credit cards in case, as duly happened, he got away with nothing else. Looking on from the corner of the room, lying on his cushion, his large round eyes staring at me, was Jasper, Pat's recently acquired Pekinese dug. As I walked past to continue my inspection, I said, 'Ye're some guard dog, you!'

On the carpet in the hall was a large towel from the kitchen, and on it were laid out silver forks and knives and spoons. Little did he know that they were not solid silver, but only plated. At the bottom of the stairs were two steps and a small landing. From this a door led to my office/studio, and on the landing lay my electric typewriter and other small objects from my desk.

He had been into both Maurice's and Gavin's rooms upstairs and on a Victorian chair between the rooms, was a pile of used cheques from Gavin's room. Proceeding along the landing he had entered the bathroom. The sink taps and plug were of gold coloured material, but certainly not real gold. In a later, more thorough, search we discovered that he had forced the plug from its chain and pocketed it.

I've no doubt he opened the door of the next room, which was Lauren's bedroom. Thank goodness he had nothing but thieving in mind, because Lauren was lying there asleep, and the next room he tried was ours.

You might wonder about my recall of all of this, but I can assure you, when you've had the kind of fright we had that morning, you never forget.

When the police arrived, swiftly following my call, we discovered that the burglar had taken, as well as Pat's cards, her purse and cheque books and Lauren's purse. His *modus operandi* was, obviously to jog round a district during the kind of very hot day we had had, and to come back that night to try any open windows he had seen in the hope that they hadn't been locked again. We had missed one of ours before we went out.

In the age-old fashion of locking the gate after the horse has bolted, that afternoon we went to the dog home to try to get a dog, but were out of luck. Back home we telephoned people in Aberdour, and before the evening was out had acquired an Alsatian pup whom we called Tara.

A few months later, during the Edinburgh Festival, I was walking her in the front garden at 11.00 pm when I noticed a

Left: 'O.K. Roy, so it's a combolin! Now, do you really expect me to actually play it?'

Bottom: Lee, Roy and me at Eyemouth Harbour.

Above: I wonder if this was 'Killiecrankie'?

Left: 1991. My first solo publicity shot.

Top right: The Java St Andrew Society Ball, 1993. Pat, (purple gown), is led to the top table on the arm of the Canadian Ambassador.

Bottom left: 'My hero!' I wish.

JAVA ST. ANDREW SOCIETY
BOROBUDUR INTER.CONTINENTAL ON NOVEMBER 27TH,1993.

Left: Work in progress.

Above: The family. Standing, (l. to r.), Maurice, me and Gavin. Seated, (l. to r.), Kate, Maurice's wife, (divorced), holding their second, Michael, Lauren, holding Gavin's first, Rebecca, Pat, holding Maurice's first, Karlyn, and Michelle, Gavin's wife (heavily pregnant at the time with Jessica, their second). Confusing, isn't it.

Above: With Craig Brown in Vienna, 1996, for the world qualifier versus Austria, when the S.F.A chose 'Flower of Scotland' as their anthem for the first time.

Left: I know you'll never believe it, but Stephen beat me.

Top right: At a charity event with Brian Leishman, a real gentleman in the Rog Whittaker mould and business manager of the Edinburgh Military Tattoo for 25 years.

Bottom right: Pat and me with Prince Philip for the Duke of Edinburgh Awards.

Top left: Oliver Reid 'disrobes' in Peebles.

Bottom left: I sing 'Flower of Scotland' in 1998, at the Ross Bandstand with the Royal Scottish National Orchestra and Chorus, conducted by a very excited Jerzy Maksymiuk.

Above: 'Hey you wi' the Hong Kong tartan jacket, ye've had enough tae drink. Ye're gettin'
no more.'

Top left: Lauren with Paulo Nutini.

Bottom left: (l. to r.) Rebecca, Michelle, Gavin and Jessica.

Right top: Maurice with Karlyn and Michael.

Right bottom: Lauren with her 'Sunshine Project' children.

Left: The Black Douglas.

Above: Robert the Bruce in my car.

'And we'll all go together, to pull wild mountain thyme.'

Overleaf: Pat and me. Guess where?

young man skulking in the drive of our neighbour's house. I didn't like his body language and stood quietly behind one of our trees to watch through the railings. Eventually, he walked our way. I showed myself as he passed, making sure he saw Tara. I asked if I could help, at the same time calling Pat to the front door. He said he was looking for a party to which he had been invited, which sounded feasible. During the Festival parties abound all over the city. Just the same, when Pat came to the door, I asked her to call the police. I thought I had misjudged him when he didn't immediately take to his heels, but when the police arrived, again swiftly, and questioned him, the identity he gave led to a phone-call to Liverpool where it was found that he had form. Finally the police escorted him to Waverley Station and put him on a train, with the warning not to come back to Edinburgh.

These two incidents left a sour taste, particularly for Pat. Our children were now young adults and in the habit of staying out to all hours. Fine and to be expected, but it meant she was often on her own, with only the company of Mrs Mac her cleaning-lady for a couple of hours, and on many nights when I was away, in a huge and what now seemed a spooky place.

You know what's coming. Yes, in October we were on the move again. We would however be in the next place for twenty-two years.

The buildings on the odd-numbered side of Mayfield Road were terraced blocks of three flats per block. We went to look at number 131, comprising ground floor and basement, with garden back and front. On entering the large front lounge we were met with a tragi-comic scene. The previous owner had been an old lady living on her own with visiting carers and had left handwritten notes pinned on the walls. The one I remember most clearly said, 'Mrs Fulton, if the tray is empty, you've had your tea'. Attached to the back of the front door leading to the garden and the street, one read, 'Mrs Fulton, you really don't have to go out'.

To cut a long story short, on November 29th, the house was ours, but not before we discovered that, only two days after the burglary, a woman had tried to pass one of Pat's cheques at the Trustee Savings Bank. A vigilant employee quietly raised the alarm and kept her occupied until the police arrived. When she was apprehended, it was discovered that she was a known criminal. On July 30th another woman was caught in an off licence in Hammersmith trying to pass Pat's credit cards. Another time, the police waited in the foyer of a theatre in London to see what would happen when two seats in the stalls, taken from Pat's purse, were given to the commissionaire, but nobody turned up.

In August we had an alarm system fitted which connected directly to the police and Roy, who had also been made to think by our experience, did the same.

I was singing in St Albans on December 2nd when I learned that we had sold Wester Coates for £100,000, which was perhaps as well as we were already in the throes of work at Mayfield Road. Mrs Fulton had let the house go as she had progressed into old age and, sadly, dementia. We now tried to bring it up to date with damp course, a new kitchen and bathrooms, re-wiring and plumbing and, one which was new to me, asphalting of the whole floor throughout the basement. Pat and I didn't object to all this work because its sorry state was how we got the property for the low price of £41,555.

Towards the end of February, 1985, before we moved in, our sums told us that, with purchase price and legal fees totalling £45,000, clearance of our £25,000 mortgage, and nearly £25,000 refurbishment bills, we were left with a small sum, for the first time in what seemed a very long time.

After the fields of grass at West Buccleuch and the large, awkward garden at Wester Coates, I was determined to remove the bane of my life, the Flymo, from my existence. Therefore, the first big job I undertook on entry was to dig up the grass in the back garden and get rid of it, laying slabs in its place but leaving an earthen border for Pat's precious green fingers. Half of the front garden became a drive-in and the other half a large plot. A border beside the long path from the road meant she could keep roses growing from early spring to the end of autumn, mainly by regularly spreading liberal layers of chicken manure.

The Corries were now doing only one tour in the year. The revenue from that, and my portrait commissions, meant that we were again living comfortably and I had more time to enjoy family life. By the time of the 1989 tour Gavin had moved out, married Michelle and they were moving towards giving Pat and me two grandchildren, Rebecca and Jessica. Maurice had also flown the nest and married Kate and they would produce another two, Karlyn and Michael. Lauren, although not married, was surrounded by children at Watson's College where she had become a nursery nurse.

Having sung together for so many years, and having become used to highly successful appearances with, in the main, packed houses, The Corries had become just our job. Just our job, but I don't want to give the impression that we went to work with anything other than a completely professional approach in preparation, rehearsal, and execution; and if you ever attended one of our shows, I'm sure this must have shone through.

After work Roy and I reverted to being two Joe Soaps, just like normal guys in the street. I was painting as well, which was also a job, but I was engaged in ordinary things most of the time. When Pat did a piece of tapestry and wanted it stretched over a foot-stool, it was Joe Soap Ronnie who did the stretching. When slabs had to be laid it was Joe Soap Ronnie who laid them. Don't think for one minute that I objected to these domestic tasks, I was delighted to be there with the ability and desire.

That said, when something comes along to break what might be called 'normal', it's quite exciting, provided of course that nobody is hurt by it.

Lee, as our 'roadie', had certain tasks to perform, the main one being driving, getting us from point A to point B. He also helped Roy set up the sound, and placed the instruments on stage after they were tuned back stage. Whenever we could get home while on tour it was also his responsibility to take the instruments out of the bus and store them in his home, just about ten yards down his garden path. Unfortunately, the Hardengreen Social Club, Lee's local, was also just a few yards away.

One night, when we were particularly early in getting back to Edinburgh, Lee succumbed to the temptation of one wee drink and a chat to his pals before unpacking and storing the instruments. The inevitable happened. Someone who had probably 'cased' his habits, was around, the van was broken into and every instrument stolen, including the priceless, unique, combolins built by Roy.

When Lee got back to the van and discovered the theft, he immediately phoned me. His one wee drink with his pals must have extended to two or three because it was two thirty in the morning when he called. I was in no condition to hit the roof because I, too, had sampled a few wee drinks before going to bed, but I had to phone the police. It was suggested that I go early next morning to the station at the end of Mayfield Road, where nowadays stands the Braidburn Inn, and leave descriptions. This done, Roy and I frantically shopped around Edinburgh for replacements where possible, at the same time wondering what we could sing without our big guns, the combolins. After the next two nights' concerts I was again in bed when I received another late night call.

This one was neither from Lee nor the police, but from a man who was obviously a fence. In the most pleasant of tones, he told me that he was sorry he hadn't been able to get all of the instruments back, but that he had recovered the big green cases that housed the combolins and laid them in a back-green in the Craigmillar area, not far from Mayfield Road. Even the densest thief would realise that they couldn't possibly off load them, with only two in existence and associated with nobody but The Corries.

He explained that he was a fan, and was delighted to return them to us. In my excitement and relief, and it could also have been something to do with the wee drinks I had swallowed, I thanked him politely and asked his name. He showed remarkable presence of mind by saying, 'Oh! Ye're no' gonnie catch me that way, Ronnie'. I couldn't help but smile.

I put the phone down and called the police, saying that I was on my way to pick up the instruments. 'No! No!' I was told. 'Don't go on your own. Come down to the station and a couple of constables will go with you.'

This I did, and while we were on the way to the back green they explained what should have been obvious, that this could perhaps be a ruse to get me on my own and rob me. Of course, they were right. They also said that, when we arrived, I should look around carefully. I would probably notice that every curtain was slightly drawn to watch our progress towards the instruments. Again they were right. I told them that I would accept the responsibility of opening the cases lest they were booby-trapped. As it happened, they weren't, and I took the instruments home, thankfully undamaged.

To this day when I drive through Craigmillar I imagine some of the local villains smiling and saying to themselves and saying, 'Ah remember him, that guy fae The Corries.'

Chapter Twenty Six

1989 started well. We celebrated Pat's birthday by spending the weekend at the George V Hotel in Paris, and followed that a few months later with a holiday in Penang, having discovered the island a couple of years before. In an interesting talk with the manager of one of the jewellery shops in the Golden Sands Hotel, she suggested that, since we had visited for the last couple of years, we must be very rich. When we said this was not so, and that we had to save every year to come, she explained that if she saved all her life she couldn't afford to visit the United Kingdom. This was, and remains, a sobering thought, and speaks of the huge difference between the two halves of our world.

Another local man told us he was Christian, Muslim and also Buddhist. When we asked him to explain he told us he was hedging his bets.

That was the year I brought back some frames of tropical beetles, no longer possible since they have been declared an endangered species. The frames were sealed and contained a small bag of chemicals to preserve the samples. One was a Big Headed Jewel (*callopistus castelnaudi*), about one and a half inches long with emerald green, iridescent wings. Another, the White spotted Longhorn (*cerambycidae batocera*), was again green, but not iridescent, with white spots on its wings, the spots surrounded by black. The Green Banded Jewel, Single Horn Rhino and Three Horn Rhino were nothing compared to the Stag Rhino beetle with one small horn, and a huge one, sticking out the front of its head with small 'antlers' at the end.

One evening on holiday in the Gambia, we were dining in the open when Pat suddenly grasped my hand and gazed longingly into my eyes. She thought I was playing footsie with her until she looked under the table, there to see a Stag Rhino beetle slowly crawling over her foot. Passion was never more quickly dispersed with a scream.

So the year progressed until The Corries embarked on our autumn tour, our longest, and that proved to be the most financially successful. There was no hint of impending trouble until, during the last two nights, Roy experienced a sort of vertigo, staggering a bit on stage at the end of the two-hour show. It was very noticeable to me, if not to the audience, but we managed to finish the tour, go home, and wind up the business end in the usual way. After this we parted, planning to meet again the following autumn, which was our pattern. We did not live in each other's pockets. I put Roy's problem down to the additional stress of a longer tour, or possibly the glare of spotlights set too close to the front of the stage. It might have been caused by Roy's asthma as he did not usually use his spray when we were touring.

For whatever reason, I didn't pay too much heed. After a long time on the road we were both tired.

Our business procedure was to take a monthly salary, which meant a monthly session for the countersigning of cheques. I was surprised in early January, 1990, when Roy arrived at our home to say that he was suffering from dizziness and impaired vision, accompanied by pains in his head. He had come to suggest that we each take a lump sum in lieu of the next few months as a precaution against his possibly becoming worse and not being able to see to write.

His premonitions were proved correct when, on January 29th, 1990, he had an operation for the removal of a brain tumour. The operation seemed to have been successful as, immediately after coming round in the recovery room, he called for his guitar and fired off a series of complicated runs and riffs. His smile was large then, and he said that everything was all right after all. After the operation radio therapy was recommended, and Roy was admitted as an outpatient; in fact, he insisted on being an outpatient. I speak in ignorance of technical knowledge of the treatment procedure when I say that a plastic helmet was fabricated so that the radio beam would always land on the spot where the tumour had been, but possibly you get the idea.

As it happened, Pat's mother Violet was also in trouble. Advancing years had not stopped her from taking foreign jaunts, possibly they even whetted her appetite. She planned to embark on a holiday to what had become our favourite place in the world, the Golden Sands Hotel on Ferringay Beach, Penang, but only a couple of weeks before departure, stomach pains followed by tests meant she was summoned to the Western General Hospital. It was recommended that Pat be with her for the results. As Pat and Violet faced the surgeon, and he told her that she had bowel cancer, she exclaimed that that was something, since, on her last visit to Penang, a palmist had told her she would live until she was 96. Pat said, 'Well, Mum, you're going out there next week, you go and see the palmist and get your money back.'

The surgeon was flabbergasted, and asked if they understood the full import of what he had said. When Pat and her mother agreed that, because the holiday had already been paid in full, Violet would go to Penang and see him on her return, he gave an unbelieving shake of the head. They left the consulting room and went home to pack Violet's case.

She experienced no difficulties on holiday and, upon her return, became an outpatient at the Western General Hospital. When we told Roy he said that she would be fine since he would know when she was coming and would have a word with the nurses about coordinating their visits. As it happened, because of her age, Violet's outpatient visits became too stressful and she was admitted full time. So it came about that Violet took the reverse role of looking after Roy when he came in.

Soon afterwards, Roy elected to go home to Forres, where he died on August 12th, 1990.

Roy's death came as a shock to many. Less so, perhaps, to those of us who were close and knew how his cancer had travelled despite the treatment he had received. However it struck us though, the reality of loss had to be faced, as it does for all of us and probably several times in the course of any one life.

After he died I was asked to participate in a television tribute. What I had to say ran as follows.

'In cases like this you derive a great deal of comfort and help from your family and I'm no exception. My wife, Pat, said to me that, obviously, it is right to mourn his death but it's also right to . . . celebrate his life.

'I think that what we managed to do was capture the eternal essence of Scottish music and Scottishness. That is certainly what I felt, and I know Roy did too. I've given some thought to what Roy might like as his epitaph, and I'll go away back to the old days of Barney McKenna, the late Luke Kelly and the early days of the Fureys. I remember that it was once said to Roy, by Barney McKenna, that Roy had educated fingers. I think he would love that to be his epitaph, which in fact is true. He had very educated fingers. If we did capture the spirit of that age I am delighted, and I'm sure Roy would say the same.

'Although we created something unique we didn't see ourselves as superstars or anything like that, the big theatrical thing. We were very homely. We didn't analyse ourselves an awful lot because we thought that's dangerous. Henry Moore once was given a book by a psychologist, and I think he read the first two pages and it explained too deeply what his motivation was for creating the shapes he did, and he thought that, "Well, if I know why I do it I may not want to do it anymore." Roy and I were very much the same way, reason didn't come into it a lot. Obviously, we had to follow certain patterns, but the motivation was mainly feeling: feeling for the songs, the country, and the music. That was of prime importance to him.'

Violet, on the other hand, responded well to very powerful treatment, although the treatment itself nearly killed her. She recovered and years later died as a resident in care at the age of, yes, 96.

The 1990 Rugby Five Nations Championship was on the horizon when I was summoned to the offices of the Scottish Rugby Union to listen to a request which had come directly from the Scotland captain, David Sole, and his teammates.

Bill Hogg, then the secretary of the SRU, explained that for the past two seasons' internationals, the team had adopted the habit of singing, 'Flower of Scotland' under their breath when God Save The Queen was being played before kick-off. They had grown tired of this surreptitious practice and wanted FoS to be played as their anthem. Could they have permission to do so? I said that no permission was required and that both Roy and I would be over the moon if they went ahead.

Bill also told me that The Corries' recording of Flower of Scotland was always played on the bus taking the players from their hotel to Murrayfield, that it was timed to end just as the bus stopped inside the stadium and that the players sang along all the way. Since Roy was now in a much reduced condition at home, I took it on myself to agree that the first verse should certainly be played before the games as our anthem.

I phoned this news to Roy, and will leave it to your imagination to think what his reaction was. It was played for the first time ever as the Scottish National Anthem at the first game of the championship at Murrayfield against France. I'm told that Roy was well enough to watch on television and that he had a broad smile on his face.

Not long afterwards, I was again summoned to Bill Hogg's office where I was told that, two weeks after the French game, when we played Wales in Cardiff, David Sole and his team noticed that the Welsh anthem was twice as long as ours. What could we do about it? Again I had to take it on myself to decide whether to add the second or the third verse. I chose the third since its opening lines of 'Those days are past now, and in the past they must remain', have a more conciliatory feeling. Then again, when you think about it, what should a national anthem be but fiercely patriotic, especially sung at a rugby match where the combatants are steeling themselves to knock seven bells out of each other . . .'

At this point, let me make something clear. 'Flower of Scotland' is constantly criticised as being anti-English, but what could be more anti-Scottish than 'God Save The Queen' which we, as the Scottish nation, have been forced to sing over many years. Let me give you the words of one of that song's verses:

'God grant that Marshall Wade, may by thy mighty aid,
    victory bring.
May he sedition hush, and like a torrent rush,
Rebellious Scots to crush, God save the King.'

When FoS was aired during that Five Nations, it came under such fierce criticism that one of our most widely read national weekly newspapers conducted a poll naming other contenders for an anthem, songs such as, 'Scotland the Brave', and others which had been rolling around in the national collective psyche for a lot longer than FoS. The resulting 31% *in favour* of Roy's song was streets ahead of anything else.

Not long afterwards, Ernie Walker of the SFA announced that, at a forthcoming football international, Scotland's anthem would be 'Scotland the Brave'. Immediately, the editor got on the phone to ask Ernie if he hadn't read about the poll. What did Ernie think was going to happen when the band struck up 'Scotland the Brave'? The fans would be singing 'Flower of

257

Scotland'! To which Ernie replied, 'I don't know, because I'll be singing 'Flower of Scotland' as well.'

I have lost count of the number of songs that have been presented for the public to choose from, and the number of polls, but I can tell you that in every survey taken, over a twenty-four year period to date, 'Flower of Scotland' has come out on top by a wide margin.

'Flower of Scotland', in the form finally settled on for that momentous Grand Slam winning year of 1990, has now become accepted, the world over, as Scotland's national anthem. The memory of 'God Save The Queen', often sung reluctantly, frequently under protest, suggests a second meaning for Roy's words, 'Those days are past now'.

Thank you, Roy Williamson.

Chapter Twenty Seven

Saturday, March 17th, 1990 was one of the most exciting days of my life. Not just my life, but that of every other patriotic Scot, whether they follow the round or the oval ball. As our rugby boys sang their way into the Murrayfield stadium, they fired themselves up to face a super, but possibly over-confident, England team. Both had come through the Five Nations Championship defeating all before them to meet each other on this momentous day in what, for the first time in rugby history, was a Grand Slam in the true sense of the word. The Calcutta Cup, Triple Crown and Grand Slam were all at stake in this one match.

Excitement had built throughout the country, as what the result would mean dawned on even Scottish football supporters. When I say 'throughout the country', of course, I mean Scotland. Not so in England where, of course, the result was never thought to be in question. This would be just another steamroller win for a vastly superior England side. It was accepted that the Scots had done very well to have battled their way into this position but, alas for them, here was where it stopped.

Walking down Mayfield Road that morning I couldn't believe the sight of so many Scottish flags and so much bunting, hanging from what seemed like every window casement. My newsagent's shop was at the bottom of the hill, and my view carried on towards the city centre to where Mayfield Road joined Ratcliffe Terrace, and further on to Causewayside, an ocean of St Andrew's crosses and rampant lions and Scotland banners as far as the eye could see, which I knew would be the case throughout Edinburgh, and no doubt every other town in Scotland.

When Pat and I reached the stadium we entered an atmosphere, now widely documented by spectators, players and media alike, as something which none of us had experienced before, and none would again. That atmosphere mounted to fever pitch just before the start when, after the England team burst from the tunnel (to the usual very polite applause from the home crowd), the Scots didn't follow suit, but simply walked on, led by their captain David Sole, in the most menacing fashion you could imagine. As we saw this unfold before us, at first we fell silent, but then the stadium rose with a noise you wouldn't believe if you hadn't been there.

In a 2014 television programme celebrating the rise and rise of Flower of Scotland as the Scottish national anthem, the great Andy Irvine says that, after that walk-on and the subsequent manner of the singing of FoS by the team and their supporters, there was a feeling afoot that the English should certainly prepare themselves to be sent homeward to think again.

I won't rub it in by describing the game but I can tell you that afterwards in the Green Room, I sat beside Bill McLaren watching a run through. When we came to the Tony Stanger try, the score which settled the outcome, Bill wiped a tear from his eye and I marvelled once again at how this most patriotic of Scots could remain so unbiased in his commentaries. I had known Bill for some time because, in his role as rugby coach at a school in Hawick, he had been my son Maurice's rugby mentor during his Balcary years.

Somehow I wasn't surprised next day, even though it was Sunday, to receive a call from the Royal Bank, through their now SRU liaison man, Alwyn James, requesting another Grand Slam celebratory painting. Alwyn had taken the place of Mike

Keohane, who had arranged the 1984 painting, and he proved to be straight out of the Rog Whittaker mould, a mild-mannered, soft-spoken Welshman with whom I made an immediate bond. It was a bond strengthened through the following years until, at one point, he suggested that he become a ghost writer for these very words I'm now writing myself.

I arranged a meeting with Alwyn for the following Monday when we discussed the details of the proposed painting, which I had already given thought to on the Saturday night. It would have to include the Stanger try, but also a depiction of the try-saving tackle by Scott Hastings on Jeremy Guscott, with a centrepiece of David Sole leaving the pitch wearing the tartan tammie that had been thrust onto his head by an excited fan.

At the meeting we also discussed the print that would be made on completion of the painting. I explained that I thought it had been a mistake to sell the 1984 print as only a Scotsman reader offer and requested, to prove my point, that I produce and market the new print myself. He took my proposition to his superiors and we closed the deal with a letter of acceptance from the Bank which Alwyn delivered by hand.

Knowing how much work I had before me, I had no guilt feelings about letting down The Corries. It had become very obvious that, with Roy lying at home in Forres in worsening shape, there would be no tour that year. Nor indeed was touring likely in any subsequent year.

Speaking selfishly, here was an opportunity to take my mind off what I had started to think of as a doubtful singing future. Was this me, once again, being in the right place at the right time?

On March 27th, Roy visited although he was not doing at all well. Unable to sit up in the passenger seat of the Volvo, he sat in the back on a large beanbag to prevent him from lolling about. Such movement brought on dizzy fits and sickness. He stayed for only thirty minutes and felt so unwell that he was forced to leave. I got the feeling this might be the last time I saw him and, in my house, it was, although I did pay him a couple of visits at his home in Forres. The second of these was the last time I saw him alive.

It was with mixed feelings that I engrossed myself in the preparation of the painting.

Before I got properly down to it I had a visit from David Sole two weeks after the victory, with the request that I join the team in recording a single of FoS to be sold in aid of a Melrose rugby player paralysed through a rugby injury. I agreed and organised the recording in the STV studios in Edinburgh. All STV personnel volunteered their time off one Sunday to do the recording.

The players arrived, as you might expect, still in high spirits, and lined up for a team shot. The camera moved down the line to catch each player as it passed, but the boys only saw this as an excuse for a joke and every second player dropped out of sight as the camera moved along. Funny the first time, but the crew had to stop in the middle and start again. When the same thing happened, I could see that they were becoming a bit annoyed. Running on stage I demanded, forcefully, that they desist. I'm afraid that I may have used expletives. When I said that everybody was there in their own time to help them in their charitable endeavour Scott Hastings saw my point and took over until the job was done.

The recording was completed but not, unfortunately, to everyone's satisfaction. When it came to reducing their voices, under scrutiny, onto the master tape, it was found by the technicians that, although they might all have been dab hands with a rugby ball they were nae singers. I had deliberately taken a back-seat in the recording, not wishing to give the impression that I couldn't wait to start recording on my own. I may have been misguided in that. I therefore brought in Gavin and his friend Murray McKie to assist. We went into STV and they added their voices to the mix, the engineers 'dropping' them in at different places in the recording. The result was that we finally made a passable single which went to the shops. It didn't reach the top of the hit parade, but I hope it made a bit for their cause.

In the midst of all of this, and continuing talks with the BBC regarding more television series to be done when Roy was well again (we were still living in hope then), I started to photograph the players for the painting. We also set up a business exclusively to handle print sales when they eventually became available. We called the firm Mayfield Prints and put it in Pat's name.

On the same day that we received a cheque for £8,500 from a matured insurance policy, I received an order from the bank for 1150 prints, which we would call 'deluxe', to be printed on extra special paper and distributed to all their branches. This order meant that, even before I had started the painting, I was guaranteed the agreed fee, plus the profit on the order and any other sales accruing to Mayfield Prints from our own sales. I was confident of producing a successful picture and, since I was now working in oils, had no need to worry about any last minute mistakes. I was also confident that we would have sufficient money to embark on an adequate advertising campaign and at least give Mayfield Prints a good chance of success.

I worked on the painting through May and June, hearing from time to time about Roy's worsening condition. At one point, after he had been put on a course of morphine, he rallied from a very low period but, unfortunately, that didn't last and he lapsed again.

By the end of May, I was done. On June 4th, W. Gordon Smith came in with a photographer to do a piece on the painting for the following week's Scottish supplement of *The Observer*. What better publicity could we have?

On June 6th, my friend from schooldays, Bert Brown, came with his photographer from Alna Press to take shots for the printmaking and, next day, I was choosing from the transparencies. Two days later we ordered 5,000 cardboard tubes for the prints.

The Bank had already paid what they owed for their order and, on the day we received the VAT number for Mayfield Prints, delivered 980 labels for their internal distribution. In fair exchange, I delivered the framed picture to them at Head Office in St Andrew's Square.

From the day on June 21st, when boxes of canisters arrived, together with post office bags I had ordered, the house was a hive of industry. So much so that Lauren's friends all came in to help load, cap, label, seal and stamp the orders which had arrived after our first advertising shots. These amounted to, on the first day, 940 of our own orders and 300 for the bank. The bank would collect theirs, and a post office van would collect ours on the afternoon of Wednesday, June 27th. Pat's diary tells me that the first van that came was too small and another one had to be ordered.

At 12.30 pm on June 28th the painting was unveiled at the Bank and at 5.00 pm Pat, Lauren and I left for a holiday in the Gambia, where we received regular reports from Violet, whom we had left in charge of the assembly line. When we got back on July 21st, Gavin had just returned from the bank where he had deposited another £1,000 for that day's orders alone.

Sales did inevitably drop off, picking up again at Christmas and during the next Five Nations until, in spring of 1992, Pat wound up Mayfield Prints. She presented her books for inspection by the dreaded tax authorities who questioned very seriously how just one print could have generated so much money. Her book-keeping impressed them though, with the result that, when tax was duly paid, we found that we had cleared £37,000.

Chapter Twenty Eight

When Roy died on August 12th, 1990, so too did The Corries. The extremely strong image we created in the public mind lingered for some time and, to a certain extent, still does.

Not long after he died, BBC Enterprises produced a couple of commemorative Corries' videos which did very well at the box-office. My half-share of that, and the revenue from the tour of 1989, together with what I was earning from my prints and portrait commissions, meant I was in a very healthy financial position. Grand Slams are not won every year though, and images fade in time, so what was I to do for a job? I was still only fifty-three years old.

In the television tribute to Roy I made it clear that I would not be taking another singing partner. However, I did assume that perhaps my half share of what we had achieved might be enough to draw an audience. Although confident of my voice I have never been so in my instrumentation. What I had been doing on guitar, banjo, mandolin, moothie, combolins, etc, was all right behind the strength of Roy's musical lead. Never did I attempt to make myself his equal on instruments. Even assuming I could, it would be far too much like hard work. I am nothing if not practical though, and it seemed silly not to give solo performing a try.

My first foray into the blue was at a charity concert in the Caird Hall, Dundee, when I was invited to close the first half with a spot of about twenty minutes. Surely that would not be too taxing, and so it proved.

I don't remember the content of the whole twenty minutes, but I do remember starting with a medley of up-tempo Corries favourites, stringing together a couple of verses each of songs such as 'Killiecrankie', 'The Lass of Fyvie', 'The Lammas Tide', and probably a couple more. If you were at the show that night in late 1990, and I'm wrong I accept your judgement. Frankly, with it being my first ever solo stage appearance, I'm surprised I remember anything at all.

I might have been a bag of nerves, but Pat was worse. With the show being for charity, at the interval there was a bigger crowd than usual in the green room. I walked in to see Pat standing rigidly with her back to the wall and tears running down her cheeks. When I asked her what was wrong she told me that she was just overcome with seeing me out there on my own, having been for so many years used to the duo. I will confess to becoming a tad emotional too, but more with relief than anything else. We both recovered quickly and, when we got home, started to plan my solo career in earnest. Let me give you a couple of quotes from the newsletter we sent out in the summer of 1991, informing the public of my forthcoming Autumn, 1991 tour.

'Dear People,

Here I am, bothering you again. Of course, you've only yourselves to blame for making this year's shortened spring tour a huge success. A huge success it most certainly was, and, early on, I took the opportunity to gauge reaction, to which I responded by starting to book these autumn dates.

The tour itself is somewhat spread, this being due to the decision only a few months ago to obtain dates, but this seemed to me to be the best opportunity to get back to an annual autumn tour, which is my intention.

You will notice from the list that I'll be in the Glasgow Royal Concert Hall three times during the tour. November 6th is my solo concert, the other two just being short spots of about two or three songs apiece. The appearance with the City of Glasgow Philharmonic Orchestra in September should be interesting, with two of my songs in the spot being fully orchestrated.

The Aberdeen date in His Majesty's happens by chance to fall on Burns' Night, so BBC Television (Scotland) plan to come in and take 30 minutes of the show and transmit it live. The 8.30 start is there to accommodate the BBC. His Majesty's Theatre Club members are allowed to book for shows one week earlier than the public, but if you show this list, you can also take advantage of that facility. Theatre Club booking opens on September 30th.

Following my live TV broadcast from Aberdeen in January, I'll be recording a television series in the spring of 1972 for transmission in the autumn. It'll be a series of six half-hours with myself and guests. I'm looking forward to that.

Right, I'm off to learn some new songs, and brush up on some old ones, so it looks as if it's now very much . . . business as usual.

I thank you for your continued support and . . . I'll see you on the night.'

My thanks for their continued support was a bit of an understatement. I was more than grateful. I think my first solo appearances relied heavily on the public's sympathy but, having continued, I hope that I was actually entertaining them as much as Roy and I had done in the past.

Whatever the reason for the full houses and truly fantastic reception I received, it just went on and on. My confidence was boosted by the fact that Pat was now my 'roadie', as her presence and undying support were invaluable. I found very quickly that, after performing with Roy on stage for so long, doing it on my own was more than twice as difficult. In a two hour solo concert, I didn't have a moment's respite. With two of you there, it's easier to hold an audience's attention, particularly in the breaks between songs. Taking turns with your stage companion speaking during these breaks gives you the chance to take a breather and think, 'What's next?' Without that presence you have to be careful to take time for an extra breath or another thought. A whole new way of pacing is required.

It's only in reading through Pat's diaries for this book that I realise how close I came to losing her support. She had taken over Lee's job of placing the instruments on stage, which was fine where there was a stage front tab. In a lot of the smaller venues though, such as Cumbernauld Village Theatre, she had to walk on in full view of the audience, which she felt nervous about doing in the early days.

On the night our grand-daughter, Rebecca, was born, I announced quietly in the first half that Pat had become a grandmother. She was unaware that I had done so and, when she walked on-stage with the instruments for the second half, she was met with a fantastic shout, much applause and good humoured 'grannie' comments. In her diary she says, 'I could have strangled that bastard'.

Proceeding in the same professional manner as The Corries, Pat bought some clothes and shoes to use in her stage appearances with the instruments. They were used for nothing else, but when she presented the receipts in our accounts the tax man wouldn't allow them, not believing that they were used for that sole purpose. She argued to no avail. Inland Revenue was adamant and refused to budge.

They have a strange way of thinking, these people. We bought a beautiful antique couch for the window of the lounge, and when we claimed it as a prop for the portrait-painting, it was allowed.

My 1993 autumn tour newsletter, describes what I was up to between times.

'Hello folks,
Sorry I'm a bit late with this leaflet, but I've been very busy since we last met. What with Burns' Suppers, after-dinner

speeches, cabaret appearances and, och aye, singing for the World Boxing Championship aficionados, I've hardly had time to turn around. As well as all this, I've been in America and Canada for the first time in 17 years, appearing at the Boston Celtic Festival, then on to Philadelphia and Virginia, and then out to Vancouver and Vancouver Island.

My first ever solo concert in Canada was promoted by The Vancouver Moray, Nairn and Banff Association who had this to say in their newsletter after the show . . .

'Like a good malt whisky, the maturing process has mellowed and smoothed out his voice and performance to give us a unique product with a distinct flavour all of its own.' (Isla Robertson, President.)'

Because Pat and I were now so together in this endeavour, our life had become a sort of holiday.

Chapter Twenty Nine

Lauren was still at Broughton School when she expressed a desire to meet Hercules the Bear.

Having met Andy Robin at some engagement or other I chanced my arm by phoning him at his base at Sheriffmuir Inn, where he was living with his wife Maggie and their 'son,' Herc.

When Pat and I, Lauren and Lauren's friend, Pauline McDonald, presented ourselves at the door of the Inn Andy answered and, after a hand-shake that nearly broke every bone in my hand, showed us into the kitchen to see Hercules for the first time. What a sight he was, this huge grizzly, seated upright on a reinforced bench at the kitchen table. This would have been strange enough, but sitting on his knee was Maggie Robin with a tin of Heinz beans in her left hand and a spoon in the other, telling him to be 'nice' and to be a good boy when he was eating. Herc was having none of that. He spurned the spoon and reached right into the can with the claws of one paw, while the other paw was placed, unbelievably, round Maggie's waist. So, this was what one of the most ferocious animals known to Man did between mauling lumberjacks and terrorising the whole of the Canadian populace.

Andy and Maggie Robin's life with Hercules the Bear is well documented. They first bought him as a cub for £50, and their relationship with him developed over some twenty five years until he was an international star.

Andy that day explained that Hercules was no 'Performing

Bear,' but simply a big, daft laddie who enjoyed playing and wrestling with one of Scotland's champion professional wrestlers, Andy Robin himself.

In the early days of their life together, in the hills around Sheriffmuir Inn, the bear was muzzled for Andy's safety until, one day on an exercising run, Andy stumbled while jumping a stream and fell into the water, knocking himself unconscious. He came to on his back with Herc trying to lick his face through the muzzle, having obviously pulled Andy out of the water and dragged him onto dry land. As Andy gradually regained his senses, he realised that this was no wild beast trying to eat him, but a friend trying to save him. He vowed then, in the recumbent, vulnerable position he found himself, that Hercules would never again wear a muzzle, nor would he ever remove the bear's claws, as he had been advised. Witness to this are the many scars on his body from accidental scratches received in play with his pal.

Andy laughed out loud as he told me of the day, many years after that decision had been taken and Hercules had become a star, that he suffered a visit from an income tax inspector who was incredulous, and a tad suspicious, at the bear's financial success.

They were still at Sheriffmuir when the tax-man called. He was politely shown into the kitchen and, coffee in hand, taken upstairs to the family lounge and seated on a bench in front of a large open fireplace. Andy excused himself to go and get some logs. Now, when Andy goes for logs, he doesn't hang about. Not for him the small net bags purchased at the local garage, but huge limbs wrenched from the surrounding trees. As the flames began to rise, Andy excused himself again, suggesting that the man might like to meet Hercules face to face. As Mr Taxman sipped his coffee, after a few minutes, he became aware of a dark shape approaching his bench. Andy had deliberately sent Herc into the room on his own, to approach his favourite seat in front of the fire and plonk himself down beside the unsuspecting inspector. The reaction was exactly what you would expect. The gentleman gave a couple of nervous coughs and told Andy that everything seemed fine and that he would be hearing from him in due course.

I next met Hercules in Edinburgh when he and Andy were putting on one of their wrestling shows in their large ring erected in the car-park outside Meadowbank Stadium.

I missed the show, but went to the Robins' huge tour bus for a cup of coffee. It was the first time I had seen the bus and it was certainly very impressive with all mod-cons and conveniences. Seating myself in an easy chair with a curtain behind it, I asked after Hercs' health and Andy, in his usual jocular fashion, suggested I see for myself and pulled a tab to open the curtain. There was Herc behind a wall of thick iron bars, his snout poking through the gaps not a foot from my face. The bus was rigged to take the whole family, with Andy and Maggie's living quarters cheek by jowl with Herc's. Why was I surprised? This, after all, was family.

We got to know this family quite well over the years. After they moved from Sheriffmuir to their Great Bear Ranch, near Gleneagles Hotel, Maggie opened a shop in Auchterarder selling choice ladies' clothing. Pat bought some of the smart dresses Maggie specialised in and, at one point, I bought a few choice pieces myself. One suit in particular proved worth its weight in gold when Maggie asked me to compere one of her annual Charity Fashion Parades in the Hotel. It was a creation by designer Alexander McQueen, single-breasted in a grey tweed. What made it special was the one-inch yellow stripe that was set into the middle of the shoulder pads and ran right down the sides of the sleeves to finish at the cuff. The same yellow band ran down the side of only one trouser-leg. Very fancy, very expensive, but just right for that occasion. Now that I come to think of it, I'm still waiting for another such special occasion to wear the bloody thing again.

I have another jacket, this one by Moschino, which I bought

in Jenners of Princes Street, and it is often the source of some amusement. It's covered in cartoon characters in the brightest of primary colours and could by no means be called 'camouflage'. At a reception during the Edinburgh Festival of 2013, I wore it and managed to raise a few smiles without even opening my mouth. At that reception, the Kinloch Andersons, Scotland's premier tartan manufacturers, were displaying Mrs Anderson's latest book illustrating every tartan in the world. I flipped through it quickly and surprised her by saying that she didn't have my jacket design in its pages, because mine was made from Hong Kong Tartan. She disdainfully replied that there was no such thing as a Hong Kong Tartan. Therefore, just to tease her, I launched into a completely fictitious story about the jacket's origin, which goes as follows:

On a visit to Stanley Market in Hong Kong when I was there for a St Andrew's Night Ball, I asked a local Chinese tailor if he could make me a tartan jacket as quickly as possible. 'Tatan?' he questioned, 'I not know tatan. Wha' is tatan?' I told him it was a cloth with bright patches of colour and lines going up and down all over it. 'Ah, So!' he said with a delighted smile, 'Ah so! I ha' tatan'. And he rushed into his back shop and brought out the cloth with the cartoon characters all over it. And there I had my jacket.

Mrs Kinloch Anderson wasn't amused.

If you ever find yourself in Stanley Market and somebody tells you not to buy one of the many silk shirts at £1 a shot you'll find on sale there, because they'll fall apart in a couple of weeks, don't believe a word. I bought a whole bunch and they lasted for twenty years.

Many years ago, on a visit to Bangkok, on the concourse of our hotel, a tailor's shop advertised two suits (made to measure), two pairs of trousers, two shirts, a belt and a tie, all for £50. Nothing ventured, nothing gained; I popped in to speak to the proprietor, saying that I would be delighted to take up his offer but we were leaving in a couple of days. No matter, he said, he could fulfil the order in that time. I duly underwent the measurement process and asked what material would be used. He nodded towards shelves and shelves of cloth and asked me to choose, promising to deliver to my room the next night in time to be packed and ready for our departure the next day. Not really believing him, I left him to his work. If he didn't turn up in time, it was worth £50 for another holiday anecdote. Needless to say, I did get them and, like my Hong Kong bargains, wore them many times over the years. Great value, and to be recommended.

All a far cry from The Great Bear Ranch of course.

The Great Bear Ranch is the last place I saw Hercules alive, at a party in the lounge. Pat and I had driven up through snow to join him and his guests and had embarrassingly run off the road on our approach to the Ranch, having to be dug out by some of the other guests before the party proper got underway.

There were many people present, all impatient to meet Herc, the star of the evening. I had my cine-camera and started filming as Andy slid open the glass doors of the lounge to go and rouse the big boy from his den, positioning myself at the other side of Herc's swimming pool, immediately outside the party-room. As Andy came out, he turned to his right and walked up the side of the pool to where Herc's 'hoose' was. As he slid open the heavy iron-barred gate, he shouted, 'Okay Hercy, get up off yer arse, ya old bugger. It's party time!' A few minutes later, Herc emerged and lumbered after his pal, catching up with him just as he opened the glass doors to make a grand entrance together.

By the time I got back inside, Herc was the unrivalled centre of attention, in the middle of a whole gang of incredulous, many of them nervous, humans. He was sitting on the floor with Andy astride his shoulders, left hand clutching the thick hairs of Herc's neck, his right hand high in the air, holding a stetson hat, very much in a sort of 'ride 'em cowboy' pose.

When he was asked how safe it was to be in this wild beast's presence, Andy would reply that there was no danger as long as he or Maggie was present. Otherwise, be prepared to run a very long way, and fast.

As if to prove the point, Pat took up a position on the carpet at Herc's feet. His huge head was inclined down towards her face and I like to think he was saying to her, 'What de ye think o' this silly bugger on my back?' As they transferred thoughts, I panned my camera down to film a close-up of Pat's hand gently sliding over the rough, hairy paw of Hercules the Bear. As she curled her fingers round his claws, he responded with a slight turn of his hand to allow her to do so, a gesture which meant, 'You are all right, dear.'

Pat and I felt truly privileged to be so close to one of a unique love story.

Chapter Thirty

'What's it like to stand up there and sing in front of all those people?' has been an oft-asked question throughout my long career. I can't speak for any other performer, only repeat: for me it was a job. Not so when I was singing Josef Locke's 'Hear my song, Violetta' as a daft wee scout in the annual troop concert. That was just something we did as part of the year's events and we all mucked in together. Perhaps that experience, however, prepared me for when I first appeared as one of the Corrie Folk Trio and Paddie Bell at the Tryst Coffee House in 1962 when I took on the job to earn a few extra pounds. Not one of us gave any thought to the possibility of that three week engagement extending into a lifelong career.

So, I'm standing in front of all those people, but how many actually constitute 'all those people,' and how do I handle their presence?

Let's go back to the smallest audience I ever sang to which, undoubtedly, was the eight people on that first night at the Tryst, but let's say Roy, Bill and Paddie aren't there. On my own, looking at their expectant faces and singing away to my heart's content, I can see and gauge their reactions to every word at a forward glance with the use of minimal peripheral vision. If you multiply eight to eighty, that number of bodies inevitably spreads outwards so that, to make eye contact with them all in turn, I have to start looking to the sides and to the front. Keep adding bodies and I have to make more movements if I am to look at them and keep in touch with them all. Now, think of a large theatre where they are more widely spread in the stalls, but they are also in the circle and the gods and my movements are no longer only side to side, but also up to the heavens. I believe this is called 'quartering' an audience.

(A detail of the process of 'quartering,' especially when Roy would take a verse of 'Johnnie Lad' as our first song, would be my scanning of the complimentary seats. If any were empty, I would have a pretty good idea who hadn't come and made a mental note to take them off the comps list. And you thought I wasn't watching!)

Now, that's all fine, even in the biggest theatres where everybody has paid to see only me in solo concert and I have to assume that they are all looking in my direction (in, what I would hope to be, rapt attention). So, what happens when I find myself in a stadium, standing on a pitch and surrounded by upwards of 50,000 football or rugby fans who aren't there to hear two hours of singing?

In my first experiences of this situation, I did my sound checks and stood between two monitors on the ground with a microphone rooted to a spot in front of me and 'quartered' only the stand in front of me. After many such experiences, and having watched television playbacks, I became aware that I wasn't singing to all of my audience. Most of them were seeing either only my back, or one of my sides. I therefore adopted the practice of using a hand-held microphone and, while singing, moved from my central spot and walked round in a small circle to take in all sides of the stands and terraces. If you like, a much more vast 'quartering'.

Such a movement away from the monitors made a bit of a nonsense of my sound checks in the empty stadium earlier in the day. At first I worried about that, but then realised that as soon as the opening strains were heard, 50,000 voices took over. I was not there as the singer, Ronnie Browne, but as the embodiment of The Corries, who had become deeply embedded in their psyche. Did I mind that? Not one jot. Had I not been half of that and was I not lucky enough to be there feeling the utmost pride in leading them?

Now, when you ask me the question, 'What's it like to stand up and sing in front of all those people?' maybe you'll appreciate my answer: 'Bloody hard work!'

With the technicalities of the performances explained and out of the way, I'd like to relate a few anecdotes.

The first appearance I made to sing for the Scottish rugby team at Murrayfield was March 1st, 1997, in a game against Ireland. I did my usual sound-checks at about 12.30 pm, before the crowd started to come in, and eventually led the anthem and returned to my seat in the stand behind the Royal Box.

Not wishing to risk my voice by partaking of the complimentary pre-match lunch in the President's Suite, Pat had prepared a flask of soup for me to have after singing. I decided to wait until half-time to do so.

Callum Entwhistle was a police detective, first encountered in the Dalkeith area when we had the instruments stolen at Lee's house in Eskbank. By March 1st, 1997, he had been elevated to the security squad guarding Princess Anne at her numerous Murrayfield appearances and he was on duty that day.

When half-time arrived we all stood up to stretch our legs. Even the members of the Royal Family can become stiff watching a game, and the occupants of the Royal Box joined the rest of us. At that point, the princess's security team sprang into action. Only then do you realise just how many there are as they stand to attention, usually with hands crossed in front of them, ranged on all sides of the Princess and, with their backs to her, scanning the surrounding crowd.

At that point I took my soup flask from my overcoat inside pocket. Made from aluminium it looked for all the world like a mortar shell. Callum, standing not far from me, saw the glint in my hand as I unscrewed the cap and, instinctively, his hand dived inside his jacket. I noticed his movement and realised what was happening, while at the same time wondering what kind of weapon he had concealed in there. The incident was over in a flash as he simultaneously recognised me and understood the situation, his hand slowly returning to the clasped position. I consumed my soup and put the flask away, thinking no more about it as we watched the rest of the game, which we won 38-10.

As I preened myself, thinking that my singing possibly had been a contributory factor, the Royal party, together with the Union Presidential party, made their way downstairs into the President's Suite for the official dinner. We all dutifully waited before we followed. On my way inside I noticed that Callum had taken up a stance against the wall on the right. As I walked past him I suddenly felt a steely hand grasping my collar-bone through my coat. Immediately, I remembered the flask incident and closed my eyes, imagining myself on the way to the Tower of London, accused of attempted assassination. Half-way through the thought, Callum whispered quietly in my ear, 'England 20, France 23. Ya Beauty!' In the same movement that he gave me the score from the afternoon's other game, he was back on duty against the wall.

There was an incident at another game in which I was involved with both Callum and the princess.

I had taken the trouble to change out of my kilt after singing. The match was over and so too was the official dinner. The tables were clearing and we were all milling about the Presidential Suite, socialising. It is usual practice for the princess to have her meal in an ante-room off the suite and be entertained with some other VIPs, and her party must leave the premises before the rest of us can depart. I was deep in conversation with Mr Jinkie himself, Jim Renwick of Hawick, with my back to the ante-room when, unaware that the princess was making her way to the exit, I suddenly broke off our conversation, whirled round and banged into her. Again, Callum was on hand to apprehend me when Princess Anne, completely unabashed, exclaimed, 'Oh my gosh, it's our singer,' and extended her hand in greeting. This stopped Callum in his tracks. He stepped back, gave me one of those brows down, quizzical, looks, and removed his hand from inside his jacket. I took the opportunity to thank Her Royal Highness for always singing Flower so well and so vociferously, thereby helping its acceptance as the anthem. She said not at all, it was a marvellous song, and keep up the good work, and then floated on her way.

We've all heard of the big business deals that are concluded on the nineteenth hole. The SRU President's Suite is similar. It can be a hive of business brains.

My son Gavin created the official Corries website, www. corries.com, in the early 1990s and runs it with the utmost precision. As an off-shoot, he owns another couple of companies which deal in tourists' souvenir goods. His partner in one of these is Mike Graham who, at one time, was the Scottish representative for Gilbert Rugby Balls, a splinter company of Gray's of Cambridge. Through Gavin and Mike, I did a deal for CML where I licensed the words of Flower of Scotland to be printed on the side of small souvenir Gilbert balls. As a result, I was invited to one of the Scotland Internationals at Murrayfield by Richard Gray, one of the family owners of the company.

Sitting at the dinner table after the game I noticed at the table beside us, David Murray of what was at the time Murray International Metals, now formerly of Rangers. He was in the company of Alex Salmond, now a former First Minister of Scotland, and a few more bigwigs. Richard was intrigued when I told him that I knew David of old and said that he would be delighted to meet him. We sidled over to David's table and I leant forward and said, 'Hi David, I've a feeling you might like to meet this man. You happen to have balls in common.' He was slightly mystified until I explained that he had the round ball and Richard had the oval one, adding,

'You see, this is Richard Gray from Gray's of Cambridge, who is also Gilbert Rugby Balls.' David leapt up and exclaimed, 'You're joking, how many of these do you sell in a year?' 'Oh, probably hundreds of thousands worldwide,' says Richard. 'How much do you charge for them?' asked David. '£70 each for match balls,' replied Richard. 'Hey,' says David, 'That's some business to be. . . .' At that point he stopped in his tracks, extended his hand and said, 'I'm David Murray, by the way. How d'you do?'

Business always comes first.

A pleasant interlude for Pat and me occurred on August 12th, 2002 at the Edinburgh Book Festival. This was not from my singing of Flower, but from the author Diana Gabaldon's use of it in one of her famous Outlander series of novels. She had applied for a CML licence to publish the words and, when she was booked for the Festival, knowing that I lived in Edinburgh, invited us to attend her appearance. When I told Diana that a friend of Lauren's, Kath Grandison, was her biggest fan, she suggested that maybe she would like to come along as well. Kath was so excited when I told her who she was going to meet that she was thrilled. When I followed up by saying that she would also have dinner with Diana, she couldn't believe it. When Diana rounded off the evening with us at home for coffee and drinks, and she actually sat on the same couch as her heroine, she was beside herself.

Here, in Diana Gabaldon, was another internationally famous personage in the Rog Whittaker mould. She displayed grace and charm from the moment we met, and all of us who were in her company that day are delighted at her continued success with her worldwide television series.

Between the years of 2007 and 2009, I sang for the Scottish Football Association twelve times consecutively at Hampden internationals and once at Pittodrie.

Colin Spence, the son of our sound man, the late Allan

Spence, ran the Events company in charge of organising these games. You might think that my being invited to sing so many times hints at some kind of insider dealing. Not so. My performances were requested especially by the Tartan Army who, it seems, wanted no other singer to lead them. I can't brush over that statement without saying how proud I feel to this day to have been so favoured. Most singers would give their eye teeth to find themselves in the position of singing an anthem just once in their career. How, then, do you think I feel at having done it so many times?

My contracts with the SFA illustrate their exquisite professionalism in their handling of guests invited to Hampden Park. Not only was I given a generous fee for my performance, but I was also allowed to invite six friends, in addition to Pat and Allan Spence who came with me to supervise sound, to enjoy each and every one of the games. I am eternally grateful to Scottish Football for this.

On the day of a game, Pat and I would probably take a couple of passengers with us to Glasgow in our car, the rest making their own way. We would congregate in the car park, our spaces reserved immediately in front of the steps leading up to the front doors. We would enter as one group and be met at the main reception desk by Colin's team. As I was led straight out to the pitch for a sound check with Allan, my guests were taken into the building and shown into a private suite where champagne was served by two waiters who were there at our disposal. When I came up to join them, lunch would be served. As I was called downstairs for the start of the match, a curtain opened behind the dining table to reveal a private box where my excited guests sat down to watch me go to work. The singing over, I would repair again to our room, change from the kilt, and join my friends to enjoy the match.

At half time, glasses were re-charged and coffee provided, and the traditional Scottish football half-time repast of meat pies was served. When the game was over we were invited to stay in the room for at least an hour, again with a couple of drinks on hand, to await the clearing of the supporters and the roads, before making for our transport. So, keeping that pattern of events in mind, you will see how I was able to repay some personal favours done me by family and business friends alike.

In the first few games in the sequence I accommodated the full circle of my family in turn. They all enjoyed the experience, but throughout the years had perhaps become used to unusual settings like the Green Room of the Usher Hall, or the control room of BBC Television, or a reception on the Royal Yacht *Britannia*. Not so people like my roofer Stewart, who has kept me warm and dry in the many homes he has looked after, or my postman, Kenny, who was the talk of his sorting office when he appeared for work on the Monday after his 'turn'.

Dave Clemenson, as the then IT director of Wiseman Dairies, who was well used to hospitality suites, marvelled at the SFA's attention to detail when I invited him along in small return for his allowing us the use of his holiday flat in Nice.

On a personal note, we were all flabbergasted on August 20th, 2008, at the game against Northern Ireland, when we sat down to lunch. It was my 71st birthday. The door opened and a cake was brought in aflame with candles, maybe not quite seventy one of them, but enough to heat up the room. I was presented with a bottle of Highland Park, two crystal glasses and a signed, framed international jersey. Before I sang, my birthday was announced over the public address system. I don't know if you've ever heard 60,000 voices singing, 'Happy Birthday to you,' but I can assure you that it's quite stunning to be on the receiving end.

Chapter Thirty One

My grandson, Michael, is a gifted footballer and an avid Scotland supporter. He was only sixteen years of age the day he arrived at Hampden with us. I allowed arrangements to proceed as normal until I was on my way to the pitch when, as the rest of the party was led upstairs, I called Michael back and said he could possibly be of assistance to me. We threaded our way through the maze of corridors in the bowels of the stadium, passed innumerable security men, officials and even one or two of the squad as they prepared for the game. Michael's eyes opened in wonderment as recognition dawned and, when we finally stepped onto the hallowed turf, could hardly contain himself with excitement. I could just imagine him saying to himself, 'One day, I'll be playing here'.

As if it wasn't enough to be allowed by the groundsmen to actually walk on the pitch, (these guys are notoriously protective), suddenly he was surrounded by a couple of linesmen, two or three of our hosts from Colin Spence's firm and a few others, all of whom engaged him in football banter as if he was Ally McCoist himself. I remember that sight with gratitude. Here was a young man, not being ignored by these important people, but completely accepted and welcomed as 'one of the boys'. Mentioning Ally McCoist reminds me . . .

My early association with the SFA brought an invitation to a home international game. As usual, the invitation was extended not just to Pat and me, but allowed for us to bring two other companions. My daughter, Lauren, had a couple of school friends, Carolyn and Clark Ballantyne, who eventually married and named their first girl after Lauren. They have remained close friends since schooldays and, indeed, have holidayed with us in our property in Luxor.

The Ballantynes also have a son called Alex. Now, Clark is intoxicated with the whole atmosphere of football and football stadiums, the smell of the grass, the gathering spectators, the warm-up preparations. Anticipating 'like father, like son,' I thought that they would be ideal candidates for the two extra seats.

As we sat in the centre stand, I could see the smiles on both their faces grow wider and wider as the kick-off approached until, just before the whistle blew, the two empty seats next to young Alex filled with none other than Ally McCoist and his own young son, who was probably of an age with Alex. Having been to Austria with Ally in '96, we exchanged greetings as he took his seat. He was sitting right beside Alex and, to the wee boys' amazement, he was actually touching thighs with his footballing hero. He dug his father in the ribs and, in silent mouthing, said, 'D'ye see who that is?' and gave a wee point with his finger. I noticed his excitement and stretched over to ask Ally if he would say hello to my friends. Of course, it was no bother and hands were shaken. For the whole of the match, the four of them exchanged shouts of encouragement, or boos of dissent, as the case may have been, and I know that Clark and Alex have never forgotten the grace and charm of this sporting legend.

Another offshoot of these appearances was being requested, this time by the Tartan Army Club, to sing for them in a Glasgow pub before their departure by train to Paris for an international. The date was September 10th, 2007. To be surrounded by the fans in a stadium, separated from them by many yards of space, is entirely different to being squeezed like a sardine in their midst in a pub. Their enthusiasm was boundless, and to have my hand shaken almost without pause (there's a pun in there somewhere), to see tears in the eyes of men who have been brought up with Corries' songs and loved them, and to be crushed to death in the warmest of embraces, is a remarkable experience. Being the object of such unabashed affection and admiration makes me one of the luckiest men in the world and you have my assurance that I fully appreciate every manifestation of it I encounter.

My last singing for the SFA was at the Netherlands game at Hampden on September 9th, 2009. It could not have been in sharper contrast to my next engagement ten days later when I found myself doing the anthem at the final of the Scottish Shinty Championships in Oban.

The Hampden audience of well-nigh sixty thousand had shrunk to less than one thousand, congregated around a small football pitch in the town. What made matters awkward was the fact that I was required to sing with my back to the fans, but facing the television cameras, so that the audience I had to sing to was the invisible one sitting in the comfort of their armchairs at home. Earlier in the afternoon, I had spoken in the stand to that ace accordionist and musician, Phil Cunningham. He has many hobbies, one unusual one being the recording of bird-song, but that day he was engaged in photography. He was tinkering with the preparation of his zoom cameras for the photographing of the shinty, and, as I sang, I visualised him practising his notorious sense of humour by taking close-ups of my bum in its swaying kilt.

My penultimate performance of Flower of Scotland took place twelve days later at the Scottish/Irish Shinty/Hurling international on October 31st, 2009, in Inverness. It was the same set-up as Oban and awkward to undertake for the same reasons.

This brings me to what I think will be the very last time I will ever perform the song. At a ceremony on July 21st, 2014, in Scotland House at the Old Fruitmarket, Glasgow, the

Scottish Commonwealth athletes chose their standard bearer for the opening ceremony of the Commonwealth Games 2014. Immediately after Sir Chris Hoy handed the saltire over, I was called to the stage to sing Flower to the entire Scotland team of athletes. It took a huge effort of will to get to the end without tears as I looked down on these eager faces giving full voice in anticipation of giving their all for their country. This statement will perhaps become clearer later on.

Some months earlier, Jon Doig, Chief Executive of Commonwealth Games Scotland Ltd, had approached me with an invitation. I had dealings with Jon years ago at the Delhi Commonwealth Games, and now he informed me that, as in Delhi, Flower of Scotland would be used as the anthem for the flag ceremony should we win gold. It seemed that the Games committee wanted all of the anthems to be the same length if possible, and Flower of Scotland required an additional fifteen seconds to comply. Since it's not a good idea to just play and sing it that wee bit slower, lest it become the dirge many people have accused it of being, I was asked to sit in with the Royal Scottish National Orchestra's arranger, John Logan, to lend my opinion.

Since Roy died in 1990, I have been at pains wherever possible to explain that, although I am now inextricably associated with Flower of Scotland, and it is assumed in some quarters that it was I who wrote it, this is by no means correct. The song was written, words and music, by my late partner in The Corries, Roy Williamson, and I have become its 'guardian,' if you like. It was an honour to be asked to work with John in this new arrangement.

The word 'unofficial' is used regarding the anthem, but I can't help feeling that with an arrangement by the Royal Scottish National Orchestra, itself backed by the Commonwealth Games Association, it couldn't be much more official and, perhaps, the 'unofficial' tag should finally be dropped. Or is that controversial?

Whatever the future holds, neither the words nor the melody could be changed in any new arrangement. So what was to be done?

I worried that, if it was purely orchestral, when played at the ceremony to a world-wide audience it would have no particularly Scottish identity. My first comment therefore, when I sat down with John, was that the anthem start with the sound of a pipe-band being predominant. There was no argument with that, and so we proceeded through the work. The pipes were integrated with the orchestra throughout the unchanged melody line until at the very end, the orchestra came into its own with the addition of a few bars of crescendo, adding the seconds required by the Games people.

Anyone who heard the arrangement played behind the many gold flag ceremonies with which our highly successful athletes honoured themselves and the nation will surely agree that it was stunning.

Lyle Borland was a young dental student who gave unstintingly of his time through the early days of The Corrie Folk Trio and Paddie Bell. He didn't do quite as well in his studies as he would have wanted, but well enough to eventually take up a job as a world representative for a dental equipment manufacturing firm. At the time we all agreed that this seemed like a very glamorous job, travelling from one country to another and staying in some of the finest hotels in the world. He very kindly developed the habit of sending a couple of postage stamps home to my children from all of the countries he visited which, for a while, strengthened that supposition. It didn't take too long though, for that belief to be shattered.

He came home with stories of unstable and delayed flights, dicey hotels, long periods of waiting in airport lounges, missed meetings resulting in flight changes, etc. To a certain extent, foreign engagements for St Andrew and Robert Burns turned out to be the same for us. I speak from the experience of having now done, as well as Jakarta, two Hong Kong St Andrew's celebrations, one in Singapore, and one Burns' Supper on a Caribbean cruise ship. As with Lyle's experience, it all looks very glamorous in your engagement diary.

All the people involved in such enterprises bend over backwards to make you feel at home. Like Sheila and Stuart Walker in Singapore, a couple originally from Comrie in Perthshire, who had travelled the world through Stuart's employment as a Marine Insurance Inspector. When I went out, Stuart's main cause for concern was shipping piracy. It wasn't until the Somalian piracy of recent years that I finally understood the nature of his job, in spite of his explanation whilst Pat and I stayed with them in their flat in Singapore. I just couldn't come to grips with the idea of a small band of people seizing a massive ship, steering it to a neutral harbour, repainting it and giving it false identification and then selling it on under another country's flag. That was my interpretation of what Stuart was investigating, not just once in a while, but on a regular basis.

After negotiations of fees and expenses were agreed, always with a bit of argy-bargy over whether Club class was necessary in addition to a handsome remunerative package, we found ourselves in Singapore and taken to the Walkers' flat on the top floor of a circular building in the middle of the city. The views were stunning with a window looking out on Singapore from every room. The inside of the lounge was a sort of little Scotland, with tartan furnishings and pictures of shepherds with their dugs and views of Comrie and Edinburgh. Scottish dance music was piped through a sound system in welcome and the party they threw for us that night was second to none.

The night of the St Andrew's celebration went as well as all of them do all over the world, again proving that the occasion marks the height of the social calendar, wherever it takes place. After my spot, we danced the night away and didn't manage breakfast until 7.00 am.

There was a grannie flat in Sheila and Stuart's place which

was given over to us during our five night stay. On the morning of our late-night flight back to the U.K., we woke to find Sheila sitting alone in her lounge. Stuart had been called away on yet another mission to find a ship. She was on her own quite a lot with Stuart away for sometimes days on end. With a house-keeper in attendance and regular laundry-maid services, she admitted that sometimes time hung heavily on her hands. I only mention this to illustrate that even her apparently glamorous lifestyle could at times be just as boring as anyone else's. Later, she took us round Singapore, visiting some of her favourite haunts.

On our first visit to sing for St Andrew in Hong Kong, we were taken to the Hong Kong Racing Club. As well as being the home of horse-racing in Hong Kong, the Club was the home of Hong Kong Rugby Club. Our host was the Captain of Rugby and he provided me with another example of how the so-called glam-orous aspects of life may not necessarily make for a better one.

The Racing Club had decided to make improvements to their facilities which inevitably would upset the amenities of the Rugby Club. As far as I remember, the race-track which encircled the rugby pitch was to be either raised or lowered which would cause major upheaval to the rugby boys. To compensate, the Racing Club promised to improve the rugby amenities by providing up-dated, modern facilities to the rugby clubhouse. One improvement which springs to mind was a golf room. I'm not into golf myself, but I'm sure those of you who are will understand what I'm about to describe.

In a very narrow room I was confronted by a patch of grass on which lay umpteen golf balls and clubs. On my right side was what I can only describe as a camera contraption with, about eight metres ahead, a large screen. The idea apparently was to whack your ball as if in play and, as it passed through the camera's range and hit the screen, the camera gauged the ball's trajectory and speed. When it hit, the screen lit up with a picture of a golf course and where on that golf course the ball had landed. You again whacked your ball and the process was repeated until your round was complete.

This sounds now, as I describe it, pretty daft. Maybe not so to a golfer who, by using the facility, could perhaps improve his game.

There were many more 'improvements' promised, but the captain explained that he had warned his fellow members that, if they accepted them, they should be very careful. Although the initial costs would be met by the Racing Club, the upkeep and eventual servicing would be the responsibility of the rugby fraternity. Could they see themselves in the future being able to afford to maintain them? The Racing Club would have achieved their aims but perhaps in the process would have left the Rugby Club with an albatross round its neck.

I don't know what the membership of the rugby club decided to do in the end, but it seemed to me to be a pertinent warning for the future.

Our second visit to Hong Kong proved to be amusing to me, if not to the St Andrew's Society who booked me. In our first telephone conversation I stated my usual terms of engagement and the call ended with their promise to get back as quickly as possible as the date for the Dinner was fast approaching. A few days later I picked up the phone to listen to an improved offer of only one club-class air fare, either Pat or myself to travel in comparative comfort, and the other in steerage. Immediately I rejected the offer and replaced the phone. A few more days later another offer arrived. Club-class could be paid for two, but the fee for the performance would have to be reduced. Another refusal from me. More days later I refused their next offer of Club for two, full requested fee, but reduced quality of hotel accommodation. Again, no thanks from me, and perhaps we should forget the whole idea. Four days later their final call came offering everything I had requested in the first place if I would come out to entertain them.

Mystified, I asked their reasons for the about turn. It seemed that, through the negotiations, word had gone round the Scottish community in Hong Kong that I would be coming. They were actually selling tickets for the event on the strength of my appearance, and were now left with no choice but to comply with my original terms.

No hard feelings were harboured and the engagement went well, with further amusement resulting from the fact that it was while I was there that I discovered Flower of Scotland was known to the membership as 'No. 37 in their songbook'. The Society had adopted Flower of Scotland many years before there was any hint of it becoming the anthem of our country. At that time, it was just another popular Scottish song.

On the home front my life was equally interesting, more in my capacity now as a Scottish 'personality', than as a singer.

Annually, Alan Noble and his wife Marna did a fantastic job organising what was called the Orchid Ball, a charitable evening in the Sheraton Hotel in support of Muscular Dystrophy with the usual dinner, speeches, after-dinner auction and dancing. My first Orchid was in 1991. Pat and I attended some of them at the top table.

On one occasion, the then Lady Provost of Edinburgh, Eleanor McLaughlin, attended as principal guest. I sat on her left and Pat sat beside her husband on his right. As the evening progressed with introductions, speeches and the auction, Pat kept being nudged on her left side by the Provost's escort who finally, I suppose in embarrassment, told her that he was not trying to be over familiar but that, every time he said something Eleanor deemed was inappropriate, she would either kick his foot, knee him, or drive her elbow into his side. This prompted an involuntary twitch from himself which made contact with Pat. He apologised and complained that he was black and blue down his left side. Apparently this happened at every official engagement he attended with his Lady.

On another occasion Stephen Hendry, seven times world snooker champion, was the subject of an auction item. A frame of snooker with Stephen was on offer to the highest bidder and, when the bid reached £900, Pat nudged me and said, 'Go on, you know you'd like that'. I put up my hand to bid £1000 thinking that I was only helping the bids on and, to my chagrin, that's where it stopped.

I went along to Stephen's practice-rooms in Stirling to play the frame and would like to say that Stephen took pity on me and let me win hands down. That's not the way champions operate though, and I was soon on my knees, crying for mercy, with Pat laughing her head off in revenge for my announcement in concert of her first grandchild.

The night I became an auction item was not quite so funny.

Sitting talking to the actor Matthew Kelly, a genial giant of a man, who was the principal speaker that night, Alan Noble came up behind me and whispered that he and the orchestra leader had come up with the idea that someone would surely bid to sing 'Flower of Scotland' with me on stage. Was I game? Nothing ventured, nothing gained. I said it was worth a try.

As I stood there feeling somewhat embarrassed and, I must say, spare, the bidding started at £100, as is normal at the Orchid Ball. When it reached £3,000 I was surprised and flattered at the same time. It was at £4,000, with a sense of amazement having crept in, when a voice shouted, '£6,000 pounds!' Not surprisingly, the bidding stopped, a gentleman was announced as the winner and invited to join me on stage.

To thunderous applause from the audience, even before he started to sing, he stood beside me and we shook hands as the band struck up the intro. Starting exactly in unison, as if he were Roy Williamson himself, throughout the song he proved his worth as a word perfect and grand singer with harmonies to boot. The applause at the end matched his efforts. Over the noise I asked why he was prepared to make such a bid. When he said that he had always wanted to sing with The Corries and that he had been told only the week before that he had cancer and had but a few months to live he knew this would be his last chance. I'm still moved by this memory.

Sir Tom Farmer was plain 'Tom' the night he won a hooded Orkney rocking chair at the auction. As he sat beside me after his win, I asked him how his wife would react to yet another acquisition for her house that was full of Tom's famed collection of wins. In his position, it is expected that he bid in auctions, and he never disappoints. On this occasion, he explained that he wouldn't take it home: his plan was to see if Edinburgh's society photographer, Trevor Yerbury, could make use of it as a prop in his studio for his portraits.

He went on to explain that, yes, there was little room left in his home for his fast mounting collection of trophies, like the one he was given when he was voted 'Businessman of the Year', a giant Edinburgh Crystal bowl. Tom was honoured to accept it, but in the knowledge that he didn't know where on earth he would display it. Finally he opted for a shelf in the office of his Edinburgh headquarters, the same place where he had kindly agreed to pose for my Edinburgh painting of celebrities.

It was a striking piece of glass, so much so that everyone who entered his inner sanctum immediately asked why it was there. Tom became so fed up with relating the same story that, in the end, he arranged for the side of the bowl to be made smooth, and the explanation engraved on the blank area of glass. This was all very well until, exactly one year after his acceptance, a telephone call from London requested its return for presentation to the next year's recipient. At great expense to himself, and (to his credit) his great amusement, he had a new one made.

Chapter Thirty Two

In 1991, at the same time as we were adding a conservatory to the property at 131 Mayfield Road, we bought the flat above us. I used it as an office and studio for a couple of years before we decided to let it, choosing an Edinburgh Estate Agent, a family friend, Brian Adair of Kenneth Ryden & Partners, to handle the lets. We did this for a very good reason.

When we split the ground floor and basement at Henderson Row and moved upstairs, all those years before, we let the bottom flat. The first tenants were no bother, except that they had a thing about collecting milk bottles. When we let for the first time, we didn't insist on inspection rights and it wasn't until they moved out after six months that we discovered their collection piled up in the coal cellar. In the Sixties, milk came in glass bottles and the ones they left were immaculately clean. We had no problem with all this, but why not hand them back as they bought new supplies? Beats me.

Anyway, our next lot were a party of six female Edinburgh University students. We thought we did everything the right way by approaching the University letting authorities to select the party of girls, and we assumed that that office would vet them and take responsibility for their actions. The let was in the name of one of the girls, whose father was a Church of Scotland minister in Alnwick, who assured us of her best behaviour.

Again we did not build in inspection rights and, living above them, noted that they were certainly not over noisy, nor did they have too many loud parties. After all, who were we to speak about loud parties?

On one occasion, however, I had to take them to task. We had not yet sunk the bath in the stairway and still had access to the flat at the bottom of the inside stair doorway, which could be opened only from our side. One weekend, we were informed that the ladies would be going home for the holiday period and that the flat would be empty. It was with some surprise, therefore, that, on the first night they were to be away, I heard noises from below, but not the noises we had become used to. I went down to investigate, to hear shouting from one end of the flat to the other. This seemed very strange, so I opened the door and walked into the hall to find myself in the middle of a gang of about ten people whom I had never seen before.

I asked very politely, as is my wont, what the hell they were doing there, to be informed that the girls had told them that they would leave the window open and that, if they wished, they could make use of the flat while they were away. When I informed the gang that they were in fact trespassing, they asked me who the hell I was. I answered, 'I'm the wicked landlord, and I'm about to call the police to have you all arrested.' They soon cleared out and I snibbed the window behind them. The girls were amazed that I had taken exception but, conversely, I couldn't understand their way of thinking. Maybe it was because of this difference of opinion that they decided at the end of their First Year to give up their let and move to somewhere more amenable.

The six girls were assembled together in the flat on the night we accepted the keys, and we were shocked to find how much damage had been done. We had a mantelpiece of Piranha pine, stretching the full length of the room, and cigarettes had been allowed to burn out along its full length. The marks were so evenly spaced it seemed they must have been made deliberately. On looking behind cushions and furnishings, we discovered more burn marks and tears. When I was a boy, doors usually consisted of six panels with raised moulds round them. By this time, fashion had changed and the moulds had been removed and the doors covered with a sheet of hardboard, which was what ours were like when we bought the property. Now the panels had been removed for some reason and were hanging, literally, by a tack. When we complained to both the father and the University Letting department, and requested payment for the damage, we were informed by both that the girls were under age and therefore not responsible.

The corner shop immediately across the road from our front door was run by a middle aged couple who, at all times, were impeccably dressed. The lady always wore rubber gloves when handling food and her coiffure was so perfect that it made you wonder where she found the time to attend her hairdresser. They went to work dressed as if they were going out to dinner. When the flat became vacant, and they requested that they take over, we thought that here would be clean, quiet and respectful tenants. With them in house, the flat would certainly be kept well. So, again, we didn't give a thought to inspections of the property. Big mistake.

They eventually gave up both the shop and their tenancy, leaving under cover of darkness, with the keys having been slipped through our letter-box. When we went down to have a look, we understood the cloak and dagger.

The front door opened on to a long, narrow hall with a bedroom leading off on both sides. As we opened the bedroom on the left, which had been theirs, we nearly fell through a hole in the floorboards, caused by the rotting of the planks which were covered in red dust, the tell-tale sign of dry-rot. The whole flat was riddled. This does not happen overnight but must have been progressive during their stay. I can't understand why they didn't leave every morning with this dust on their clothing, and it beats me why they didn't inform me of its presence when they noticed the early evidence. Their bed, which hadn't been made up on their departure, had sheets dangling to the floor and was covered in spoor.

I knew enough about rot to immediately call my friend Bill McFadyen of McFadyen Preservations, who advised that my joiner, Bill Philp, should start work as soon as possible. Every floor board in the flat had to be removed and carefully destroyed. Before doing so, Bill took up a few and invited me to look under them to see what I hope none of you encounter in your life, a creeping fungus that filled the space from the foundations right up to the bottom of the boards. After removal, all of the plaster on the walls had to be taken off to a height of one metre. It was like rebuilding the whole flat. Many weeks later, when the remedial work had been done, we were short in our bank balance by £7,000, which was a lot of money in the Sixties.

Our last tenant in the flat was my brother Ian and, on our frequent visits to him while he was there, he must have thought it strange my looking behind doors and under carpets when his back was turned.

Having learned from all this, at 131 Mayfield Road it was definitely Kenneth Ryden & Partners for us. They imposed a £600 deposit against damage on prospective tenants and made regular inspections. The result was some years of trouble-free letting.

One of our clients was a Muslim gentleman and his wife and two children. He must have been a lecturer at King's Buildings which was a stone's throw away at the top of Mayfield Road. King's Buildings is part of Edinburgh University's many departments, dotted throughout Edinburgh, and the reason I assume he worked that close was because he popped into the flat five times daily to pray in the back bedroom.

We had done our best to furnish the place adequately and one of the pictures on the wall was a full length portrait of my friend Mike Killey. Mike had kindly agreed to act as a model in one of my practice portraits, but didn't have room in his own home for the finished picture, which was why it had been left in what had been my studio. I'm sure you've experienced looking at the eyes of a portrait where they follow you round, and Mike's assuredly did that. This was probably why the picture was covered with a sheet, so that no other man than her husband could gaze upon my tenant's wife.

Another University lecturer who tenanted the flat was Japanese. He had been there for only one month when, it seems, he was sent to work in New York. He was gone for nearly a year before he returned, and only then to collect whatever of his belongings he had left behind. All of the time he was away, we continued to receive the rent in full.

Freda Tchaikovsky (yes, related to the great composer), used the premises once a month to stay over before catching a regular London flight, with only now and then a shopping visit in town.

The last tenants we had before finally selling the property were a young American couple, and we became friends more than business associates when they dropped in on more than one occasion to share a meal and a film with us. They had a habit of laying loose change in a large tray behind the front door when they came home and, after they left, they didn't collect it. Pat and I had a dinner out on it and there was even enough for a bottle of wine. A cheap one.

In conclusion to this perhaps useless collection of information, those of you out there contemplating the letting of property, be advised to use an agent for a grief-free existence, it is well worth their commission.

The first time I sang Flower of Scotland at an international occasion was not for rugby or football, but in the Kelvin Hall, Glasgow, in the boxing-ring when Pat Clinton won his world fly-weight championship. On Wednesday evening, March 18th, 1992, he defeated the Mexican WBO defending champion, Isadore Perez, over twelve rounds. And I was there.

Pat and I presented ourselves at one o'clock at the Kelvin Hall to rehearse with the pipe-band. The pipe-major had experience of the hall and warned that the crowd noise would be such that I might not hear the band starting up. We therefore decided that I would watch the big drummer's foot and he would exaggerate his count-off for the band, and me, coming in. That rehearsed, we went off to the Albany Hotel to join Stephen Hendry, Mark McManus, Andy Cameron, Ken Buchanan and Jim Watt for a champagne reception, before buses took us all to the Kelvin Hall. We watched three fights before the main event.

We thought that the noise at Murrayfield when we won the Grand Slam was loud, but at least it was dissipated in the open air of the stadium. At the Kelvin Hall it was cacophonous as the boxers were introduced. In an enclosed space, the noise had nowhere to escape, but just went round and round, growing louder and louder. The pipe-major was correct, but he hadn't accounted for the fact that, as the boxers and their retinues made their way to the ring, where I was stationed, the crowd rose, some of them spilling into the passageways. A couple of them even shadow-boxed along the floor in front of the combatants' parties. The result was that I could neither hear the pipes nor see the feet of the bandsmen. Tommy Gilmour, the boxing promoter, reckoned that, because of a confusing start to the anthem, I had 'lost my bottle,' as he put it. Not so, I was simply unsure when to start singing.

There was no such confusion after twelve rounds of boxing when both of Pat's hands were lifted in victory. He and I sang Flower once again and I suspect the fans joined in. I don't know, because in the middle of the ring it was bedlam. There's a nice shot of that scene where Tommy is gripping my hand as we both stand in the centre of the ring behind Pat.

I sang for him again one year later at the defence of his title, but only once that night because, unfortunately, he lost the fight.

It was June 23rd, 1996, before I sang it again. Not for

rugby fans, but for the followers of the American Football team, the Scottish Claymores, 38,982 of whom crammed into Murrayfield Stadium to watch them contest the World Bowl '96 against Frankfurt Galaxy, which they won 32 - 27. Just one year before they had been bottom of the heap but in 1996, under their coach, Jim Criner, they bounced back to the top. Jim asked me to lend a hand by leading the singing and I was delighted to oblige.

It was a big occasion and Pat was nervous for me, but at the same time as proud as punch and we joined in the celebrations with the best of them. The entry for the next day in her diary says, 'Ronnie did the ironing and hoovered all of upstairs.' How were the mighty fallen!

I was hoovering again on August 28th, a couple of days before my next big Flower of Scotland appearance, this time for the fitba' fans in Vienna. The SFA had decided, for the first time ever, to use Flower as the anthem for their game against Austria and they invited Pat and me to travel with them on their Caledonian Airways chartered flight out of Glasgow, myself to sing before kick-off on the Saturday.

We were met at Glasgow Airport by Jim Farry, then the Secretary of the SFA, who handed our cases, passports and tickets to a young man, told us that we wouldn't see any of them again until we reached Vienna, and rushed us to a VIP lounge. The plane had on board: the Scottish squad, together with the Scottish Under 21 team; the Committee, physios, doctors, coaches and managers; and a full complement of press and media. Being of the oval ball persuasion, I felt slightly guilty being photographed with Craig Brown, but I soon got over that. That evening in the Holiday Inn Plaza Hotel on the outskirts of the city, we relaxed with a meal and drinks with the committee in Suite 330 overlooking the Danube.

Next day I went to the stadium to rehearse with the Tyrolean band. You know the guys with the lederhosen? It was as well

I did because they struck up 'Scotland the Brave'. The television director was present and she was in consternation when I stopped them to explain that it was the wrong song. Although a tape of Flower had been sent over for our use, the Austrians had assumed that we would be using what had been played three years before on Scotland's last visit. We soon got it sorted out and I did my sound check with the tape playing, leaving the Austrian singer to do her sound with the band.

This lady was from Viennese Opera, taller than I and somewhat disparaging when I told her that I was just a simple folksinger. She drew herself up to even more imposing heights as she waited for her band to start. However, when she heard the triple echoes from the empty stadium, she stopped them and hurried them to a small room within the stadium for her check, the whole exercise defeating the purpose. Ah well, that's opera for you.

Not wishing to intrude too much as strangers within a whole group of people who already knew each other well, Pat and I organised our usual City Bus tour for the next morning. This didn't sit well with the committee who were doing everything in their power to make us welcome and had waited for us to join the official tour. They were kind enough, though, to congratulate us on our professional attitude and later, at 5.30, we all left for the stadium and an 8.30 kick-off.

After changing into my kilt and Prince Charlie jacket, I walked to the track side to meet my operatic counterpart and walk with her onto the pitch, to our separate podiums for the singing. She was dressed in Valkyrie black and thigh high boots which made her look even taller. Right on cue, we started out together. As I took her arm, up in the stand, Jim Farry nudged Pat's arm and said, 'Well, Pat, we've certainly won the first round'. 'How so?' asked Pat. He replied, 'Ronnie's got better legs than her'.

Although the stadium was hardly full of Scots, there was a fair complement present and they were all in one group, which made it easy to sing to them instead of trying to circumnavigate the terraces to search for them. The anthem was well sung and received. The result was a goalless draw, which seemed to please everybody, the feeling being that they had both won, a feeling completely alien to me. In rugby you either win or you lose.

After the game, it was straight to the plane and we were back in Glasgow by three in the morning.

Chapter Thirty Three

The Boston Celtic Festival of 1993 did not go well. I was invited with the Alexander Brothers from Scotland, Paddy Reilly from Ireland, whose recording of 'The Fields of Athenry' was at the time a huge hit (to this day it bursts out spontaneously on the terraces of rugby and football internationals), and a whole array of American folk artists of whom I had never heard. Also, many retailers took stalls at the venue for the week-end's proceedings.

Unfortunately, it seems the organisers forgot to advertise, because the event ran for three days to the complete indifference of the people of Boston. Nobody turned up. I know of one Scottish company who attended with case-loads of records and Scottish goods and had to pack them all up and take them home unsold. Nobody was paid. I think I was probably the only one who came out of it with anything since I had insisted on receiving our air-fares before I left home.

One young couple in the American contingent pawned some of their possessions to kit themselves out for what they thought would be a major showcase for their talents. It was they who gave me an insight into the American folk scene when they told me that in some parts of the country, the clubs they sang in were pretty rough, performers having to sing behind a metal netting to protect them from flying cans and bottles if the audience disapproved of their material.

Pat and I, together with Tom and Jack Alexander, booked

into a good hotel where, after the first night's 'performance', we entertained some of the less fortunate acts who were in rather seedy digs, by breaking out the drinks from our room hospitality bars because the night porter was not allowed to serve us drinks from the bar proper.

When Tom and Jack finally discovered the organiser's home address and paid a visit, to insist on their fee being paid, they found only her old mother in the house. She told the boys that her daughter had been taken to hospital.

It was fortunate that Pat was with me because, if it had been The Corries returning home with no money I'm sure her right eyebrow would have been raised in question. 'So, you pissed your fee up against a wall then?'

I had arranged an engagement in a folk-pub called Brittingham's Irish Pub in Philadelphia to follow Boston. The venue was the equivalent of Sandy Bell's in Forrest Road in Edinburgh, where Roy had first encountered Fin and Eddie Furey.

Bill and Karen Reid took me in the afternoon to do a sound check, only to discover a pretty doubtful prospect. There was a horseshoe bar, which in itself was very nice, but the top price seats were the ones round the bar, my performance area being in a room off, with two large doors held open wide. This took me back to the old days when we had insisted on the bar being closed for our performance. There was no way I could have done the same in this situation, but I did insist that the audience was brought into the room beside me. The deal was that I should take the ticket money and the proprietor got the drink money. The proprietor agreed, and it actually turned out to be a great night.

Our next stop was Virginia Beach, Virginia. I hired a van to take us to the south and Bill Reid agreed to drive.

Eileen Hetterley, the lady who so kindly lent me her Corries' scrapbooks, which have supplied so much detail of The Corries' early days for this book, is undoubtedly our greatest fan.

Running a close second to Eileen is Miss Charlotte Grahame-Clarke from Virginia.

Charlotte went on an annual pilgrimage to Scotland to follow us on tour, usually attending every show for the fourteen nights of her holiday. She sat in the front row of the audience, resplendent in tartan and tweed, no doubt annoying the people behind her with the eagle's feather in her bonnet sticking straight up in the air.

As I write these words, I'm sitting in my flat in Luxor, Egypt. A couple of days before I left I had lunch in Edinburgh with Charlotte where we shared a smile or two recalling her youthful exuberance. She toured Scotland in a hired car with a special number plate displaying the word CORRIES partially obscuring her real number plate. I don't know how she got away with that one. To this day she wears a silver pendant fashioned and made by herself showing adjoined portrait heads of Roy and me.

When Charlotte heard that I would be coming as far south as Philadelphia, she suggested I continue south and she would arrange a show for me in her home town. I was doubtful if anyone in the Deep South had ever heard of The Corries, let alone Ronnie Browne, but I agreed. It wasn't the biggest audience I had ever played to, but the enthusiasm of Charlotte, her mother and their housekeeper, the bubbly Beckie, more than made up for numbers and again, we had a good night.

John and Helen McCuaig were in Vancouver to greet us and we had a relaxing meal with them the night before the concert. It was nice to go all that way to be met by friends and not just business acquaintances. Bill McLeod was also with us. He had visited us back home when we lived at West Buccleuch and, together with the president of the Moray, Banff and Nairn Society, Isla Jamieson, and her husband, had a grand evening.

We had a full-house of 400 at the Cultural Centre, but the Society seemed a bit taken aback by my attention to detail in the afternoon sound and lighting test. They were further taken aback at my astonishment at their charging an extra five dollars per ticket for anyone who wanted an autograph after the show. I'm afraid I rode roughshod over that, and signed for anyone who requested it. Maybe it was because the show went so well, and there was a full house, that I was forgiven for doing so.

I did notice something strange during the show. Out of the corner of my eye, I caught sight of a man drawing up a chair in the wings. He must have been known to the staff, because nobody questioned his presence. Causing no trouble, he sat without saying or singing a word, but seemingly in rapt attention. I didn't see him at the end, but Pat did, just for a few minutes. He introduced himself to her and simply said, 'Now I know the secret, you can make out the words', and then he was off. The only conclusion we could come to was that he was a Corries fan who had been puzzling over our success and had now found an answer that satisfied him. He didn't even wait around to say hullo to me. Some people who did wait were a family called Bentham. My cousins, they were the offspring of my mother's sister, Jane Stuart, who emigrated to Canada before World War Two and was responsible for our food parcels during the war. I don't remember what food was in the parcels, only that it was always wrapped in newspapers. All I remember of the newspaper content was the cartoon character, Li'l Abner. But then, I was only wee at the time.

After Jane's Canadian husband died, she returned to Methilhill in Fife where she remarried, in her late seventies, her schooldays sweetheart, Bob Salmond. Now there's patience for you.

Our final stop on this jaunt was in Vancouver Island, in Qualicum Bay. This one was nice for Pat because, upon our arrival in our hotel the day before the show, we found a request to visit the home of the shopkeeper who had been selling the tickets. No explanation, just the request to visit. Imagine Pat's surprise when, on arrival at their door, it was opened by a woman whom she immediately recognised as the girl who had been her best pal at Gilmerton Primary School, and who had been brought to Canada almost immediately upon leaving school. All that evening, the star of the show had to take a back seat whilst memories were exchanged.

Roy and I, and then me on my own, paid a great deal of attention to every aspect of our career to make it a success. This show in Qualicum was a prime example of how not to do it.

When I arrived at the Civic Centre where the concert was to take place, I discovered that the Musicians' Union ruling, that had marred our abortive Australian tour, was obviously in force here in Canada. Or possibly the organisers didn't think I could sustain two hours of singing on my own. Thinking I would be appearing solo, I discovered that a local group had also been booked.

This was upsetting enough, but other concerns soon became apparent. As Pat and I entered the large auditorium, we both raised eyebrows when we saw, ranged along the floor beneath the stage, a huge sound desk, with a couple of people manipulating a deck of flashing lights and buttons as they listened to . . . nothing. A whole line of microphones stood on stage, but there was nobody behind them. At the door end, inside the hall, a gang of people were setting up tables and transporting boxes and tins of crisps, biscuits, and bottles of beer and coke etc. Urns and coffee machines were apparent. Pat and I exchanged frowns.

I went down the centre aisle to the young sound man, asking him if I had come to the right place. He removed his earphones and enthusiastically pumped my hand, confirming that of course I was in the right place and he was delighted to meet me. He wasn't quite so pleased when I informed him that his array of technical equipment, sitting where it was, would conflict with any atmosphere I tried to create. If I was going to sing into his mikes that night, it would have to be me who was the centre of attention, not him. So, he would have to strike his stuff and relocate behind the stage curtains, out of sight.

When I also explained that I required only two microphones, and not the fifteen he had set out, he told me that the backing-group needed all of the fifteen. It was only then I realised that I was to be joined by other singers.

There wasn't an organiser around with whom to remonstrate, and it was getting perilously near doors opening time. Then a straggling group of what looked like gypsies ambled on stage. Finally all personnel were in place behind their microphones and their sound test began, but my patience was running out.

I interrupted the test to ask who was listening in the hall to ascertain that their group sound was what they wanted the audience to hear. Their apparent leader, a guy bashing a bodhran, stared in disbelief when I suggested that I stand in for him to let him go around the seats and listen to their balance . . . and please be quick about it, as I hadn't yet struck one chord on my guitar.

Meanwhile, at the back of the hall, Pat was explaining to someone in authority that the vendors had better sell a lot while the backing group was on because they certainly wouldn't be selling anything while I was on stage.

You get the picture!

The show was late in starting, the group overran their spot and it was even later in the evening before I made my appearance. So, the dreaded clock-watching for ferry times took place under my gaze, and the most unsatisfactory professional appearance of my career thankfully drew to a close in sheer frustration and exhaustion.

Our scheduled flight home from Vancouver to Prestwick via Chicago was changed to the very first flight from Vancouver to Scotland, flying over Greenland. During that flight I made up my mind that it was the last time I would appear in that neck of the woods.

Chapter Thirty Four

Towards the end of November 1993 I took on some club appearances in Holland, and was surprised at how well I was received in spite of the language difficulty. Then again, it seems to me that just about everyone in the world speaks a bit of English. It's we in the British Isles who are very lazy with languages.

The patrons in the clubs were surprised at my practice of changing clothing for the second half of the performance, but this harked back to my Corries' days when Roy and I did the same in concert. Had this been another small contributory factor in what must be admitted was our huge success?

In Amsterdam I took the opportunity to visit ardent Corries' fans Ko and Ria Spoor, who like Charlotte in Virginia, had spent many a holiday in Scotland following us round the country. They had become more like friends than fans and Pat and I stayed overnight with them.

It was on this visit that, to my surprise, I found that the Dutch people are perhaps not as benign as I had thought because, before finally turning in for the night, Ko pulled metal blinds down on the windows and locked them securely with padlocks. Either there was constant danger from the outside, or Ko and Ria were particularly security conscious.

The snow was on the ground when we got back to Edinburgh but we didn't mind as we were immediately bound for the sunnier climes of Jakarta, Indonesia, where I had agreed to give an after dinner speech at the Java St Andrew's Society Dinner, and a half hour's singing at the ball following.

It seems that all over the world the St Andrew's Day Ball is the highlight of the social calendar. The dinner starts early and the ball goes on until breakfast time. These folks just cannae get enough of the jiggin'. My lasting impression is how well the colours of the tartan zing out against the dusky skin colour of the locals.

If The Corries had taken on such an engagement it would have been a case of getting there and back as quickly as possible, certainly from my point of view as a married man with a family at home. Now that it was just Pat and me, we could afford the luxury of taking our time. On this occasion, we broke the journey in Singapore and arranged to fly yet further to the island of Bali for a one week holiday. This seemed to me to be a fitting end to what had been a strenuous working year.

We could now be a bit more flexible on fees. There still had to be an element of profit of course, but, in negotiations, I insisted only on Club Class airfares and respectable accommodation and subsistence. No doubt if I had had an astute agent, he would have gone for first class fares, but I'm not greedy and Club was fine for us.

As I remember it, the St Andrew's Society was very fair with us. We were met by Jim Malcolm from the British Embassy, billeted in the Mandarin Oriental and given a suite on the top floor. A fascinating feature of the rooms was, on the left hand side as you entered, a wall covered in hinged, louvre-panelled doors which, when opened, revealed a fully equipped kitchen.

After such a long journey, first stop for me was the luxurious toilet. It was huge, and as I sat there attending to Mother Nature's needs, I heard a strange clicking noise coming from under the long, double basined washstand. What must have been the world's biggest cockroach was marching towards me over the tiled floor. Now, I can appreciate the Management view that it should be nothing but the best for the Four Seasons, but how could a cockroach get up forty floors to greet a guest?

There were two double bedrooms in the suite and a comfortable lounge with a room safe. Unfortunately, I couldn't work out how to open it, and called reception for assistance. In a trice, there was a knock on the door and a tiny housekeeper entered to instruct me in the use of the contraption. She noticed my white hair and asked my age. When I told her I was fifty-six, she said, 'But where is your stick?' It would appear that, in Indonesia, if you are of my age and hair colouring, you are presented with a walking-stick to designate old age. The cheeky buggers.

I had agreed with the Society that we would arrive a couple of days prior to the Ball to acclimatise after what was a stressfully long journey. For the next couple of days, between putting finishing touches to what was my first major after dinner speech, and being driven round the Jakarta sights in a limousine, both Pat and I became more relaxed.

A young married couple from the British Diplomatic Corps were assigned to look after us, utilising a limousine that was available to them twenty-four hours a day, with three chauffeurs working in shifts. They told us that they were dreading their term of duty coming to an end, when they would no doubt be returned to England where no such perks would be theirs.

The day of the Ball dawned and that evening Pat and I spruced ourselves up in best bib and tucker. I had on the kilt and black Prince Charlie jacket, and Pat wore what I can best describe as a gownless evening strap as we entered the elevator to begin our descent to the mezzanine floor. About two levels from the bottom, the lift stopped and, as the doors slid open, a local Indonesian man entered. His eyes opened wide in astonishment when confronted with the sight of us in our finery, and he said in perfect English, 'Oh! Are you going somewhere special?' Not knowing if he would know what a St Andrew's Ball was, I replied, 'Yes, we're going to a party.' He thought for a couple of seconds and then replied, 'Well, I hope you win.' And there presented itself the opening of my forthcoming speech.

All the guests were assembled in the dining room as the top table guests were piped to our places on a raised stage at one side of the room, facing a bandstand which would be used for the dancing after the dinner. Pat swanned to her place on the arm of the Canadian Ambassador, who was Chieftain for the night, and I escorted his wife, walking behind them.

The speech went well enough, although speeches are not the strongest part of my armoury, and very soon we were all dancing. I couldn't get nearly as strenuous as everybody else, because, during the break in the middle of the Ball, I was to do my half-hour's singing. I therefore had a chance to spectate, and noticed something funny.

I'm sure you must have seen these small dance instruction books you get with illustrations showing the sequence to Scottish Country Dances by foot shapes and arrows guiding where the feet should go. There was a Japanese man on the floor during the Lancers who was holding such a book above his head and following the pattern of the dance from its pages. I'm pretty sure he did it as a joke, and it certainly worked with me as I laughed out loud. It put me in a good mood for my spot, which I enjoyed doing.

This performance signified, finally, the end of my 1993 professional commitments. So, it was away with the guitar, off with the jacket, unbutton the waistcoat, and down to some serious celebratory drinking in which I indulged with gusto. All very well until after a short spot of tunes from the small visiting pipe band who had come over from Pitlochry. They were lined up to be presented with a tot of whisky from a quaich when, all of a sudden, the pipe-major came to attention and marched across the now empty dance-floor to the top table where I was languishing with a glass of Drambuie. Stopping right in front of me he drew himself up to his full-height, snapping into a formal salute and asking in a loud voice, 'Mr Browne, would you honour us by leading us in Flower of Scotland, Sir!'

I was taken completely by surprise. This wasn't in the

contract, but what could I do? I shrugged on my jacket (the tie was lost somewhere under the table) and, without even trying to do up the buttons of the waistcoat, lurched behind the pipe-major to the microphone on the band-stand. I don't know if it was the drink, tiredness, relief at the tour being over, or just the emotion of all this Scottishness so far from home but, as the pipes struck up the introduction to the song, I just couldn't get a word out. The whole room burst straight into the first verse while I closed my eyes and knocked my forehead against the microphone, saying to myself, 'Come on, man, you're a professional. Sing!' Finally I caught up with the rest and forced myself through to the end, whereupon, to my eternal shame, I descended into sobs and ran from the stage. In floods of tears I looked desperately for some refuge where I could recover, eventually finding myself in a public toilet where I locked myself into a cubicle. After what seemed a very long time I felt ready to face the world again. I opened the door and walked out to the basins to splash my face. As I raised my head, thinking I was okay, I caught sight in the mirror of the pipe-major coming through the door. I was off again, and dashed back into the cubicle.

Back at the top-table the Ambassador was expressing concern to Pat who explained about Roy's death, my starting out on my own and the resulting trauma we had both experienced over the past two years or so. My actions were simply the release of emotional build up and I would be fine, not to worry. The Ambassador, probably in an attempt to alleviate any worries for me Pat might be stifling, launched into his story of the year before when he had been the Chieftain of the Java Highland Games, another 'must' in the Indonesian social Calendar.

In an attempt to lend some authenticity to the Games, the Ambassador ordered a caber to be sent from Scotland. Wood, however, was the biggest export from Indonesia at the time of his stewardship, and importing the stuff was against the law. To circumvent this he arranged for the caber to be smuggled ashore, tied to the side of a boat under the water line. It lay under the boat for a whole day until night fell and a team of men then untied it and took it under cover of darkness to the field where the games were to take place. Come the time of the caber competition, nobody could lift it off the ground because it had become waterlogged. The Ambassador laughed loud and long with Pat at the memory of his abortive plan.

My commitment to St Andrew being over, a day later we flew to Bali, presenting ourselves at a hotel which had been recommended by the people in Jakarta, a large complex of recently built concrete blocks with walkways connecting the various sections. On leaving Reception with our room key clutched in my hand, we followed a porter through a maze of corridors, finally coming out into the open where we thought our room would be. Not so: we continued our trek through an architect's dream of squares and small villages, passing more blocks of flats until we finally reached our accommodation. The room continued the concrete theme, not with comfortable couches on which to lounge, but lumps of stone with thin slabs of cushioned material atop them. The headboard of the bed was again in concrete and was part of an open plan bathroom area. I won't go on, because, even as the porter dropped the cases, I asked him to pick them up again and take us back to Reception where we apologised, and checked out, explaining that this was not quite what we had expected.

A taxi took us to a few smaller, more traditional hotels until we finally settled on the Bali Tropic Palace, booking into a small bungalow in its grounds. Even this place didn't bode well since, on our first evening with Pat sitting relaxing on our small verandah, she sustained fifty-two mosquito bites on her back, and still counting. The heat of the sun on the Island of Bali doesn't come on its own, but is accompanied by an equal amount of humidity, ninety degrees of both next day. The result was that, even with air-conditioning at full blast, we just couldn't keep our bodies dry.

Our first lunch of the holiday was marred, not by the food which was actually excellent and beautifully presented, but by the fact that, although we were the only patrons in the dining room, the management still deemed it necessary to provide entertainment in the form of a young singing duo. Although they did very well with covers of popular standards of the time, it meant that at the end of every song we had to lay down our eating irons to applaud.

We were also the only patrons to languish round the large swimming-pool, with rather embarrassed attendants trying hard not to overdo their ministrations. In the end we became very friendly with these gentle young men who were intrigued by my removal of the false nails I had been wearing on my right hand all through the tour.

In playing the guitar, it's necessary to keep the nails of your left hand very short and allow the tips of the fingers to become like small hammers of toughened skin. The nails of the right hand, by contrast, must be kept fairly long to facilitate the plucking of the strings. Women can tell us of their constant attention to the protection of their nails, sometimes by the addition of false ones. Roy and I did the same, and I noticed, when Paco Pena stayed with us, that he reinforced his right hand nails by sticking on layers of toilet paper. We used straightforward false nails bought from hairdressers' suppliers.

I learned from our pool attendants that, on the island of Bali, if a man wears his pinky nail long, this signifies that he is either a poet or an artist. They were disappointed to learn that my long pinky nail was used merely to pick the wax from my ear.

In any new place Pat and I visited, like most tourists, we made a point of taking the city bus tour. In this case it was the island bus tour. Setting out early one morning to pick up from other hotels we were soon at full complement to the sound of many different languages. After visiting various beach resorts we cut over the hills at the centre of the island, where, in the square of a mountain village, the bus drove through a cock fight which was in full swing. There was the sound of a few *tut-tuts* in the bus, but people must be allowed their own idiosyncratic customs. Visits to batik, wood-carving and jewellery factories led on to rice fields and a monkey forest. Packed lunches were consumed during the day because the highlight of the tour was to be an evening banquet of local delicacies. As dusk fell, we entered a temple to be entertained by the priests and local children in a mammoth cabaret show, which was a celebration of their Temple Monkey God. The priests wore lavish costumes and monkey masks and performed dances to the chattered accompaniment of the monkey-masked children.

As the evening wore on we reached banquet time. We had all been looking forward to this and now sat at long tables festooned with floral decorations and plates of exotic fruits. The main course, of a local curry, was placed in front of Pat and me in a huge silver salver. Unfortunately, before we had a chance to lift the lid and get tucked in to what the smell promised to be a tasty dish, three cockroaches slid from under the lid and scuttled over the table to disappear into the dishes of fruit. We went to bed hungry.

Apart from the tour, we spent our time relaxing either on the loungers beside the pool, or swimming across the water to sit at the pool bar and listen to the bartenders' version of 'Lock The Door, Lariston', their favourite from a cassette I had given them. Explaining in our conversations throughout the week what I did for a living had been made easier by just handing them a tape and saying, 'Listen to that and you'll see.'

After Roy died in 1990 the BBC issued two commemorative videos. The second one was called 'Years Must Roll On' and traces The Corries from our early days of black and white television to near the end of our career together. It also traces the development of the changing colour of my hair. In the first clips it is seen as uniformly dark, but as each clip progresses, first one streak of white appears and then another, and another, until towards the end of the video my hair is uniformly white, although my beard remains dark.

In Bali, I didn't realise that the pool water had been over-chlorinated until I was sitting on the plane on my way home; now the centre of attention not as that guy fae the Corries, but as 'that guy wi' the pea-green hair.'

Chapter Thirty Five

BBC Enterprises first tribute video for Roy was called 'A Vision of The Corries'. This came on the market in late 1990, and in 1991 was followed by 'Years Must Roll On'. In London in a consultative capacity I met Iain McLay, the mild-mannered, quiet-spoken Scot in charge of the whole operation. Once again in my life, it was a case of being in the right place at the right time.

Iain was a man of huge experience in the record industry with whom I struck up an immediate bond of friendship. We talked at length about The Corries and, in the course of these conversations, I explained my aversion to the whole process of recording music. Since that side of our business had been Roy's baby, I was now left in charge of our recorded catalogue. Iain explained that he was about to leave BBC Enterprises to set up his own label, Moidart Music Ltd, and that he would gladly take our output under his label's wing. This was manna from heaven as far as I was concerned. A deal was struck, Iain took over our catalogue and managed it immaculately until his retirement in 2009. On March 1st of that year my son, Gavin, took over under his own label, Gavin Browne Productions Ltd, (GBPLtd).

I have explained how much more difficult it is to perform a two hour long concert solo, more than twice as difficult as doing it with someone on stage beside you, but I did keep going for a couple of years after Roy died. It would appear though, that, as with the recording business, it was too much like hard work for me. I stopped the tours in 1993, although I did continue to perform the odd solo concert. Singing to a full house in the King's Theatre, Edinburgh on October 29th, 1995, was a huge success and, as late as May 20th, 2000, I was still at it.

The year 2000 was the 175th Anniversary of Standard Life, who planned a programme of events called LIVE 175, and I agreed to do a solo show in the Edinburgh International Conference Centre. This was in support of their charity, the Standard Life Anniversary Appeal and I'm pleased we kept the programme because it reminds me of what I was up to at the time. For instance, in the years 1998 and 1999 I closed the Royal Scottish National Orchestra's Prom Season with Flower. I nearly went to Monaco in late 2000 to do it with the Monaco Symphony Orchestra and Chorus for a huge European Television Charity Show, but that didn't come off. If it had, who knows what direction my singing might have gone and I might now be writing, 'Once again, in the right place at the right time'.

In January of 2000, I had already been in the EICC for a Royal Mail Burns Supper where the haggis had been piped in bearing its own post code printed on the skin, 'PUD 1'.

On November 5th, 2000, I went to London to sing for Richard Susskind. Richard was an IT expert in the legal profession and a crazy Corries fan, as was his whole family, young and old. I had done a Burns Supper for his legal firm when he was responsible for its arrangement but, in November, I appeared in his home at a Bar Mitzvah for one of his children. As I sang, I noticed him signing frantically that he and his brother would like to join me at the microphone and sing along. No harm in that, I thought, and up they came, soon to be joined by more members of the family. All of a sudden, I was surrounded by a group. Every member of the group sang better than me, so I handed over the guitar and sat down. It's the easiest money I ever earned in my life. Richard didn't seem to mind because I was invited back for two more Bar Mitzvahs.

I produced a live album called 'The First Time' in 1992 on a label I created for myself which I called 'Reekie,' and followed that in 1995 and 1996 with two albums on the Scotdisc label.

Dougie Stephenson and Bill Garden, two of the kindest men you will ever meet, (I've never seen Dougie without a smile on his face), offered me the chance to record for them in their BGS 'Scotty's Sound Studio' in Kilsyth. Both of them knew of my dislike of recording studios and my lack of confidence on instruments, so they suggested that I lay down voice tracks and they would have them backed by a small orchestra later. While I did that Bill, manipulating the sound-desk, was patience itself and made my hesitant efforts so much easier.

The first efforts resulted in 'Scottish Love Songs' in 1995. The backing orchestration was sympathetically arranged by Lena Martell's musical arranger, Peter Day, and we filmed the result on the West Highland Way. In 1996, 'Battle Songs and Ballads' was filmed all over Scotland with orchestration by Paul Farrer, who is best known as a producer of film scores.

In 1988, 'Tumbledown,' not a film, but a BBC Television drama, was screened, telling the true story of Robert Lawrence MC and his battle with injury sustained when a sniper shot him in the head at the end of the Falklands War. Robert's father, Wing Commander John Lawrence, another Corries fanatic, was involved in the making of the drama and approached me in its early production stages to write the musical score. I explained that I neither read nor wrote music and so couldn't oblige. In the final analysis, he insisted that some Corries' music be included because Robert's regiment, 2nd Battalion Scots Guards, had played our stuff nonstop on the way to the Falklands as the second wave of British land forces committed to the war.

Although I couldn't help him with the music, John and I became friendly through our mutual interest in rugby. John was a British Lions selector. We attended some international games together and, because of our friendship, I performed at a couple of Wooden Spoon Society charity events. At one I stayed with him and his charmer of a wife, Jean, and after dinner gave them a few songs. John said that never in his wildest dreams would he have imagined that he would receive a personal audience with a Corrie, and he wept with pleasure. Now, that's the kind of show of affection I find hard to bear. I keep telling you, it was just a job.

Talk of rugby and affection and emotion brings me to Nancy Ovens, the mother-in-law of Scott Hastings whose family portrait I had the privilege of painting. I attended a surprise birthday party for Nancy, and how surprised she was when she heard me burst into song, just for her. It was a well kept secret and she, like John Lawrence, displayed her emotion after I sang. On that occasion I told her 'No tae be sae daft'.

When Gavin and Scott Hastings were simultaneously selected to play for the British Lions, another surprise party was in order, and on that night I discovered that their mother was a dab hand at 'the spoons,' which she played with style to my guitar.

When I sang at Nancy Ovens' funeral though, I couldn't muster the same good humour. Her favourite song was the Robert Burns classic, 'Ae Fond Kiss', and her husband and daughter Jenny, Scott's wife, were sitting in the front pew right ahead of me. I was fine until I came to the line, 'Nothing could resist my Nancy,' when I all but broke down. As I went back to my seat beside Gavin Hastings, he whispered, 'You're a hero'. I accepted that accolade, because I felt like one.

My visit to the First World War cemeteries at Ypres and Flanders, sealed forever the knowledge that I will never again be able to sing one particular song. 'The Green Fields of France,' which some call, 'Willie McBride', and some 'No Man's Land'. It was written by a Scot, now resident in Australia, Eric Bogle, and

Eric took as his inspiration the gravestone of a fallen soldier, Willie McBride.

Des Brogan, a former principal history teacher, and the creator of Mercat Tours, invited Pat and me to accompany him on one of his visits to Ypres. It's a fascinating experience, and highly recommended, but make sure you take many boxes of tissues with you. I enjoyed the whole trip, if 'enjoyed' is the right word for a sometimes harrowing few days. It became slightly uncomfortable though, when Des, another Corries buff, played our version incessantly during his running commentary all the way to France. He also said that it's played every night to schoolchildren, as they settle in their dormitory at lights out. Of the many songs played, that one seems to hit the hardest, and I'm not surprised given the setting.

A battalion of soldiers was raised in Nova Scotia to come to Europe to fight in the Great War. In their very first encounter, as they crossed a field of grass, they were caught in a cross-fire and, in less than thirty minutes, 95% of their number were mown down. They lie there to this day in what is a designated war grave. There was no chance to recover their bodies as dead horse after dead horse fell on top of them. Rats and other vermin took their pleasure on rotting flesh. Rainstorm after rainstorm descended before more bodies were added eventually to the pile. It is one of the most sobering events of my life to stand on that grass, knowing what lies beneath.

I am told that their community back home in Nova Scotia refused point blank to raise a battalion to fight in the Second World War. Is it any wonder?

To stand in front of Willie McBride's gravestone now makes me realise that it's as well Roy and I recorded his song when we did, because, I repeat, there is no possible chance I could even begin to sing it now.

Willie French is a very good friend of my family whom Lauren first met when he arrived at Watson's College to take up a post as a teacher. He was a member of an amateur dramatics society and we attended many of their productions where we discovered that Willie is a fine singer who also plays drums. It's fair to say that he is passionate about music and, yes, he's another Corries' fan.

Willie is now a head teacher, and another of his interests is the work of Robert Burns, so much so, that he hosts a small Burns Supper in his home every year with just a few chosen guests. I have been one of these guests on quite a few occasions. At first when I was invited, Willie would ask me to sing but I always said no, that I don't sing anymore. He now doesn't ask, accepting that I will say no.

When the invitation arrived last year I said to Lauren that, this time, I would surprise him with a couple of songs, and proceeded to practise and get my voice back in shape. Do you know, even in practice, I can't get through without starting to weep? This is not just in sentimental songs, but in any song. To think that during all these years of singing, of harnessing emotion to wring it out of an audience, and I've seen evidence of it in the open shedding of tears in a theatre, I can't now control it. It is a strange phenomenon to have to accept.

That is why, after being accorded the honour of singing Flower of Scotland for our Commonwealth Games athletes, a request I couldn't refuse, I realised that, after nearly breaking down once more, I should not try to sing again.

Let's not end this chapter on a low point. Instead, I'll take you back to August 27th, 2008, and a very happy night at the Corn Exchange, Edinburgh, where I attended a concert by Paolo Nutini.

When this young man first hit the headlines there were constant references in articles and interviews about the influence our music had had on him in his childhood, since we apparently were firm favourites of his family. Knowing his agents from the past, I phoned their office to pass on my congratulations on his blossoming career. The result of my call was that, since he was about to perform in Edinburgh the agent wondered if I might like to come along and say hello. I thought that would be very nice, and promptly accepted, knowing that Lauren particularly would like to meet him.

Lauren has to this day in our freezer an apple with one bite out of it, but this is no ordinary bite. It is Bono's imprint. When U2 were not as big as they are now, they came to Edinburgh to perform in the Playhouse, at the top of Leith Walk, where the manager was Ted Way. Ted had been the manager of the Odeon Cinema when we performed there, and he kindly allowed us to attend U2's sound check in the afternoon. It was then that Lauren met Bono and asked for this unique autograph in her apple. Bono agreed and bit deep.

We kept my forthcoming attendance at the Corn Exchange a secret from Paolo and his family and, to spring the surprise on the night, I arrived after he had started his set. The Corn Exchange has a gallery at the end facing the stage, and it was there that the Nutini family gathered *en masse* to support their laddie.

I suppose I caused a wee bit of a stir when I started to mingle with them, but nothing to the surprise Paolo got at the reception backstage. I waited until his back was to me and quietly walked up to him and tapped him on the shoulder. His shocked gaze of recognition soon broke into one of his fantastic smiles, which we quickly captured in a photograph.

Chapter Thirty Six

In early 1995 I was invited to take part in a low budget film called 'The Bruce'. It was produced by Bob Carruthers, and starred the Glasgow actor, Sandy Welch, as Robert the Bruce. Also in the cast were: Oliver Reed, Brian Blessed and 'Wolf,' who was the bad boy star of the popular television series, *Gladiators*. I took the part of Maxwell the Minstrel, for which I received the princely sum of £400. According to an article in the *Daily Record* on May 20th, 1995, Sandy was paid £2,000 and a slice of the profits. I don't know what Oliver, Brian or Wolf put in the bank, but nobody was making any fortune. Certainly not the majority of the rest of the cast, who I believe actually paid £200 each for the privilege of taking part.

My grandfather, Albert Browne, was born in Blackness Castle when his father was a soldier and Blackness was an arsenal. By coincidence it was there I did my first stint as an actor and where it quickly dawned on me that I wasn't a good one.

My first entrance as Maxwell the Minstrel, in the guise of a messenger from the south to report that one of the Bruce's castles had been sacked by the English. The whole garrison had been killed, sparing only me to take the warning to the King that a large force was on its way north to put him to the sword.

In the make-up room they did a real job on me. My hair was tousled and splattered with a red dye which they assured me would wash out immediately. The assurance was necessary because, right after filming inside the castle with the King, I was due to follow the crew down to the foreshore to sing a song called 'The Black Douglas' as the man of that name, who was the Bruce's 1st Lieutenant, rode out to battle to the cheers of his followers. Corny? Yes. The problem was that the singing scene would be before my bloody entrance and of course my hair would have to be its natural white.

There was consternation in the make up room as more and more angry calls came from the shore. My non-appearance was holding up the filming schedule but I couldn't leave because, as in my pea-green experience in Bali, they couldn't get my hair clear of the dye. Not a good start to my film career.

My next scene was a non-speaking part at Talla Reservoir, a background shot as the old retainer frolicking with the King's children. The scene where I was pledging fealty to His Majesty was cut because it followed my doing another song to the accompaniment of the bodhran. Again corny? Again, yes.

Cut to June 1st at Dunfermline Abbey where I squeezed into shot crying 'God save the King' twice at his coronation. Neither a singing nor a speaking but a shouting part. I had really come into my own the month before on May 21st at Neidpath Castle, during the Battle of Bannockburn where I fought in the Bruce's army. The parts of the army were played by the Wallace Clan. I had met Seoras Wallace, the Clan's leader, before, and he now instructed me in the wielding of a large hammer to knock spots off a recumbent wounded English soldier.

Seoras and his band of warriors give displays of armed combat. Their skills with broadsword, claymore, spiked targe, lance and battle-axe, and any other weapon of destruction you care to mention, are as near the real thing as you can imagine. When they fight, they don't hold back, and that was what he encouraged me to do to my Englishman. The shaft of my hammer was wooden but the head, although it looked real even close up, was actually foam rubber. I therefore had no compunction about laying in to this man's chest, arms and head. Time after time, I brought the weapon down with full force as my destruction of the man was filmed in close up. Small sacks of the red liquid used on my hair had been attached to add authenticity, bursting all over my poor victim's body.

His token resistance was soon broken down until he finally lay with arms akimbo and my final, killer blow descended. Half-way through its arc the head flew off the shaft and disappeared into the battle raging round us. The shaft, however, kept on going and landed full force on the soldier's chest. With a shout of pain, he forgot that he was acting and leapt from the ground, his head coming into contact with mine, 'gaein' me the heid'. My shout of pain echoed his and we ended up in a knot on the ground but, once again in my life, laughter over pain saved the day.

Bob Carruthers, however, was not amused as he counted the cost of stopping filming. Another delay caused by this bloody old folk-singer! Word must have spread around the film world, because I've never been asked to take part in one again. Compensation was granted, though, when, at a nice wee ceremony later in the filming I was made an honorary member of the Wallace Clan.

Later that day the final scenes of the battle were staged, which was when, as you will remember from your history lessons, the camp-followers were called upon to run down the hill to help finish off Edward's fleeing forces. Not being as young as I once was, I was sensible enough not to overdo the running. Even so, in mid-stride over the small hillocks, I felt a muscle pull on the inside of my left thigh. I had no choice but to stop in my tracks, exit the battlefield and eventually limp to my car and drive home.

After a couple of days, the pain subsided and I thought no more of it. A few days after that, though, I noticed a large bruise that started under my thigh and crept up and over it. Over the next few days, the bruise continued to grow until it covered my thigh completely. As with the broken hand sustained in my Range Rover crash, the bruise was not accompanied with pain, which surprised a therapist at the Thistle Foundation in Craigmillar, Edinburgh.

Pat had been attending the Thistle for therapy to a shoulder injury and when I had taken her in that day I was wearing shorts and the bruise was in full sight. I was surprised to feel no pain as the therapist kneaded the leg all over. The bruise took some time to disappear and I'm pleased to report that it has never caused any ill effects. I must say that I will always feel proud when I look at my photograph of the wound sustained at Bannockburn. That makes me a true Scot does it not?

My involvement with 'The Bruce' did not end when filming stopped. After editing and the addition of music, which included an orchestral version of Flower of Scotland arranged by myself and Paul Farrer over the closing credits, it was ready for distribution. As part of the distribution process, showings were arranged around the halls and cinemas of Scottish towns, and I was asked if I would host these showings by giving a short introductory talk, highlighting some of the incidents that occurred during filming.

The whole world knows the reputation of Oliver Reed on and off a film set and I was on several occasions a victim of his antics. I will guardedly remain silent on all but one, because I have photographic proof of its crass nature, which leaves me in no doubt that the man's name will not be joining my Whittaker Club.

After I had officiated at the World Premieres in Glasgow and Edinburgh on March 1st and 2nd, 1996, we moved to Peebles on March 3rd. In Edinburgh the film was supposed to screen at 7.00 pm but was delayed for nearly three quarters of an hour because of the non-appearance of Oliver Reed and Bob Carruthers. I was therefore in the position of having to entertain an increasingly restless audience without having any explanation for the absence of the two main guests.

As 7.00 pm approached in Peebles I remained unconcerned

because I knew Mr Reed was in his favourite hostelry in the town. Not late for his appearance at the hall, he had in fact arrived early. I had another five minutes or so to speak as he burst through the door on my right hand side and pulled himself up onto the stage where the film screen had been erected. All attention immediately switched to him and it was obvious to everyone that he was not what you might call sober.

After a couple of minutes of pretended interest in what I was saying, his dislike of not being the centre of attention got the better of him. He took off his jacket and tie, pulled his shirt open and slid the sleeves down to his wrists. I couldn't believe what I was seeing as he did a seated jig to draw further attention to himself. But then again, why should I not believe? This was the famous Ollie Reed was it not, in full flight? I wound up what I had to say and left the hall to the gyrations of this goon.

My opinion of the film world and the actions of some of its stars descended still further when, a few minutes later, I overheard a telephone conversation by one of the film's publicists. He was speaking to a newspaper and saying, 'You should get down here quick, Ollie's up to his tricks again'.

Chapter Thirty Seven

Roy and I had worked for Denis and Denise Snowdon of Toronto in years past, and now here I was working for them again. This time, though, it was the kind of engagement The Corries could not have undertaken because what was on offer was a Burns' Supper Caribbean Cruise lasting for a week. Under the auspices of their travel agency, the Snowdons had gathered a party of 100 Scots Canadians to go to the Caribbean in January to celebrate Burns Night. What they invited me to do was perform a concert in the on-board theatre on one of the nights of the cruise, and a spot at their Burns' Supper on the 25th of the month. These performances were open only to the 100-strong Scots party and not to the general public on the cruise.

My Far East singing for St. Andrew had involved me in short half-hour performances for which only my guitar was enough, but this would be different. I couldn't sustain a full concert with only the guitar and had to think carefully if I wanted to accept the attractive offer. I would definitely require both guitar and banjo, but also the bodhran. This would provide sufficient variety but would present a bit of difficulty in transportation, because the instruments would be in addition to at least one suitcase. A further problem would be the bodhran itself. On tour with the instrument in home engagements it went into the car unprotected, but could not travel to the Caribbean without the protection of a case. Such a case would of necessity be big and bulky. I should have no difficulty in borrowing a guitar since there would be a proliferation of performers in the various lounges and theatres. I therefore accepted the engagement on the condition that a guitar would be provided. When acceptance of this condition came through, I set about arranging for a bodhran case to be made and it became available long before we took flight.

Neither Pat nor I had experienced a cruise ship like the one we boarded in Miami. Travel brochures and television shows give you no idea whatsoever of the real thing, which is a floating five-star hotel, and a big one at that with lifts and staircases and endless corridors. When we finally arrived at our cabin we were delighted to find that Denis had booked us 'a room with a view,' to coin a phrase, with a large picture window looking onto the ocean. We were soon unpacked with the duty free broken open to celebrate the start of what was going to be, not just another professional engagement, but a holiday for the two of us.

I couldn't foresee any difficulties with my two forthcoming performances and, with neither housework nor cooking looming their ugly heads, Pat and I settled to a completely indolent way of life for the first three days at least.

Between many cups of coffee in the various lounges of this floating palace, cocktails and other refreshments in umpteen bars, sumptuous meals and snacks and sundowners in our cabin, and watching the sun set out to sea, we made contact with Denis and Denise and most of the members of their party. In making their acquaintance, I knew that the shows would go well because I was now to perform for new found friends and not strangers.

In my wanderings, I was surprised to find so many Scots amongst the bands and stage performers. One lady in particular, who was originally from Glasgow, was in tears when I complied with her request to attend my concert. She explained that she had been a lifelong fan of The Corries but, in her twenty-five years working on the cruises, had little chance to be home for any of our live concerts, relying instead on tapes and cassettes. To attend my show, even though it was only a half-Corrie concert, would give her the greatest of pleasure.

A quiet wee coffee bar in the lower decks was serviced by another Scot, a young man from Glasgow and another Corries fan. He too came to the show, and before disembarking at the end of the week, when I had my last coffee with him, he presented me with a bottle of Drambuie in thanks. It was a touching experience because as I was the customer, I should have been tipping him and not the other way about.

During the various emergency drills we were required to undergo, I discovered that most of the musicians were doubling as stewards. Obviously that was built into their contract of employment.

There was a fantastic pianist/singer who gave regular performances in the main lounge bar, a great musician. One evening he called for requests and, when a lady at the table next to us shouted one out, he launched unhesitatingly into it. When she immediately turned her back on him and resumed her conversation I mentioned to Pat how lucky I was that my musical career left me perched on my branch of the music business and not theirs.

I was, however, reminded that, way back in the early sixties, my friends The Seekers rose from their humble beginnings as cruise entertainers such as these, on their trip from Australia to London, to the very pinnacle of success. They sustained their position at the top for fifty years, singing even better now than in their early days, as they proved in their fiftieth anniversary concert, which I attended. Hope springs eternal.

My shows and the cruise over, we disembarked early in the morning and, since our flight home was not until the evening, we arranged another cruise of a different kind. This was on a speedboat that skited us over the Everglades in search of crocodiles. The only one we saw was so small you could have put it in my back pocket and so our 'holiday' ended in slight disappointment.

Arriving home, we contemplated the whole experience and concluded that, the indolent living apart, the inconvenience of transporting the instruments and baggage with possible delays in flight was a bit too much for us, and decided to think very, very carefully about any such offers in the future.

Another foreign engagement which gave us food for thought was to Moscow in 1998.

The Caledonian Society of Moscow was organising a Highland Games in the capital city, intending to bring a group of athletes, craftsmen, musicians and dancers to enlighten their fellow countrymen. Their representative, Vitalli, asked me to come along as part of that group. I knew it was an ambitious project and that there was no real money in it but, given the popularity of the works of Robert Burns in Russia, I thought it stood a chance of success and agreed to participate. Besides, Pat and I had never been to Moscow, and here was the ideal opportunity.

After protracted negotiations I said I would go out but, as with the Boston affair, would require flight tickets bought and paid and in my hand before I would leave the country. Due to fly to Russia on June 18th, we still did not have our tickets as late as the 17th. I phoned the agency who were handling the business and we were requested to fly to Heathrow next morning where we would be met by someone from tele-sales at the Lufthansa desk. This person would hand us our tickets to Frankfurt and Moscow. I emphasised again: no tickets, no Ron in Moscow. The chap arrived at the last minute and we were on our way, although this did not augur well for the trip.

When we finally arrived at a late hour, we were met by three young Russians, Demitri, Ivan and Svetlana, and were taken to our accommodation in what had been the athletes' village during the Moscow Olympic Games. To say that the complex was run down is putting it mildly. The bulk of the party were billeted in dormitory buildings, but we were given a small bungalow to ourselves.

Tiredness from the long flight, together with lack of light caused by half the bulbs in the place not functioning, metal bedsteads with ultra-thin, dirty mattresses laid on uneven springs and wallpaper hanging in shreds from the walls, sapped us of enthusiasm for the forthcoming event. You will think I exaggerate but I do not. Pat lay down, fully clothed, and tried to sleep, whilst I awaited the arrival of one of our hosts to explain that there was no possible chance of us staying there and to, please, find us a hotel which I would pay for myself.

We hadn't bothered to unpack our cases and so were ready to move out immediately. Our initial contact, Vitalli, arrived and very reluctantly agreed to my request. Before leaving, we were offered a breakfast of dry bread, cherries and yogurt. None of this was particularly appetising so we declined and were soon relaxing in the Metropole Hotel very close to Red Square. A young man, Mikail, had been assigned to us as interpreter and guide, and we all walked through the foyer, passing a couple of ladies who left us in no doubt which profession they followed.

The hotel was built between 1899 and 1920 in the Art Nouveau style, with photographs of diplomats and celebrities who obviously frequented its portals, hanging on the corridor walls. The whole feel of the place was in the sharpest contrast to what was outside the building and Mikail was amazed by his surroundings, particularly when we opened the courtesy bar in our room and he took out a couple of whiskies. It was obvious that such luxury was alien to him and later, over the next two or three days, he apologised profusely for taking the drink when he realised we had had to pay for it on our bill.

He picked us up next day to take us to the stadium where the Highland Games part of the celebration was to take place, the music and dance section being scheduled for the next day into evening. It was then we discovered that, when we vacated our bungalow the night before, most of the rest of the group had taken it over for a party where, it seems, all of their duty free was consumed. Unfortunately that night, while they were all in the bungalow, a hurricane hit Moscow and lightning caused great damage including to the fusebox which exploded and caught fire. They fled the building and returned to their dormitory, which they had now christened 'The Gulag'.

Our party got off lightly. We watched reports of the hurricane on World television and phoned home to report that we were safe. Seven people had been killed and hundreds injured. 67,000 trees in the city were damaged or destroyed.

In the Standard Life 2000 show, the script-writer who compiled the programme mistakenly wrote that Pat and I had remained in the bungalow when it went on fire and that Pat slept through the whole thing. He said that it was her snoring which helped extinguish the flames. Incorrect information, but a good line.

The stadium was in the same sorry state as the athletes' village, as we discovered when we lined up behind a Russian pipe band and made a circuit of the crumbling track. We ended up at a podium facing a stand which was devoid of spectators, the Russian locals evidently indifferent to the whole thing. I sang 'Flower of Scotland' on guitar to the backing of a valiant Scottish presence, and the games began. I use a lower case 'g' deliberately because the whole thing quickly descended into disarray with some of the younger members of the group taking the microphone for a karaoke session. Pat and I were grateful finally to take refuge in our hotel room and await the next day's developments at the open air singing festival.

We had the morning free and so arranged for Mikail to pick us up at 11.00 am for a lightning tour of Moscow City Centre including the Bolshoi Theatre, home of the Bolshoi Ballet, and Red Square. It was interesting to note that in some of the many underpasses leading to underground trains, members of the Russian State Orchestra were busking feverishly. In attempting to purchase some typically Russian lacquer boxes, we discovered that credit cards were not acceptable in the city, but were fortunate to find one of the few ATMs available and to acquire enough roubles to buy what we wanted.

We took our man for lunch at a new restaurant near Red Square, each of us grabbing a tray before passing the glass-fronted cabinets that held the food, finally paying at the cash desk. We were well used to this procedure, but, judging by his wide-eyed response, it must have been the first time our guide had been in the place. The meal finished, he told us about his life, mentioning that what we had paid for our not too lavish lunch was more than his father's monthly pension. His father was a retired university professor.

I went into a surprisingly up-market shoe shop where the assistants were completely taken aback when I bought *two* pairs of shoes, not just one. As we three walked across Red Square to our hotel, a shower of rain descended, not quite soaking us, but wetting Mikail's clothing. The smell rising from it confirmed that, as he had told us at lunch, they had no running water in the crowded flat he shared with his large family.

Mikail then took us in a car to Sigorsky Park where the folk festival and crafts' exhibition were to be held.

When I accepted the engagement, I prepared a short introductory speech for my spot. An interpreter in Edinburgh translated it into Russian and gave me some coaching, but left me to hone it with a taped version. This I did assiduously in the weeks prior to my visit and, on the evening of my performance, I asked young Svetlana to listen and give me her opinion. I shouldn't have bothered. She did listen until the end but with a growing smile. When I asked her what she thought, she said I sounded like a Scotsman trying to speak Russian. That's exactly what I was, but her reaction was enough to put me off, and all of my work went by the board as my confidence disintegrated. I just couldn't do it. I do feel sure though that had I gone ahead, the locals would have appreciated my trying and, in Pat's words, it would have been one hundred percent for effort. The singing went well enough, and blended satisfactorily with all of the other singers from various parts of the world, although while the official singers were performing, splinter 'buskers' set up stalls to sing over what we were doing.

We did more sight-seeing the next day and in the evening our Russian hosts entertained us to a ceilidh in a school complex, including a mix of Scots' songs and Corries material, all of which sounded like Russians trying to sing Scots. That afternoon Mikail sat with us in a cafe-bar. Strangely enough, when I asked him what he would like to drink he declined, but said that he wouldn't mind a cheese sandwich. How hard were things actually in Moscow? As we sat there, one of the young Scottish artists walked past and, as I called him over, readily accepted my invitation to have a whisky which he downed with a shaking hand. His complexion was rather pale and when we asked if he was alright he shook his head. He wished we had been with him half-an-hour before when he was accosted by two Russian policemen who asked to see his passport, declaring that his visa was out of order and he should accompany them to the police station. All this was done more in sign language than anything else, and it must have seemed the more confusing. There was no confusion, however, at the station where it was made obvious that his visa would only become valid upon payment of two hundred pounds. He explained that all he had was twenty pounds. This was taken from him, and he was released.

Our fascinating experiences in Moscow were crowned by a conversation at the airport with a Chinese businessman, an engineer working for a German firm in Russia to service machinery under contract to them. When we told him of our young artist's experience, he said he was not at all surprised, since he too had been accosted in Red Square by two policemen who were holding back a fierce-looking, muzzled Doberman on a short leash. They said not a word as they stopped him to open his jacket, take out his wallet and remove all of his money, replace the wallet, and walk away. This followed a strip search at the airport upon his arrival, that search including his rear end, even though he held on his person official papers bearing Russian Government stamps authorising his visit. He had already telegraphed his superiors in Hanover informing them that on no account would he return to Russia at their behest.

Although Pat and I wouldn't have wanted to miss this trip, it has to be admitted that it was at times harrowing.

Chapter Thirty Eight

After I cut down on work, we didn't wait around for engagements to provide us with foreign holidays. We found ourselves at times in Bangkok, Budapest, China twice, in India, back to Hong Kong and Penang and began what has been a protracted courtship with Luxor in Egypt.

In Bangkok Pat nearly died from heat exposure on the roof of a temple. The domes of the roof were covered in glazed ceramic tiles, and walking between the domes in the reflected heat from the fierce sun, she fainted. Covering her in soaked towels, we managed to get her into shade where she recovered enough to go shopping in the Souk. Women!

The busking fiddlers of Budapest, I must admit, were easier to listen to than Chinese Opera in Beijing, although their costumes were absolutely fantastic in colour and form. The yards long, 'peacock-tail' feathers were particularly impressive.

On our first day out in China, we visited a street market opposite our Lido Hotel. It was there I discovered souvenir painted scent bottles. The technique of painting them is extraordinary. The small bottles come in various shapes, but all have an opening in the neck about one centimetre in width. The artist takes his small, L-shaped brush and paints his design, not on the surface of the bottle, but on the inside of the glass. When the painting is finished, a small jade stopper is inserted in the opening to seal the work. I can hardly believe the skill of the artist who, very slowly, inserts his loaded brush through the small opening and paints in reverse. I know the difficulty of painting, in traditional style, a miniature on the outside surface of wood, glass or ivory. Watching this reverse process takes my breath away.

My breath was taken away again when I sat on a stool on a pavement in Beijing to have a neck and shoulders massage administered by a tiny Chinese girl you could have blown away with a whistle. But, did she have vice-like fingers? These girls stand beside the shops with stool in hand and charge passers-by, locals and tourists alike, the equivalent of only fifty pence per torture.

In Xian to see the Terracotta Warriors we opted out of the formal dinner where the Chinese delicacy of duck's feet didn't sound very appetizing. An ice-cream at the 6,000-year-old village of Ban-Po made up for it.

Our first visit to China was for only one week in October, 1999. We saw the Great Wall, the Temple of the Jade Buddhas in Shanghai, and the garden a son lovingly planted for his mother. It has a dragon crawling round the entire length of the top of the wall, its tail appearing at one side of the gate and snaking round until it stops with the head at the other side. We saw enough, in fact, to want to return for a longer period in September 2004.

On the second visit, I made a bee line for the market and was pleased to see it was still there. The reason I was so keen was that I had been told I had missed out on some master painters' scent bottles which were kept under wraps and had to be requested to be seen. Fortunately, there were still some for sale and I was lucky enough to buy a couple showing much more complicated designs than the simpler tourist efforts.

I won't describe the Great Wall, nor the rickshaw ride to an old lady's house on the way to the Ming Tombs, nor the visit to Tiananmen Square. Such sights are well documented in travel brochures, as are explanations of the city of Chongjin over the border in North Korea. This city is home to more than

30 million people, many of them displaced by the flooding of the Yangtze River.

Instead, let me tell you of our cruise up the Yangtze, not so much the main river itself, but a gorge whose waters run into it.

'Located in the Changjian River, Three Gorges, the Shennong Stream is an overflowing brook in Badong County,' says my postcard reminiscence of our trip. It's the strangest boat trip I've ever experienced, because a lot of the time we weren't actually sailing, but being pulled upstream by the oarsmen. These men are from a local tribe whose livelihood has come, for centuries, from taking tourists upriver in their long, flat bottomed peapod boats to witness breathtaking scenery.

What amused me was that, having been part-rowed, part-dragged by ropes attached to the side of the peapod, further and further up and into the wilds, at the very end of the trip we entered a shallow lagoon where the boat had to turn to take us back down to the Yangtze. At this point, as we were facing into the jungle, out of nowhere, a wee man came walking towards us, waist-deep in swirling water. He had a tray full of postcards slung round his neck, and the biggest smile you could imagine. However, when we purchased the cards, he said he didn't have change for the notes we gave him. What a chancer! By now, I'll bet, a wealthy one.

We felt like intruders on the many visits to roadside Golden Buddha temples where we stood cheek-by-jowl with local people trying to force their way between ogling tourists to light their incense sticks and bow in reverence and prayer in front of their God.

As adoptive parents ourselves, we were saddened but, at the same time, heartened to watch convoys of tourist buses full of infant Chinese, in the hopeful arms of prospective American parents, plying between restaurants and play parks.

I hope the restaurants they went to were better than the ones we visited. The hotels we stayed in were of the best, but we always made sure of a hearty breakfast to sustain us through our day of strenuous, busy excursions. Otherwise we had to dine and have tea in local eateries which served their food in platters placed on a rotating tray in the centre of the table, Chinese-style. We, the diners, sat round the table taking turns at forking what we could onto our plates.

My father's words from all those years ago in the Indian restaurant, 'They gae ye far too much,' echoed in my ears. No chance! I now know why you don't see too many fat Chinese people. There was never enough food to satisfy the eight or so people round each table, mainly greens, and slimy greens at that, and very little meat. Towards the end of the tour, our guide adopted the habit of phoning ahead to have at least fried or scrambled egg on the table. Even when she was successful, some of us went without, sitting watching the small supply vanish before our eyes as the tray rotated.

It's as well Pat couldn't eat much because a note in her diary about the toilet facilities tells me they were, '2 for 80 people and a hole in the floor'.

On the way home from China, we stopped in Hong Kong for a couple of days before paying a return visit to the Golden Sands Hotel on the Batu Ferringhy beach in Penang, Malaysia. This had been our favourite, and regular, holiday destination, but we were sorry we went back. It is a truism that things change, but the changes we saw there were a shock.

The road we used to travel through the resort had had on one side the beach and attractive hotels, on the other, a few shops at the roadside, with virgin jungle stretching as far back inland as could be seen. At night, the noise of baboons, night birds and other animals, although at times disturbing sleep, was a unique and atmospheric characteristic of a far eastern, never-to-be-forgotten holiday. Now, the beach and hotels didn't look as inviting.

What had been a green mass of forestry was now a hill of concrete with blocks of flats, and the sound of wildlife was replaced by loud disco-music. It was in stark contrast to what we remembered as a paradise.

Any feelings of disappointment about holidays were washed away by our trip to India in December 2007. Backpackers we most assuredly were not on this holiday, but honoured guests on a train called the Palace on Wheels. This was one of the trains used by the Maharajahs in the days of the Indian Raj and is every bit as luxurious an experience as is advertised in the brochures.

The exclusive nature of the way we were to be treated was illustrated on our first day during a rickshaw tour round New Dhelhi. There must have been some kind of sign on the rickshaw to designate our status because, when we were delayed in an overcrowded street by a couple of passers-by, an Indian policeman shockingly beat them on the back with a long bamboo baton to force them out of our way.

Next day was the start of the railway journey proper. We presented ourselves at the station, having been taken by courier from our executive room in the Shangri La Hotel, and he accompanied us on board to the Jaipur carriage, room number 1, the best room on the train, closest to the bar and the dining-room. Pat would probably have written, 'closest to the dining-room and bar.' Everyone has priorities.

The train had a number of inter-connected carriages which were, at breakfast time, closed off to leave a small private dining area for each of the carriages' travelling companions. Since we left Delhi in the evening and went straight to our own rooms after dinner, we didn't get a chance to meet our companions until breakfast next morning. I had my video camera handy as two Italians joined us. Silvano and Clarissa took good humouredly to a filmed introduction as two English ladies also joined us. Finally, a German called Karl, who was travelling on his own, squeezed into shot with his greeting of, 'Don't mention ze war!' This set the tone for the rest of the week, travelling across Rajasthan from New Delhi to Agra and the Taj Mahal. We were greeted at every stop with the presentation of colourful garlands hung round our necks.

First stop on the line was Jaipur where we were taken on the back of an elephant, completely covered in tattoos, up a winding, craggy path to the Amber Fort.

We travelled through Sawa Madhopur to the Yellow City of Jaisalmar, and then Udaipur to visit a factory of artists where I learned that the Indian Maharajahs were not unlike the Egyptian Pharaohs. They employed families of artists who, generation after generation, illustrated their masters' exploits and achievements in building and warfare. When the Raj collapsed and the Maharajahs lost power and wealth, some of these artists formed collectives to carry on their skills. Tourists like ourselves became at least some of their customers, and I was happy to help them out by buying a detailed painting of a procession of Maharans. At first glance you'd swear that it was a photographic reduction of a large original.

Admiration of the exquisite miniature detail of this artist's work is enhanced by knowledge of the material it's painted on. This is a flat board made from pulverised camel bone, smoothed to the appearance of thin marble. It was made by the grandfather of the manager of the factory and took him two years to complete. The panel measures only 26cms by 13cms. Imagine it filled with two mounted elephants, two mounted horses and a mounted camel. It also has twelve walking human figures and behind a stone wall, a palace in a landscape containing running deer, pheasants and storks and another smaller palace in a lake with oarsmen in two small boats.

The detail is so intricate that the artist works two hours on, two hours off, to try to save his eyesight. My fellow travellers couldn't understand why I paid as much for it as I did but, conversely, I couldn't understand their blindness in not seeing its quality. There's no way I would spend two years of my life painting one picture for £600, would you?

Our penultimate stop was in Bharatpur for a 4.00 am visit to the bird sanctuary. My alarm clock, strangely enough, wasn't working so we missed it, but this left us more refreshed for our final visit before going home. This was to Agra where Pat posed like Diana, Princess of Wales for my camera in front of the Taj Mahal.

Lest you think that Pat and I were rising, as Ma would put it, 'above our station,' with all these exotic holidays, I can tell you that at the same time we had bought a tiny cottage, a but-and-ben in effect, in Morrison Street, Kirriemuir, which we used for many years as a base to explore the surrounding Scottish countryside.

Chapter Thirty Nine

The late George Weir was a prolific wordsmith. After a colourful career which included four years in the saddle battling coyotes and diamond-back snakes on the Bond Ranch in Montana, he settled in Peebles in the Scottish Borders and became a van driver for the leading baker in town, J.H.Goodman.

Vi Williamson, Roy's ex-wife, was now living in Stobo Station House and it was there that George and Roy first met when George's delivery round coincided with a visit by Roy to see Vi and his daughters, Karen and Sheena. The chance meeting blossomed into a collaboration of George's words and Roy's music, in songs like Liberty, Flood Garry, The Heidless Cross and The Black Douglas. These songs became standards in The Corries' repertoire and it was perhaps poetic that George died on February 18th, 1990, just months before Roy on August 12th of the same year.

Pop, my father, didn't quite make it into 1990. Some years before, my brother Ian took my parents to stay with him and his wife Jean in Bognor Regis. We went to visit from time to time and were glad to see them living comfortably and well cared for, finally dying at home. Ma suffered from cancer and died on May 1st, 1985; probably from cancer of the colon. Pop's cause of death on December 20th, 1989 was perhaps clearer: 'Broncho Pneumonia.' Was this a merciful release from the dementia he had been suffering? Violet, Pat's mother, outlasted both of my parents and it was not until February 18th, 1999 that I read a eulogy for her at her funeral.

Many departures and much sadness, but I'm always amazed at how life goes round and round in circles.

My son, Gavin, married Michelle, the daughter of an extremely well-known and highly respected Edinburgh Councillor and journalist, the late Brian Meek. Brian and Michelle's mother, Glenda, had divorced and both had remarried. Brian's second wife, Frances Horsburgh, was another journalist but also pursued a second career as a political aide to Lord James Douglas Hamilton. It was through Frances that I was introduced to James, as he allows me to call him, when he became interested in the commissioning of a portrait of his forebear, The Black Douglas, to hang in the Great Hall of the refurbished Lennoxlove House, now the Family Seat.

Protracted negotiations ensued until, finally, permission for me to paint the picture was granted by James' older brother, the late Angus, Duke of Hamilton. On Monday, June 25th, 2007, I visited Lennoxlove to see where the picture would hang and ascertain the size and dimensions of the canvas, which I ordered the same day.

The Duke of Hamilton is Her Majesty the Queen's representative in Scotland, stemming from the fact that The Black Douglas was the first lieutenant of King Robert the Bruce. There is no known likeness of The Black Douglas, so here I was once again in my artistic career asking why I made things difficult for myself. What was I to make him look like? By studying archive material supplied to me by James, the reading of history books, and from information kindly supplied by the Edinburgh Castle War Museum researchers, I built up a picture of the tempestuous life of the man I was to paint.

Gavin's friend from school-days, Murray McKie, immediately came to mind. He had a mass of black hair just as The Douglas is reported as having, which partly gave rise to his name. Murray had grown into a big guy whose weightlifting had resulted in a muscular body, as swinging swords and battle-axes in countless campaigns must have developed in The Douglas. When on the run from the English forces of Edward, he took refuge in the Ettrick Forest. Gavin and Murray had studied at Selkirk High School, not a stone's throw from where the forest had been, and had we not lived ourselves in the Ettrick Valley? Add to that the fact that Murray's father was a gamekeeper who ranged through the same land which bore the imprint of the feet of The Douglas, and my imagination said to me, 'Here's your model.' Murray jumped at the chance, and I was off and running.

I spent July into August drawing and photographing Murray, as the main character, with Pat and the family posing as others who would appear in the background. I did preparatory drawings of the pose and content of the picture and finally, when the canvas was prepared, started work on the painting on August 26th. It was finished in October and unveiled at Lennoxlove on October 22nd to a large press contingent with cameras from BBC and ITV. Here is what was revealed.

If you know the song, The Black Douglas, you will be aware that it describes some of his battle exploits. While painting the man, I constantly hummed the tune to myself. I like to think that you might do the same as I describe the aspects of his life I depicted.

Although known to his opponents as The Black Douglas, not only because of his hair colouring and dark countenance but also for his ferocious nature and prowess in battle, he was also called, by an equally ferocious and loyal following, the Good Sir James.

In the painting I have suggested this contrast in the armoured gauntlet clutching his long sword, but with his other gauntlet discarded and half hidden behind the foot of his shield. The open hand of friendship now holds the helmet taken off after fighting has ceased. His adoring followers are represented by the dog at his feet gazing up at him.

The black surcoat he wears was not a fashion of the times

but a garment designed for the night fighting he specialised in. He was one of the first guerrilla warriors of his time. In the days of chivalry, knights on horseback might face each other in the morning and shout, "I say, old chap, don't you think it's a bit wet and blowy today? Why don't we wait until tomorrow to see if conditions improve?' This wasn't for The Douglas. Always heavily outnumbered by a much better-equipped enemy, he devised his method of stealth fighting by night.

History books tell us that he and a kinsman, Sim of Ledhouse, invented the rope ladder for scaling fortress walls. He fought in snowy conditions when no other would, and deliberately spread stories of his cruelty as an act of psychological warfare.

To the left of the shield, a mother dressed in black soothes her baby and sings a popular Northumbrian lullaby of the time;

'Hush ye, hush ye, little pet ye,
Hush ye, hush ye, dinna fret ye,
The Black Douglas wilna get ye.'

The Douglas's father, who had assisted William Wallace, had been caught and imprisoned in the Tower of London by King Edward I, Longshanks, the Hammer of the Scots, call him what you will. The father had died in the Tower and his castle in Scotland had been taken and given over to an English garrison. The Douglas, even in flight from the English, couldn't stand the thought and gathered a small band of fighters, including some villagers, to put the castle to flame. In the background I've shown this event which has come down to us in history as The Douglas Larder. It is so called because, after all the Englishmen had been beheaded, the well was despoiled with rotting carcases and so too were the grain and wine from the castle, all to discourage any further occupation.

The gauntlets, sword, chain mail, spurs and helmet have been historically authenticated.

Since he was, by now, a constant thorn in the flesh of

Longshanks, letters were sent by the English king to every English Commander in Scotland, warning them that if they didn't capture The Douglas soon they would end their days in The Tower. I've shown some of these letters trampled in scorn under The Douglas's left foot and taken a leaf out of Diana Gabaldon's books by painting in a bit of time travel. The stone under The Douglas's right foot is one wrested from the burning castle walls but is in fact an actual 'prentice stone carved by my son, Maurice who is now a stonemason. It rests in my garden at home.

An English knight, who met The Black Douglas during one of the Crusades, confirms in a letter that The Black Douglas bore no visible scars on his face or hands. This, in the days when scars were a sign of manhood, is exceptionally unusual and perhaps bears witness to the man's skill in battle. I have transported myself in time and can be seen on the right of the picture standing above the mother and baby. I'm dressed as the English knight who made this observation and am there to show that, after all this time, there really are no hard feelings.

To atone for his murdering of John Comyn of Badenoch in a church, King Robert the Bruce wanted to fight in the Crusades. He died before he could achieve this ambition but, before he did, he charged The Black Douglas to take his heart to the Holy Land in a casket and throw it in the face of the Saracens.

The background of the picture shows King Alphonse XI of Castile's Castle of The Stars in Teba, in southern Spain, under siege by the Moors. The Douglas went to the king's assistance, and there performed his task for The Bruce by throwing the casket he wears round his neck at the Moorish hordes. Unfortunately, he was then surrounded and killed. There are monuments to his memory to this day in Teba and he is arguably better remembered in Spain than he is in Scotland.

When Robert the Bruce had come into his own and was crowned King of Scotland, it was payback time for all who had supported the Douglas's cause. Castle and lands, and revenues resulting from their management, were returned to The Black Douglas in a ceremony where a document was signed and an emerald ring passed 'from one big, sinewy hand to another'. The date was November 8th, 1324, and the event has come down to us as 'The Emerald Charter'.

Being aware of how closely these two men were linked in history and in friendship, I wanted to illustrate this in some way in the painting. The subject was uppermost in my mind one morning, and I was still thinking about it as I went out to my car to go for a newspaper.

There is a famous legend of Robert the Bruce hiding in a cave, almost ready to give up his quest for control of his country. He sees a spider trying and trying again to complete the spinning of its web. When it succeeds, it gives him fresh hope and he continues the struggle until he finally wins.

As I opened my car door and took my seat at the wheel, I became aware of a presence. I paused and looked to my left and the hairs rose on the back of my neck. Suspended between the roof of the car and the dashboard was a large spider's web, something I had never before seen in fifty years of driving. Clinging to the middle of it was a massive, red and gold spider.

I had the presence of mind to rush indoors to drag Pat and Lauren outside to witness my discovery and also to photograph it. The print I have bears witness to it and is proof to any disbeliever. Without any further thought of newspapers, I rushed into my studio and painted a spider on the canvas clinging to the shield beside the strap.

In learning about the composition of a picture, I was taught never to allow objects to disappear out of the edge of the canvas, but to keep the viewer's eye within the picture. It will be noted that the head of the spear standing beside The Black Douglas disobeys this law. I have done this deliberately because, once again, my imagination comes into play as I see the spirit of The Bruce joining the spirit of The Douglas to climb the shaft of the spear and, together, disappear into the Great Adventure.

Chapter Forty

I don't know why Pat and I became interested in going to Egypt, but in December 1995, we booked a one week Nile Cruise, followed by one week in the Mercure Hotel in Luxor. We were in Egypt over Christmas and New Year.

A Nile Cruise is a unique experience. The ship is not at all like the huge Caribbean liner we boarded for our Burns Supper with the Canadians in '97. It's a much more homely affair with only 100 or so passengers.

On our first night, as we joined the queue inside the dining room, parties of ten were counted off, shown to a table and told that was where they would eat for the entirety of the week. It's a great system, provided you get on well with the people allotted to you. We were lucky that first time because our trip became a laugh a minute as we floated down to Edfu, Esra, on to Aswan and back, taking in the sights of the temples and tombs of the Pharaohs. During the second week we continued to see eight people who had become friends, for meals and kalesh rides (a kalesh is a horse-drawn carriage), short sunset sails on the Nile in a felucca (a traditional small Nile boat with one huge sail, a design unchanged for many hundreds of years), and visits to the Valley of the Kings.

The result of this first Egyptian jaunt was, having enjoyed it so much, and the constant sunshine and heat certainly helped, we couldn't wait to book the next one. Our enthusiasm had such an impact on Lauren, that on our next year's visit, she joined us. She too, got the bug and where, years previously, Penang had been our favourite holiday destination, Egypt now took over. Visiting the same tombs and temples each time might sound boring, but with a different guide each time and his different slant on the same edifice, interest was maintained. Soon though, the lure of the swimming pool in the hotel and the visits to the jeweller, Yorkshire Bob, just round the corner from the Sheraton Hotel, took preference.

After a couple of years we discovered the Sunshine Project International. Information on this was posted on the notice-boards in hotels around Luxor. Any unwanted cosmetics, toothpaste, socks and sandals, etc, were requested as donations to the Project, which was a local orphanage. Donations of money were also welcome.

In 1992 Pearl Smith, on holiday in Luxor, was appalled by the sight of abandoned babies in a clinic for mothers and children. Eventually she sold her home and with the assistance of Dr Amr Taha, the project was born. She rented accommodation in Luxor and soon it was bursting with foundlings. That is very much the correct word for these children because they were 'found' in rubbish skips, by the wayside or in back-alleys, or sometimes simply floating in the Nile.

We, as a family, caught up with Pearl in 2002 when her Project was housed in rented rooms just off Television Street in Luxor. By then, her work was supported by UK Trustees and the Egyptian Foundation. We made donations and, during holidays, spent time helping to decorate her crowded accommodation. I helped to erect donated beds, most of which came in loose plank form with ill-fitting nuts and bolts on the corners, and Pat and Lauren spent time changing nappies and feeding the youngsters. Unfortunately, Pearl died in February, 2004, but her work continued with the addition of more rented premises in Ahmed Esmet Street.

A system of sponsorship was available. £12 a month per child helps provide day to day care, so Pat and I began our sponsorship of two youngsters, a boy called Saad and a girl called Suad, and Lauren did the same with a boy called Amr.

I also heard that in the early days of the Project, local residents would spit on these foundlings as they passed them on the street. The children were regarded as 'unclean' because of their abandoned status. Fortunately this practice has disappeared, largely because of an occupational therapist who was employed in the now custom-built accommodation on the outskirts of Luxor, when his care of the resident children was extended to those of the surrounding locals.

One day I watched as a young boy, who must have been approaching his teens, with his legs twisted in such a way that his mother had never seen him in a standing position, rose to his full height for the first time in his life. The therapist had made a simple contraption of a board with a couple of belts attached. He strapped the boy on and raised him to rest upright against the wall. As the therapist held the top of the board and pulled it from the wall, the boy's mother, sitting cross-legged on the floor, wept as she saw her son's feet touch the ground, and wept some more as she watched him smile from ear to ear.

It's very emotional to witness sights like that, but I don't have to go as far as Egypt to become involved. To quote a short passage from a pamphlet called 'Ataxia U.K.' It says:

'The ataxias are a group of life-limiting, usually progressive neurological conditions affecting over 10,000 people in the U.K. People with ataxia have problems with balance and co-ordination. They often lose the ability to walk, speak and to swallow. For some it will also damage their vision, hearing and heart. For most there is no cure.'

In 1995, I was invited to become patron of the Edinburgh and Lothians Branch of the Ataxia Group. At that time, I was still pretty much in the public eye and thought I could perhaps do a bit of good for them. There were branch meetings to attend, and cheques to receive on behalf of the group, with attendant press coverage giving a higher profile to its members, and I was also able to speak about it at functions. I accepted the invitation, and have since done what I could to help out.

I am now seventy-seven years old and, with advancing years, am less and less in the public eye. This means that when someone from a society such as Ataxia telephones the press to say that they have Ronnie Browne accepting a cheque, and could they give it some coverage, the answer more and more becomes, 'Ronnie Browne? Who he?' This I don't mind one bit. Who needs another press clipping to file away?

Because of this, though, I have been questioning my use to our branch. Recently, as I sat at a branch meeting, I was about to announce my resignation when something gave me pause. On each side of me, trapped in their respective wheelchairs, two men were engaged in conversation. Both are well advanced in their disease and have difficulty in eating, drinking and holding a pen or eating utensil. They have lost their ability to walk. And yet, I overheard them discussing their next visit 'tae the curlin'', listening in to discover that they spend a number of their winter evenings curling at the Borders Wheelchair Curling Club in Kelso.

The meeting had been discussing how we really needed an injection of publicity to revive flagging attendances, and possibly encourage other sufferers to come along for the first time. I immediately forgot my resignation announcement, and thought that here, surely, was a story the press would be interested in. I had recently been in conversation with Fiona Scott, the Sports Editor of the *Southern Reporter* and affiliated border papers, on a CML matter, so suggested that I should contact her to arrange some press coverage of one of the Wheelchair Clubs curling competitions. Right away she saw the heading on her sports' pages, 'Ronnie Browne returns to the Borders.'

Sponsorship of our children led to outings with them when we were in Luxor and this closer association led to Lauren obtaining a sabbatical from her job as a nursery nurse at George Watson's College to spend six weeks at Sunshine in 2007. She took a room in the Flobiter Hotel in St Joseph Street and on a daily basis, boarded the local bus to take her through the town to work. She became something of a local herself as the children taught her about themselves and their customs. Language was no difficulty because most of the older children had grown up with Pearl and her deputy, Lorna Ford, speaking English to them. Lorna took over Pearl's mantle when she died, and was in charge when the new building was completed. This was where Lauren worked.

Watson's weren't so daft in allowing time off because, upon her return to Edinburgh, she produced a full report. This proved to be educationally valuable to her Watson's charges, making them aware of just how much more fortunate they were in their lives compared to their counterparts in Egypt.

Lauren's sabbatical proved educational to Pat and me as well when she passed on the local knowledge she had gained, both in language and shops and places to eat other than the Hotel restaurants we had become used to.

Our visits to Luxor continued annually until, towards the end of the holiday in January 2010, Lauren announced that she was thinking of taking early retirement and coming to stay full-time, possibly to work in Sunshine or at least in work which might have something to do with the children. Pat, ever practical, asked if she knew anything about the purchase of property and, when Lauren said 'not really' in the same breath, Pat was soon searching through the various guidebooks on the tables for information. No luck there, but we visited the estate office across the street.

On January 2nd, just three days before we were due to go home, we found ourselves looking at a brochure of flats for sale. We visited a complex, then under construction, called the Egyptian Experience. Although incomplete, it had showflats for viewing. The place was disappointing in as much as it was up the river, out of town and past the bridge to the West Bank, and too much like a holiday village. We liked the more genuine Egyptian atmosphere in town, so came back down the road and looked at a couple of places before Lauren went for her daily visit to the children in Sunshine. When she went into the office and mentioned to the manager what we were about he said that, if it was property we were interested in, he could show us something really stunning. He had been watching its construction just across the fields and he knew the builder, who was in residence. Thirty minutes later we were introduced to Giovani.

The building was a block of four flats. Giovani lived in the part-furnished ground floor and showed us round before taking us up three flights of stairs and finally onto a terrace with a smaller flat. The bottom three were all of the same construction and contained a central hall with two double bedrooms off, one *en suite*. There was also a bathroom, a small 'reception' room and, through an arched opening, a dining room leading to, on one side, a large kitchen and on the other a lounge area. There were balconies off the lounge and one of the bedrooms. The building had just been completed and the first, second and terrace flats were all empty. This made them seem huge.

It was all very impressive and when on the terrace again, looking at a spectacular view over the surrounding cultivated fields, we asked the price. We fell speechless when he said £130,000. We had initially been interested in only one flat for Lauren but here, for the same price as her own flat in Edinburgh, was a whole building, with rental potential. Back in the hotel Pat and Lauren sat on our bed and I couldn't believe my ears when I heard Pat say, 'We're having it'.

I fled to the shops in panic, but when I came back, it was a done deal. My two ladies led me by the nose back to speak to Giovani and, with a shake of the hand, it was agreed that whenever we got back home we would send £50,000 and the balance would follow when Lauren sold her flat or we sold our Kirriemuir but-and-ben.

Next day was a helter-skelter scramble from Giovani, to a judge with Lauren's passport, to the passport office for Lauren to extend her visa, back to the flats to film them, a visit to a DHL office, hiring an interpreter to go at 9.00 pm with Lauren, the Sunshine manager and Giovani to a lawyer. Finally we had dinner, exhausted.

With a late flight home the next night, the helter-skelter started again in the morning with another visit by Lauren to the courts along with Giovani and the interpreter, back to the passport office, and back again to the courts. We packed the suitcases and then withdrew money to pay the lawyer before returning to the flats to take an inventory, had baths in the hotel in preparation for the flight, followed by yet another visit to the lawyer until, with a taxi to the airport, we were suddenly sitting on a plane, with Lauren clutching legal documents in Arabic and English to prove that the fastest sale of property imaginable had just taken place.

During the flight, the three of us reflected on the whirlwind events of the last two days. As I have hinted I was not keen but, given the support Pat had always afforded me without question, I gave my blessing. Anyway, it was by now too late not to. It was done.

Lauren's flat in Edinburgh was immediately put up for sale. Between us, we decided that Lauren would buy the terrace flat, where the brick domed ceiling of the bedroom had won her over, together with the ground and first floor. We would have the second floor. Part of the master plan was that Pat and I would spend winter months there. Lauren would move in with us but stay here in Edinburgh until the time came for her permanent move, when she took her early retirement in about ten years. In the meantime, she would let her two lower flats in Egypt.

Fortunately Lauren's flat in Craigmillar sold reasonably quickly and, after a bit of to-ing and fro-ing, by late spring the money side of the purchase was concluded. It was at this time that I discovered who some of my friends really were.

There was a delay in Lauren receiving part of the payment for her flat here, and so she was short of £80,000 for Giovani in Luxor. There was a decided chance that her Egyptian purchase would founder and she would lose the flats. We were in deep discussion about this turn of events when we had a visit from my friend Ron Haggerty. Ron saw the worried frowns and asked what the problem was and, as a joke, Pat said, 'You don't have a spare £80,000 you could give Lauren, do you?' Without a moment's hesitation, and without even asking why she needed it, he replied, 'When do you want it?' We couldn't believe our ears. We were only really convinced of his intention when he presented us, the next day, with a cheque for that amount.

As I gazed at it in my hand, I knew that he and his wife were cast in the same mould as Pat and me, because the cheque was signed by Rosemary.

No mention whatsoever had been made of interest payment on the loan, nor when it would be repaid but, fortunately, only one week later, Lauren received settlement and was able to give Ron his money back.

We discovered shortly afterwards that we had found another genuine friend in Luxor. In spite of the temporary glitch in receiving his balance, Giovani didn't just take the down payment and run, and continues to this day assisting us in every way he can to develop the property which, at time of writing, we are still in process of preparing for Lauren's permanent move.

Chapter Forty One

In April 2005 we moved from 131 Mayfield Road to a new home on the outskirts of Edinburgh. The property had been converted in 1996 from two adjoining farm cottages into one house and contained two family bathrooms and three double bedrooms. It also contained a separate granny flat with bathroom, kitchen and lounge. It was therefore no inconvenience to us when Lauren moved in after her flat was sold. There was ample space for all of us. Lauren chose to use one of the bedrooms in the main building, which allowed me to use the granny flat as office, studio and storeroom.

By 2010 my professional life was all but over, and I had all the time in the world to concentrate on the new Egyptian property. First thought was to send the contents of Lauren's Edinburgh flat to Luxor, but this was easier said than done. We were put off the idea of a container when the carrier warned of likely pilfering during Customs inspections, and the thought of travelling to either of the ports of Alexandria or Said to arrange transport to Luxor was daunting. We decided against, and thought about our options. Left with no alternative but to furnish the flats locally, we learned how lucky we are in this country to have so many furniture stores, especially those selling 'flat-pack' goods.

Because Lauren was still working, her visits to her prospective new home were limited to school holidays, but Pat and I were free agents and made visits to supervise the making of furniture, buying of carpets and ornaments and the other small nick-nacks that change a holiday flat into a home. Most of Lauren's big furniture was sold or given to friends, but some of the smaller things, like table lamps and pictures, kitchenware and cushions, she squeezed into suitcases. So, over the next two years the flats took shape with precedence given to the lower flats to accelerate rental potential.

Our first trip to the flats did not go well, and I suppose we should have expected, as new foreigners in town, that we would be a target for thieves. Only a couple of days after we arrived we were burgled. All the thieves took though, was a bottle of Vodka, a special bottle of gin which Lauren had bought at Duty Free, and my cine-camera which I was about to renew anyway, because it was on the blink. The day afterwards, we found in the field behind the building both the bottle of vodka, smashed, and the battery which had dislodged from the camera. Thereafter we spent more money on attaching wrought-iron fences around the building.

On April 17th 2010, airports all across Europe and the U.K. were closed due to dust clouds from an erupting volcano in Iceland. This meant that we couldn't get home for another week which, in turn, meant more extra expense and an unexpected extra week's holiday for Lauren.

The reason we were able to travel so often during that year was the flight-only bookings available from package holiday companies. Pat and I felt we were never away from the place from September until November, and were in residence in the part-furnished ground floor flat in late November when the first rental enquiry came in the form of a knock on Lauren's door from a hot air balloon pilot. She called excitedly from Edinburgh, but unfortunately the enquiry fell through. Perhaps it was as well, because the flats were still far from ready.

Pat and I spent our time buying refrigerators, air conditioning units, mattresses, light fittings, wall hangings and carpets. It was as well we sold the cottage in Kirriemuir in September for £66,000.

We visited Sunshine with gifts for the children and packed as much work in as we could to cleaning our new property. There is a never-ending battle with dust in Egypt.

During the last few days of our stay Pat complained of pains in her stomach and inability to eat, but put it down to the non-stop work. We were pleased to finally pack the suitcases for our flight home and had been back for only a few days when, on the morning of November 23rd, she reported that her pains had gone. Her diary says: 'I think it had been a slight blockage in my intestine for the past two weeks.'

By November 26th, however, she attended a precautionary appointment with her doctor who said he would arrange for a scan the following week. On the evening of November 28th, she told me that her stomach was bad. You may remember the heavy snow of the winter of 2010. Where we were, it fell to a depth of twelve inches on the evening of the 29th, and was still there the next day when Pat asked me to phone the doctor because the pain was getting worse. He brought forward her scan to the next morning at Roodlands Hospital in Haddington.

In the morning, our taxi couldn't get up the hill because of the snow, so we walked the half mile down to meet it. Roodlands was seven miles from us and, when we got there, the driver kindly said he would wait because the weather was worsening.

Pat's scan showed a lump in her bowel.

We walked back up the hill after the taxi dropped us, and she phoned her two sisters Margaret and Diana who advised that Pat speak to her doctor immediately. She did so and said she didn't want to wait until something happened and could she please be given a bed immediately in the Western General Hospital. He responded and, later the same day, we walked down the hill again for another taxi. At the hospital she was admitted to Ward 27.

On December 2nd, Pat had another scan. Over the next two days DVT injections, a biopsy, and colonoscopy were arranged for December 5th. The surgeon, Miss Collie, who happened to be one of Lauren's mums, whose children Lauren had in her care, said they would scrutinise the results urgently. As a result, she said that, far from being allowed home that night, Pat was to stay where she was and Miss Collie would operate in the morning to remove the lump.

On December 7th, Pat was taken to theatre at 10.30 am, and wakened in recovery at 4.30 that afternoon. It's no surprise that there are no entries in her diary until December 12th when notes of who had been visiting begin to appear. On the afternoon of December 14th she was home with us. Everything seemed to be settling, although one cryptic diary entry comments: 'sore arse'.

And what was I doing all this time but washing and cleaning, going messages and putting up Christmas decorations? Saying it sounds like sour grapes, but don't dare think so. I was just so pleased to have my Pat at home with me and in such good spirits.

Unfortunately, our good spirits didn't last long. On January 1st, 2011, after Lauren had returned to Luxor with her friend, Brenda, Pat complained of a return of stomach pains. On January 6th she weighed in at a mere 10 stones, fully clothed, in the Cancer Centre at the Western General. Thereafter her consultant informed us, in what I would describe as the harshest, most dismissive terms, that even with four treatments of chemotherapy she could look forward to only a few months of life. Neither of us could believe that the meeting with the consultant had lasted less than ten minutes. As we looked at each other, we gasped at the cruelty of this dismissal of a life. Only three days before, we had been celebrating Pat's 73rd birthday.

I find it painful to write of the telephone calls I had to make to the family members that evening, but some relief arrived the next day when Miss Collie phoned. She reported that she had removed all cancer from Pat's bowel and another small infected piece in her tummy fat. She thought the chemotherapy would get rid of any cancerous cells and that the outlook was very good.

This news, followed by a night at the Pantomime in The King's Theatre, bucked us up considerably as we looked forward to the coming year. The hilarious laughter at the panto revived Pat's fighting spirit and, next morning, we booked flights to take us back to Luxor for two weeks before her chemotherapy treatments were due to begin on January 24th. These were postponed and, on the 18th, we were off, knowing Gavin was to join us in the second week for his first experience of Egypt.

Giovani was waiting at the airport to inform us that the two lower flats had been rented. The ground floor had been taken by four Turkish men who had come to Egypt to set up a sun-dried tomato business, and the first floor by a couple who had visited earlier for a week. It was encouraging for Lauren, whose flats you'll remember they were, to find that the couple were moving in on February 21st for six months, as there was no predicting just how long the Turks would be there with their tomatoes.

Pat and I continued installing things like bath towel rails and sink shelves, and furnishing flats One and Two with more kitchen ware. Pat went to Sunshine with dozens of lollipops for the children and, what with meals out and buying a couple of sun loungers, all of a sudden the first week had passed and it was time to meet Gavin at the airport. For years we had been extolling the wonders of Luxor, and he had finally succumbed to our pleas to come out, fascinated to see what had possessed his sister to burn her boats, and set up here.

This holiday was our present to him for his 50th birthday. He was with us just one day when news arrived of riots in Cairo to oust President Mubarak. Trouble spread and, on the evening of January 28th, 2011, as Pat, Gavin and I stood on our terrace enjoying a sundowner, just below us on the Main Street, a demonstration gathered in numbers and made its way towards the local police station. Windows were broken, the building was torched, and armed police soon filled the road. Rifle shots rang out and tear gas filled the air, wafting towards us four flights above the road.

The crowds moved away as the police advanced and soon all was still in our area. As the noise subsided Gavin stared at us in fright. He's a big laddie, standing 6' 3", but was visibly shaken and I could almost hear him saying to himself, 'What the hell have they brought me to?'

Over the next two days, the police were withdrawn from the streets. It was said that this was a ploy to frighten the populace into a feeling of insecurity but if so, it didn't work. A day later we saw our neighbours in gangs, armed with long, thick sticks, roaming the streets and stopping all traffic through their neighbourhood to check credentials. I went down amongst them to see what was going on and they told me not to worry about a thing, Mr Ronnie. They were there to protect all of us.

Lauren's Turkish tenants took fright, leaving everything in the flat as they rushed for the first available flight home. We haven't seen them since, and her couple for the first floor never appeared. Europeans in Cairo were advised to leave the country and a curfew from 4.00 pm to 7.00 am was imposed. On our way to the Sheraton Hotel for lunch we received calls from home checking on our wellbeing, but continued to the Luxor Museum and Karnak Temple with Gavin. In all ways possible we carried on as normal until, on February 2nd, we left on what I believe was the last holiday charter flight out of Luxor, bound direct for Manchester.

While I cannot deny that there have been trouble and killings in Egypt the four years between then and now, we have witnessed no more of it than we did on that first night. There have been at least two major demonstrations in Luxor, but we have been unaffected and have been able to go about our business untroubled.

Pat started her chemotherapy on February 10th. On our

return home she was warned that she would have six treatments, each one preceded by a blood sample taken at her own doctor's surgery. She suffered the same setbacks as, I know, so many others. No doubt many among the readers of this book. Missed treatments due to low blood counts, side effects like loss of feeling in the extremities, difficulties and discomfort in walking and handling simple things like a spoon. Sore heads constantly plagued her and, when she tried to knit scarves for charity, her arms ached, sometimes aching even when she wasn't using the needles.

In April, after a couple of treatments, her blood, magnesium and calcium levels were in good shape so we squeezed in a week in Luxor, in spite of the insurance company confirming that she wasn't covered for anything relating to the cancer. We took out a large, plastic pool, and it was nice to see her relaxing in the sun. Her comment in the diary: 'The pool is great.'

Whilst we were there we had a marble bunker and splash panel fitted in Lauren's kitchen. I love to watch a good workman do his work, and these were good workmen. To cut the small holes for the taps, they turned the marble on its reverse side and made many, many angular, cross cuts until they ended up with just a pin-hole on the facing side. They then very carefully chipped at it until they made the hole exactly the size they were after. Fascinating.

On our return to Edinburgh, during a treatment, Pat spoke to a young man in a chair beside her, also wired up for his various drips. When Pat told him she was just back from Egypt he said, 'Jesus, they've just told me I shouldn't go to Montrose.'

Her treatments finally over, her doctor's examination of September 22nd was upbeat and he gave her the all clear to go away until December if she wished. So, on October 5th, we were off.

Arriving in Cairo to change flights for Luxor, we touched down in the middle of a flight-controllers' strike. Our flight was cancelled so, after humming-and-hawing with our fellow passengers about hiring a bus, we finally hired a taxi. The journey took twelve hours and was shared with a young German couple. Although perfect timing wasn't important to us, it meant that they were able to make their Nile Cruise and they were delighted.

Five days later our grand-daughter, Rebecca, came out to join us for a week. She was most put out when we told her that she wouldn't be able to wear any of the short skirts that youngsters favour these days. In spite of that, she enjoyed herself.

We too enjoyed ourselves in the middle of what had always been the master plan of wintering in the sun. This was not to be for long. On October 21st, Pat discovered a small lump in her stomach and we made hurried arrangements to get back home, which we achieved in two days.

Pat's doctor seemed satisfied with her at his examination and we found ourselves ten days later on a direct flight from Manchester to Luxor. The plane could accommodate 240, but there were only nineteen on board this time, indicative of what had happened to Egypt's tourist industry because of the revolution.

During all this time, a tenant had been in residence in Lauren's first floor flat. Her name was Bierit, a Danish journalist and author who, thanks to the miracle of the internet, conducted her business in the comfort of a seat in the sun on the balcony of her lounge. As a cancer sufferer herself she had commiserated with Pat over coffee. Now though, just after we arrived back, she left for Denmark for more treatment on her remaining breast. She went home with our utmost sympathy.

A couple of complaints of a sore stomach led to heavy sickness for Pat during the night of November 15th, but by 4.00 pm the pain had gone.

There were still constant jobs for me to do. Some varnish stains had to be removed from the terrace tiles following the erection of a massive shade we had ordered. I painted the cupboards in Lauren's kitchen, stuck decorative tiles round the bottom of the shade supports, and watered, every day, the tiny garden on the ground floor, at the same time spraying the lane leading to our property to keep down the dust.

Buying gigabytes on our 'dongle' gave us internet access in the flat so that we could keep track of banking and mail.

In these ways our short time passed.

Here are Pat's diary entries from December 1st onwards: 'In pain all day.' 'Stayed mainly in bed.' 'Not good.' 'Thoughts of maybe having to go home early.' 'The last co-codamol at 11 didn't work.' 'Ronnie looked up flights.' 'Watched *Extras*. 'Very funny.' 'Pain bearable.' 'Washed clothes.' And, on December 6th, 'Flight to Cairo.'

Pat had a scan on December 9th which resulted in another entry, 'Miss Collie came at 6.50. The cancer is back.'

Chapter Forty Two

Throughout our life together, Pat and I often found ourselves offering sympathy to families faced with this kind of devastating news, but nothing can prepare you for when it lands on your own doorstep. We had discussed the disease many times and Pat had often voiced her opinion that, 'Cancer always comes back.' Now here it was, with a vengeance. It had spread everywhere. There was no hope, and I now believe that was in her mind when she asked to go to Luxor so often after it became obvious that she was not up to it.

Informing the family of this latest turn of events, I had to keep a stiff upper lip, hearing their distraught reactions. My own upset became manifest the next day when I was driving in town and my distracted thoughts made me reverse into a taxi. Later in the day, sitting in a taxi coming home from a business meeting, I left my briefcase containing important documents on the back seat.

I make no apology for once again illustrating Pat's fighting spirit. Only one day after noting in her diary what amounted to, in effect, her death sentence, she followed with the comment, 'The Panto was great.'

During the night of December 13th she was admitted to the emergency wards of the Royal Infirmary where she was found to have blood clots and fluid on her lungs. For six days we all awaited that fateful telephone call to tell us she was gone, but no. At 5.00 pm on the 20th, she had rallied, and that night she was in her own bed at home. Admittedly, she didn't sleep much and was in pain, but it didn't prevent her getting up next day to ask me to drive her to the surgery where she presented a box of chocolates to her nurse, Linda.

It was a muted Festive Season for all of us, and when, in early January, another scan confirmed the bad news, she was at it again, booking another Egyptian jaunt for February 1st. There's no way I would have wanted to stop her but, knowing how I was afraid to take sole responsibility lest something happen, Gavin and Lauren insisted on coming with us. This was just as well, because, after spending a few comfortable and happy days, she suddenly felt excruciating pain. It took us some time to find a suitable doctor to come to her aid, but mercifully we did. A Dr Safwat was a kidney specialist at the International Hospital in Luxor, and he was soon with Pat showing her the utmost kindness. He suspended a drip from a light bracket by her bed and, in the space of only thirty minutes, she was out of pain entirely and resting comfortably.

The doctor assured us that she would remain comfortable overnight but that he would return next day with another drip which would take longer to go through her body. Meanwhile we were trying desperately to book flights home, but couldn't.

Dr Safwat came in the morning and set up the drip again, which did keep Pat comfortable. Returning that evening with a portable scanner and a nursing assistant, he performed a scan in the hope that he could offer better news than her surgeons in Scotland. To no avail. All he could do was inform us that Pat should have her kidneys looked at. Yet again in our lives, laughter proved good medicine and she remained trouble and pain free until we departed for home.

Although she tried not to show it Pat was soon in pain again, and when we arrived home late, she tried to sleep but couldn't. An appointment at the Cancer Clinic had been pre-arranged before we left. It was for the next morning and, as we entered the surgery, she didn't give the doctor a chance to speak but immediately asked to be admitted to hospital and please to be kept out of pain.

She was given a bed, and over the next few days, found herself in a ward with three other women about to suffer the same fate as herself. One evening, as Lauren and I were visiting, in the corner of the room, about ten people had congregated round another bed. The matron came in and remonstrated saying that it was only two to a bed and that they would all have to leave. Forgetful of the situation, Pat came out with, 'Come on, matron, you'd think we were dying or something.' A short, shocked silence descended until it was superseded by laughter. Even the matron joined in, and the visitors were allowed to stay.

Next day, Pat was informed that her needs would be better administered in a hospice and she was transferred to St Columba's.

After a few days there, Pat was noticeably becoming thinner and weaker. I tried to make her room more homely by putting together a portable wardrobe for her clothing, which by this time she was becoming less and less willing to change into. One of her standard lamps from the house made the night lighting less harsh.

I would spend all day with her until visitors arrived in the evening, but we couldn't stand parting. That last wave as we left her on her own for the night tore our hearts out.

I asked if I could please take her home. It seemed that our domestic set-up qualified for what they called 'The Package'. This required that room for a medical bed, wheelchair access when it became necessary, a hoist towards the end, bathing facilities, etc, should all be on one level. Our qualification was augmented by the fact that I would be with her twenty-four hours a day on a bed beside hers in her room. Lauren had been promised time off work so that Pat would always waken from sleep to a known and loved face.

I have nothing but respect and admiration for the staff and

management of St Columba's Hospice, but to bring her home was the best decision I have ever taken in my life. Lauren and I were assisted by carers coming in four times a day if necessary, and our district nurse visited promptly every mid-day to reload the pump attached to Pat's arm with the drugs needed to keep her out of pain.

I was warned on taking her into my care that she could die at any time. As it was, this fighting spirit battled for over six weeks until, at 1.30 on the afternoon of April 22nd, 2012, with Lauren and her older sister, Margaret, by my side I heard her take her last whispered breath.

It will not have gone unnoticed that I have somewhat skipped over Pat's last days with us. This must not be seen as disrespect towards her, simply that it's too painful to relate.

We didn't have a conventional funeral service for Pat. Neither of us was of a religious persuasion. We had attended many funerals where all the attention was centred round a god and his mercy, with hymns in his praise taking up most of the time, leaving mention of the deceased as only a small part of the proceedings. We believed that all of the time allotted should be spent in memory of the dead, with emphasis on celebration of their life with us. I therefore organised a gathering of friends in the small, intimate Chapel of Rest of funeral directors, William Purves, choosing their Dalkeith office because of the Elliot family's long association with the town.

As well as diaries dating way back, I had been in the habit of filming and photographing the family as it grew. The first video clips show our move from Henderson Row when Gavin was only ten years old. These clips, together with even older photographs of Pat from babyhood, were the nucleus of a video tribute to her that Gavin, Maurice and Lauren helped me prepare.

My favourite clip is of Gavin's two, Rebecca and Jessica, as infants in the bath, with Pat wetting her hands, rubbing the soap to a lather and blowing bubbles at them. The giggling and screeches of laughter were a fitting memory of what my lady stood for.

On May 1st, 2012, the afternoon was spent with many showings of the tribute. Friends took turns to sit in the chapel, with Pat in front of them in a wicker coffin bedecked with a large floral spray made up by Margaret. Behind her was a photographic portrait in a favourite ball gown. Leaning on the coffin was a wooden plaque of hers with the words, 'What if the hokey-cokey really is what it's all about'. She would have liked that.

A month later we had a gathering for her in her beloved garden at home. Guests from childhood and school days, together with friends made during her life, congregated to share memories and laughter under the cherry trees, magnolias and rhododendrons she had planted herself. We were fortunate in the weather, which must have been the best of the year, because the house could never have accommodated the number of friends who turned out.

The main part of the celebration took place in the part of the garden Pat could never make up her mind what to do with. The gable end of the building faces west and is bathed, summer and winter, in whatever sunsets present themselves. At the other end, we built on a conservatory which catches the sun from early morning till tea time.

Many years ago, when Pat and Margaret were on one of their annual pilgrimages to the Chelsea Flower Show, as they were looking at some unusual rose specimens, they overheard a conversation between two awfully posh ladies. One said to the other, 'Do you have swans on the lake?' The other lady replied, 'Only on the laaarge one.'

In August, 2012, I had another conservatory built at the west end of the house. In order to accommodate a huge boulder in the garden, it had to be not so big as the first one. So now what I have is 'a laaarge conservatory,' and also, 'a smaaall conservatory'.

The small one affords me a 180-degree view of the garden and sky surrounding me. I begin my viewing from the right hand side and slowly move my head round. I pass my sight of Arthur's Seat with the sun behind it and continue through 180 degrees and then stop. I stop only to twist in my seat to the left through a further 20 degrees and there - what a sight. The sun catches the various colours of bark on the trunk and branches of a huge eucalyptus tree. It lasts only ten minutes until the sun finally goes down, but for someone like me who loves colour so much it is breathtaking.

If I paint an idyllic picture, idyllic it is. People ask if I'm still physically painting. I look out on a garden which is constantly a changing picture so, lazy bugger that I am, except when I move pots of acer, magnolia, Pieris and peony up and down, thereby creating living still-lives, I don't paint.

Finally

I approach the end, not of my life, but of its story so far.

July 21st, 2014, heralded the end of my singing career when I sang 'Flower of Scotland' for the Commonwealth Games athletes, because I will not sing again. You have to know when to stop.

I have had a long, interesting and rewarding life, and I trust that I have a bit yet to go. I have always kept the words of my art teacher, Agnes Johnston, ringing in my ears, 'Make the most of moments.' I charge you to do the same.

These words, together with all of the other words which have formed this story of my life, I dedicate to the lady who made my life, the lady who accorded me the highest honour of my life when she agreed to change her name to mine, Patricia Isabella Elliot, my Pat.

Index

Note: In some entries, Ronnie Browne and Roy Williamson are abbreviated to RB and RW respectively.

That Guy Fae The Corries